Developments in Christian Thought for OCR

The teaching content of this resource is endorsed by OCR for use with specification AS Level Religious Studies (H173) and specification A Level Religious Studies (H573). In order to gain OCR endorsement, this resource has been reviewed against OCR's endorsement criteria.

This resource was designed using the most up to date information from the specification. Specifications are updated over time which means there may be contradictions between the resource and the specification, therefore please use the information on the latest specification and Sample Assessment Materials at all times when ensuring students are fully prepared for their assessments.

Any references to assessment and/or assessment preparation are the publisher's interpretation of the specification requirements and are not endorsed by OCR. OCR recommends that teachers consider using a range of teaching and learning resources in preparing learners for assessment, based on their own professional judgement for their students' needs. OCR has not paid for the production of this resource, nor does OCR receive any royalties from its sale. For more information about the endorsement process, please visit the OCR website, www.ocr.org.uk.

Copyright © Dennis Brown and Ann Greggs 2020

The right of Dennis Brown and Ann Greggs to be identified as Authors of this Work has been asserted in accordance with the UK Copyright, Designs and Patents Act 1988.

First published in 2020 by Polity Press
Reprinted 2021

Polity Press
65 Bridge Street
Cambridge CB2 1UR, UK

Polity Press
101 Station Landing
Suite 300
Medford, MA 02155, USA

All rights reserved. Except for the quotation of short passages for the purpose of criticism and review, no part of this publication may be reproduced, stored in a retrieval system or transmitted, in any form or by any means, electronic, mechanical, photocopying, recording or otherwise, without the prior permission of the publisher.

ISBN-13: 978-1-5095-3235-3
ISBN-13: 978-1-5095-3236-0(pb)

A catalogue record for this book is available from the British Library.

Library of Congress Cataloging-in-Publication Data
Names: Brown, Dennis, 1955- author. | Greggs, Ann, author.
Title: Developments in Christian thought for OCR : the complete resource for component 03 of the new AS and A level specification / Dennis Brown, Ann Greggs.
Description: Medford, MA, USA : Polity, 2020. | Includes bibliographical references and index. | Summary: "The third OCR-endorsed bestselling textbook for Religious Studies"-- Provided by publisher.
Identifiers: LCCN 2019041151 | ISBN 9781509532353 | ISBN 9781509532360 (pb) | ISBN 9781509532384 (epub)
Subjects: LCSH: Theology.
Classification: LCC BR118 .B764 2020 | DDC 230--dc23
LC record available at https://lccn.loc.gov/2019041151

Typeset in 9.5pt on 13pt Utopia by Servis Filmsetting Ltd, Stockport, Cheshire
Printed and bound in Great Britain by CPI Group (UK) Ltd, Croydon

The publisher has used its best endeavours to ensure that the URLs for external websites referred to in this book are correct and active at the time of going to press. However, the publisher has no responsibility for the websites and can make no guarantee that a site will remain live or that the content is or will remain appropriate.

Every effort has been made to trace all copyright holders, but if any have been overlooked the publisher will be pleased to include any necessary credits in any subsequent reprint or edition.

For further information on Polity, visit our website: politybooks.com

DENNIS BROWN • ANN GREGGS

DEVELOPMENTS IN CHRISTIAN THOUGHT FOR OCR

THE COMPLETE RESOURCE FOR COMPONENT 03 OF THE NEW AS AND A LEVEL SPECIFICATION

polity

Ann dedicates this book to her Nan, The Troll, with love and thanks for being such an inspiration and for being the best 'Nan Pat'.

Dennis dedicates this book to his cats, Bramble, Cosmo, Fizz, Ginny and Vesper and thanks them for their valuable contributions during the writing process.

Contents

Acknowledgements — vi
Foreword: What is Theology? — vii
Scholars' Timeline — x

SECTION I HUMAN NATURE

1 Augustine's Teaching on Human Nature — 3
2 Death and the Afterlife — 21

SECTION II FOUNDATIONS: THE KNOWLEDGE OF GOD

3 Knowledge of God's Existence — 41
4 The Person of Jesus Christ — 55

SECTION III LIVING

5 Christian Moral Principles — 75
6 Christian Moral Action — 90

SECTION IV PLURALISM

7 Religious Pluralism and Theology — 109
8 Religious Pluralism and Society — 125

SECTION V SOCIETY

9 Gender and Society — 143
10 Gender and Theology — 156

SECTION VI CHALLENGES

11 The Challenge of Secularism — 173
12 Liberation Theology and Marx — 189

Study Skills and Assessment — 205
Glossary of Key Terms — 218
Illustration Credits — 225
Index — 226

Acknowledgements

This book would not have come about without the support and patience of many people. We would like to thank everybody at Polity Press who has been involved in the writing process, particularly Pascal Porcheron, Ellen MacDonald-Kramer, Neil de Cort and Leigh Mueller, who have worked alongside us and shown patience and understanding when the writing process became frustrating and all-consuming. They have offered their continual support, enthusiasm and encouragement, and the book is much better for their input. We offer thanks also to Polity's anonymous readers, whose comments were helpful at an early stage of writing.

Ann would like to thank Dennis for his unwavering patience, which she pushed and tested every step of the way during the writing process. She would also like to credit her family – especially her parents, Jacqueline and Paul, who freely offered their time, reading sections of the book and entertaining their grandson whilst the writing process was under way. There are many people who offered support, laughs and understanding, and without them this book would not have been possible – namely, Alison, Carole, Fiona, Gemma, Melanie, Michael, Shona, Tilly and all of the little crazies (Simon, Daniel, Juniper and Abel) who allow her to embarrass them as much as she does her own son. Mostly she pays homage to her son, Billy, who makes her proud and makes her laugh in equal measures. All of this is for him.

Dennis would like to thank Ann for continuing to share her intelligence and understanding of the complex issues discussed in the book, and for the clarity of her writing. Her determined and practical approach to the needs and dynamics of writing under pressure have been admirable.

The authors and publishers are grateful to all who gave permission to reproduce copyright material. While every attempt has been made to acknowledge all the sources we have drawn upon, we would like to apologize if any omissions have been made and would invite any such copyright holders to contact Polity Press, so that these may be rectified in future editions.

Foreword: What is Theology?

Theology is an ancient subject, the name coming from two Greek words – *theos* (God) and *logos* (speech/thought), so theology is 'thinking about God'. The word is most often heard in discussion within monotheistic religions, but, more recently, can also relate to Hindu, Sikh and even some forms of Buddhist contexts too.

Your study of Developments in Christian Thought is essentially an introduction to Christian theology, as you will be discussing some of the main thoughts about God that have engaged Christian theologians for the last 2,000 years.

The question of what 'theology' actually is may not be as simple to answer as you might think. This is because the subject has undergone a fundamental change during the last 100 years, from being a vocational subject to being an academic one. If you were studying theology 100 years ago, you would very probably have been:

(a) male
(b) Christian and
(c) training to be a priest/clergyman.

Given these prerequisites, then, you would already have known at least some of the subject matter of theology, from regular attendance at church services. Most obviously, you would have known the Bible, but also some of the major Christian beliefs that you would have learned in church services. You would have been 'doing theology from the inside', or, as St Anselm put it, theology was 'faith seeking understanding' (*fides quaerens intellectum*), i.e. instead of simply (blindly) accepting what the Bible or priest said, some people wished to have a deeper understanding of God. They would have used reason and logic to attain this.

This deeper understanding came from studying the Bible in its original languages – Hebrew for the Old Testament, Greek for the New Testament. Theology students would study the biblical documents in the philosophical, social and historical contexts from which they developed, and reflect on the impact these had on early Christianity. They would study Christian doctrines, like the Trinity, or salvation (soteriology), and ponder the impact these have made on Christian communities over time, up to the present day.

Today, Theology is a popular subject of study at university. Most universities will offer courses in Theology, or Religious Studies or Divinity. Some students of Theology will be Christian, but many are not, and this is one of the major differences from 100 years ago, with another positive change being that women may study at this level. Non-religious theologians will be fascinated by the subject matter, having been well taught at school, or by seeing and hearing about religion in the media – for good reasons or bad – and want to know more.

As you work through this book, you will be challenged to think hard about difficult ideas. We hope, however, that by the end of your study of theology, you will have enjoyed the journey as far as we have taken it here. Perhaps you will decide that you want to continue the journey at university, where you will discover further areas of study, and new aspects of the areas you will cover in this book. Whatever choices you make, we hope that you will enjoy the subject matter of theology and find it engaging, challenging and worthwhile. Good luck!

Introductions to Theology
David F. Ford, *Theology: A Very Short Introduction* (Oxford University Press, 2013)
Alister E. McGrath, *Theology: The Basics*, 4th edn (Wiley-Blackwell, 2017)
Alister E. McGrath, *Theology: The Basic Readings*, 3rd edn (Wiley-Blackwell, 2018)

General Books on Theology / Christian Thought
Steven D. Cone, *Theology from the Great Tradition* (Bloomsbury T&T Clark, 2018)
Millard J. Erickson, *Christian Theology*, 3rd edn (Baker Academic, 2013)
Colin E. Gunton (ed.), *The Cambridge Companion to Christian Doctrine* (Cambridge University Press, 1997)
Mike Higton, *Christian Doctrine* (SCM Press, 2008)
Jonathan Hill, *The History of Christian Thought* (Lion Publishing, 2003)
Alister E. McGrath, *Christian Theology: An Introduction*, 6th edn (Wiley-Blackwell, 2016)
Daniel L. Migliore, *Faith Seeking Understanding: An Introduction to Christian Theology*, 3rd edition (Eerdmans, 2004)
Neil Ormerod, *Introducing Contemporary Theologies: The What and the Who of Theology Today* (Orbis, 1997)
Stephen Pattison, *The SCM Guide to Theological Reflection* (SCM Press, 2008)
Christopher Ben Simpson, *Modern Christian Theology* (Bloomsbury T&T Clark, 2016)
Anthony Towey, *An Introduction to Christian Theology*, 2nd edn (Bloomsbury T&T Clark, 2018)

The Structure of This Book
This book is split into six sections, which will help you to achieve a comprehensive knowledge and understanding of what Christian theology is about. Each section has two parts. You will find interconnections between topics in the different sections; this is deliberate, so that you will come to a deeper understanding of theological issues. You will be exploring what Christians believe and how those beliefs came into existence, how they developed over time and how they are discussed today.

SECTION I: HUMAN NATURE. This section begins with a study of a pivotal figure in early Christianity, St Augustine, and his views on what human nature actually is and the relationship of humans with God. The second part of this section looks at different

Christian interpretations of another important aspect of human nature, the belief in an afterlife.

SECTION II: FOUNDATIONS: THE KNOWLEDGE OF GOD. This section studies two paths that Christians believe lead to knowledge of God – one natural, one revealed. You will explore the relationship between faith and reason, and discuss how Christians understand the relationship they have with God. This leads to an in-depth investigation of the person of Jesus Christ and his authority.

SECTION III: LIVING. In this section, you will explore two major aspects of how Christians put their beliefs into practice. First, you will study Christian moral principles – where they come from and whether they are unique. The second part of this section focuses on Christian Moral Action, with a study of a significant twentieth-century theologian, Dietrich Bonhoeffer, who taught about the relationship between the Church and the State. You will learn how his principles and actions led to his death.

SECTION IV: PLURALISM. In this section, you will be studying two aspects of how present-day Christianity interacts with other cultures and religions. First, you will discuss whether Christianity has an exclusive relationship with God. Second, you will explore whether other religions can also claim to know God, or whether there are many paths to achieving knowledge of God.

SECTION V: SOCIETY. In this section, you will be studying the effects of changing views of gender and gender roles in Christian thought and practice. This will include both Christian and secular views of the roles of men and women in the family and in society. The second part of this section investigates how feminist theologians have reinterpreted the nature of God and why this is important for 21st-century Christians.

SECTION VI: CHALLENGES. In the first part of this section, you will investigate some of the most important challenges to Christian belief today, specifically those from secularism, including the views of Sigmund Freud (God is an illusion) and Richard Dawkins (Christianity should play no part in public life), and responses to these views. The second part of this section studies the debate between Christianity, in the form of Liberation Theology, and the political ideology of Marxism.

Scholars' Timeline

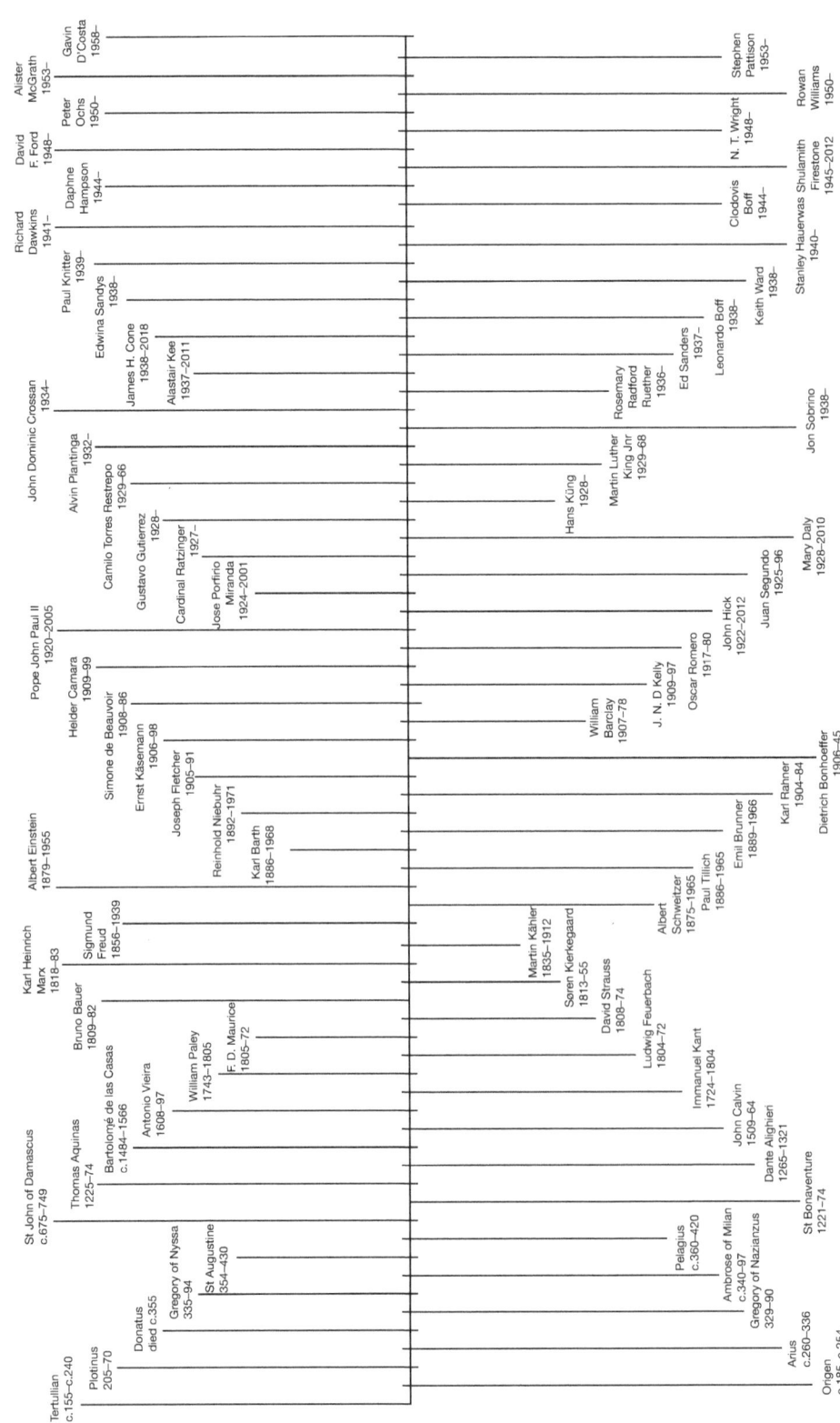

SECTION I
HUMAN NATURE

CHAPTER 1
Augustine's Teaching on Human Nature

The Fall: The account in Gen. 3 where Adam and Eve disobey God and are expelled from the Garden of Eden

LEARNING OUTCOMES

In this chapter, you will be learning about Augustine's teaching on human nature

- human relationships pre- and post-Fall
  - Augustine's interpretation of Genesis 3 (the **Fall**), including:
    - the state of perfection before the Fall, and Adam and Eve's relationship as friends
    - lust and selfish desires after the Fall
- Original Sin and its effects on the will and human societies
  - Augustine's teaching that Original Sin is passed on through sexual intercourse and is the cause of:
    - human selfishness and lack of free will
    - lack of stability, and corruption, in all human societies
- God's grace
  - Augustine's teaching that only God's grace, his generous love, can overcome sin and the rebellious will, to achieve the greatest good (*summum bonum*)

4 HUMAN NATURE

St Augustine of Hippo (354–430) Augustine was born in Thagaste in Roman North Africa (modern Algeria) at a time when the Romans were having difficulty in controlling dissident groups who were invading some North African provinces. He was educated at Carthage and Milan, and was a Manichaean for several years before becoming a Christian at age 33. He was influenced by Platonism and this comes across in many of his writings. In his famous *Confessions*, he writes with candour and insight about how he lived with an unnamed woman, with whom he had a son, Adeodatus. Augustine understood God to be the source of all goodness and no evil, but that human nature, like the natural world, had a tendency to fall away from its creator. He saw human nature to be corrupt and needing God's grace and forgiveness to be saved. Augustine was made priest, then Bishop, at Hippo, and wrote a wide range of books and commentaries. He came into conflict with heretical groups such as the Pelagians and Donatists. His writings have had a major impact on the development of Christian thought.

Introduction

Are human beings naturally positive and good, or are they negative and evil by nature? This question is the subject of this chapter and St Augustine is one of the most important Christian philosophers who have not only studied it but built the foundations of how human nature has been understood ever since. Before we discuss what

Exercise

Look at the following examples and discuss what they have to say about human nature.

- In May 2017, Islamist suicide bomber Salman Abedi detonated a home-made bomb, filled with nuts and bolts, in the foyer of the Manchester Arena at the end of an Ariana Grande concert, where most of the attendees were children. The bomb killed 23 people (including the bomber), 10 of whom were under 20, with the youngest aged 8. Of those injured, 112 were treated in hospital, several for life-changing injuries.
- In October 2017, it was widely reported in Britain that two young women verbally abused a homeless man, then urinated on his sleeping bag before setting fire to his few possessions, all of which were destroyed.
- Also in October 2017, American multi-millionaire property developer Stephen Paddock shot dead 59 people and wounded more than 500 at a Las Vegas country music festival. Around 40 different guns were found in his hotel room.
- In 2013, English 6-year-old Emmileah Anderson discovered that some children do not receive any Christmas presents. She wrote to Father Christmas saying that he should give her presents to these children. She then completed a fund-raising walk and raised £300 for a local hospice.
- In London in 2015, a cyclist was trapped under the wheel of a bus and would have died before the emergency services arrived, had it not been for the 100-strong crowd who lifted the bus so that the cyclist could be freed. The man made a full recovery after hospital treatment.
- Jon Meis, a student at Seattle Pacific University in 2014, observed a gunman shooting at other students, killing 1 and wounding 2 others. While the gunman was reloading his weapon, Meis used pepper spray to disable the gunman and tackled him to the ground. Police arrived and arrested the gunman. Meis, a Christian, who was hailed as a hero, asked that the donations of money that were made to him should be given to the victims.

Augustine's Teaching on Human Nature — 5

Augustine had to say, however, it will be useful to think briefly about some examples of human behaviour and what they may have to say about human nature.

As you will have noticed, the first three of these examples show that some human beings can be extremely evil, while the other three show that individuals or groups can be extremely unselfish and kind, even to the point of putting their own lives at risk. In the twenty-first century, psychologists attempt to unravel the intentions and motivations of such people to ascertain why they do the things they do. In the fifth century, St Augustine attempted to find out whether humans are essentially good or evil by using the means at his disposal. Before we delve into Augustine's thoughts on human nature, however, it is very important to know something about his background and formative experiences, as these had a deep impact on his beliefs concerning human nature.

> **Exercise**
> How would you define human nature?

Who was Augustine?

The Conversion of St Augustine, by Fra Angelico

6 HUMAN NATURE

His life

It is important to know about Augustine's life, as it shaped his thought and teaching. Augustine (Aurelius Augustinus) was born in the North African town of Thagaste on 13 November 354, and died in Hippo on 28 August 430. Thagaste, now called Souk Ahras, in Algeria, was an old Roman–Berber city sited 60 miles from the Mediterranean coast. It had been Christianized for at least half a century when Augustine was born. Although his mother Monica was uneducated, she was a devout Christian, while his father Patrick was not. He held minor public office and had responsibility for tax-collecting. Monica was to play a major part in Augustine's life and he mentions her often, but he rarely mentions his father.

Augustine did not like his school in Thagaste and used to play truant so he could watch games such as bear-baiting. When he was 17, however, a rich neighbour enabled him to go to university in Carthage. Here he studied rhetoric – the art of writing and speaking correctly in eloquent Latin, using as his model much of the greatest literature of his day. Mastering this subject was essential for anyone hoping to join the governing ranks of society. Augustine excelled at rhetoric and became a professor at Carthage, then Rome, and finally Milan. Milan was the seat of government for Italy and Africa at the time, so Augustine came into contact with some of the most influential and important families. He did not, though, pursue these contacts but instead became involved with a pseudo-Christian sect called Manichaeism.

Manichaeism

Manichaeism had been founded by Mani, who was born in 216 CE in Mesopotamia (modern Iraq). He was brought up in the Jewish-Christian Gnostic sect known as the Elkesaites. Mani believed that the teaching of Jesus was incomplete but that the teaching of St Paul contained much truth. Augustine may have become interested in this group because of their views on sexual abstinence. Most Manichees took a vow of sexual renunciation, which was unique to this group, as Christians did not practise monasticism at this time in North Africa. The Manichees, however, had a kind of associate membership called 'hearers' that allowed followers to continue with their careers and have mistresses. Augustine had had a mistress since the age of 16, despite the reservations of his mother Monica. Augustine may also have admired Mani's teaching that the Old Testament could not really be considered part of God's revelation, as its picture of God as a primitive, vengeful and cruel leader did not compare with the God of Love revealed in the New Testament (NT).

The Manichees believed that the universe was dualistic – there was a cosmic battle between good and evil, and individuals were made up of two opposing souls: one good, the other evil. This explained why people committed wrong actions some of the time and good ones at other times. Manichees taught that the higher human soul becomes trapped in the world of darkness because of the failings of the material body. The aim of following Manichaeism is to liberate the higher soul and allow it to reach the world of light. This can be achieved by strict abstinence from all the evil temptations, including lust, wealth, gluttony, wine and meat.

Platonism

Augustine remained a Manichaean 'hearer' for nine years before leaving the group. After his initial enthusiasm, he gradually became disillusioned with the Manichees' beliefs. He moved, first to Rome, then to Milan in 384 to teach rhetoric, where he got to know a number of intellectuals who lived according to a sophisticated form of Christianity that combined membership of the Church with a non-literal interpretation of the Bible. This suited him very well because he had become dissatisfied with the literal interpretation practised by the Manichees. The Milan group interpreted the Old Testament myths in the light of Platonist philosophy, particularly the version promulgated by **Plotinus** (205–70 CE).

> **Plotinus (205–270 CE)** Plotinus was an Egyptian mystical philosopher, who reworked Plato's philosophy in his *Enneads*. Augustine was deeply influenced by Plotinus' approach.

Plotinus was born in Egypt and educated in the Greek tradition, and finally settled in Rome. He spent much of his life reworking the philosophy of Plato (for Plato's philosophy, see Brown and Greggs, *Philosophy of Religion for OCR*, Polity, 2018, pp. 9–23), though he was also influenced by Aristotle and the Roman Stoics. His philosophical ideas are contained in the six books of his *Enneads*. Plotinus' views contain mystical ideas and practical philosophy, and Augustine was deeply influenced by this approach.

The aim of Plotinus' ideas was to assist a student to return to 'the One' or the ultimate Being. For Plotinus, there was a tripartite divinity – the One, the Intellect, and the **Soul**. Superficially, these might appear to be analogous to the Christian Trinity (Father, Son and Holy Spirit), but, while Christians understood the Trinity as co-equal, Plotinus understood the Soul, the Intellect and the One as successive stages of being. The One cannot be fully described or understood because human language is inadequate for the purpose. Knowledge of the One may only be achieved through the Soul and the Intellect. All three aspects are logical progressions.

After discussions with a group of Platonists, Augustine became very interested in their ideas. He read Plotinus' writings and was struck by his notion that there was only the Form of the Good, rather than Plato's whole realm of the Forms (see *ibid.*, pp. 9–13). Augustine also liked Plotinus' doctrine that **knowledge** of the One could only be achieved by contemplation and self-reflection, in addition to intellectual study. Augustine, however, found a problem with this, as most people would find it impossible. People live in the material world with all its stresses and

> **Soul:** For Christians, this is the immaterial, spiritual part of a human being, which is potentially eternal

> **Knowledge:** There are two kinds of knowledge - natural and revealed

The One
The Intellect
The Soul

Plotinus' hierarchical understanding of the relationship between Soul, Intellect and the One

8 HUMAN NATURE

difficulties, and these hindrances would result in the soul becoming separate and much less important for them.

Augustine's view of the relationship of the soul to the material body is heavily influenced by Platonic philosophy. In his early writings, Augustine taught that the soul could find happiness on its own. Platonism also helped Augustine in presenting a solution to the Problem of Evil (see *ibid.*, pp. 120–4). Augustine argued that evil was not a thing in itself (the Manichees had believed that it was), but was instead the privation or absence of goodness. Ultimately, however, Augustine was not convinced of the lasting value of Platonism. It may have been intellectually stimulating for him, but it lacked emotional and spiritual fulfilment. It was at this point that Augustine met Bishop **Ambrose of Milan**, a meeting that would lead to Augustine's 'conversion' to mainstream Christianity.

> **Ambrose of Milan (c.340–397)** Ambrose was born into a well-off family and studied law and literature in Rome, before becoming the Governor of Aemelia-Liguria in northern Italy. In 374, he was made Bishop of Milan, before he had been baptized. He was popular as a bishop, but was also a scholar. He wrote several theological works, and had a fundamental influence on Augustine, who travelled to study with Ambrose. It is widely accepted that Ambrose baptized Augustine.

Influence of Ambrose and conversion

Augustine continued to study the Bible during the period when he was interested in Platonism, and continued to consider himself a Christian. The Manichees, too, were seen by Augustine as practising a form of Christianity. While he was teaching rhetoric at Milan, he became acquainted with the city's Bishop, Ambrose. Ambrose had been elected as Bishop of Milan in 374, even though he was not baptized at the time. He was an outstanding preacher and staunch opponent of heretical ideas. Ambrose convinced Augustine that mainstream Christian doctrines were correct and that the Old Testament was important for Christians because of its symbolic meaning. This was a revelation for Augustine and, as he recounts later in his *Confessions* (book 8, ch. 12), after hearing the voice of a boy or girl (he could not decide which it was) repeating the words 'Tolle, Lege' (take up and read) over and over, Augustine seized his copy of the Bible and read, in the first passage he saw (Romans 13:13–14), St Paul's statement: 'Not in riot and drunken parties, not in eroticism and indecencies, not in strife and rivalry, but put on the Lord Jesus Christ and make no provision for the flesh in its lusts.'

Augustine took this as a divine message: 'At once, with the last words of this sentence, it was as if a light of relief from all anxiety flooded into my heart. All shadows of doubt were dispelled' (St Augustine, *Confessions*, p. 153).

This conversion experience was the final piece of the puzzle for Augustine: that true **wisdom** does not come from intellectual pursuit of Platonism, but requires God's

Wisdom: From the Greek word *sophos*, refers to knowledge that comes separately from sense experience and fosters an understanding of one's place in society and how a person should live their life.

grace as revealed in Jesus Christ. Augustine, along with his son Adeodatus, was baptized by Ambrose in 387. He remained in Milan until the death of his mother Monica, and his son two years later, before returning to Thagaste in order to concentrate on the spiritual life.

Augustine joined a monastic community in Thagaste so that he could devote himself to the pursuit of Christian philosophy. In this, he could use the concepts of great philosophers such as Plato and Cicero to draw out the Christian idea of human nature as created to establish union with God. This quest was to occupy Augustine for the rest of his life.

Augustine was ordained a priest in 391, and Bishop of Hippo in 396, when he was 41 years old. He remained there until his death in 430.

Augustine's time as Bishop was dominated by two important theological controversies, concerning **Donatism** and **Pelagianism**. The latter was more important and draining for Augustine, and caused him to change some of his own theological views.

> **Donatism:** A movement declared as a heresy

> **Pelagianism:** The view of a British theologian who argued that Original Sin did not ruin human nature, and that humans are still able to choose freely to do good or evil

Controversy with Donatism

Donatism is named after the fourth-century Bishop of Carthage in North Africa, **Donatus Magnus** (died c.355). In the third century, Christians in North Africa had been persecuted on the orders of the emperor, Diocletian. Many believers, including clergy, were killed. Some Christians were spared death if they renounced their membership of the Church. If they had Christian texts that they surrendered to be burned, they were allowed to live. If not, they were killed. Many Christians, including priests, surrendered their texts. After the persecution ended, the Christian Emperor, Constantine, declared that all Christians would be allowed to worship freely, and those who had left the religion because of the persecution were taken back into the Church, including many priests. This decision caused a lot of argument among the North African Christian communities and Donatus Magnus became the spokesman for some of them, and his movement became known as Donatism.

Donatus declared that lapsed clergy should not be allowed back into the Church because they had broken their vows. The Donatists argued that priests must be without fault, because part of their role was to administer the Sacrament and to pray for their congregations.

Augustine campaigned for many years against the Donatists in his position as Bishop of Hippo, and finally won the battle against them, at least temporarily. He consistently argued that it was the office held by a priest, which was guaranteed by Christ, rather than the particular holiness of the individual priest, which could not be guaranteed, that made the Sacrament and the priest's prayers legitimate. After Augustine's death, however, the Donatists became increasingly separate from mainstream Christianity and finally disappeared after the Muslim conquest of North Africa in the seventh century.

Controversy with the Pelagians

Augustine's conflict with the Pelagians, from 411 onwards, was much more serious, and caused him to change some of his theological views. **Pelagius** (c.360–c.420) was a 'British' monk, an ascetic who had lived in Rome and inspired a group of holy-minded lay-people who followed him. Pelagius believed that God had equipped humans with potential (*posse*), volition (*velle*) and realization (*esse*). These attributes were the building blocks for humans to attain a saintly, or even a sinless, life. Pelagius and his followers believed that human nature was created by God and embedded in humans so that they could make their own moral decisions. The choices they made and the deeds they committed were for their own benefit, not primarily for God's. In Pelagius' words: 'In his willing, therefore, and doing a good work consists man's praise . . . Whenever we say a man can live without sin, we also give praise to God by our acknowledgement of the power we have received from him, who has bestowed such power to us' (J. Stevenson and W. H. C. Frend, *Creeds, Councils and Controversies: Documents Illustrating the History of the Church AD 337–461*, SPCK, 1989, pp. 232–3).

Psychologically, this may be seen as normal thinking for many people – that one's character is judged by the good actions one does. For example, a person might run a marathon to raise money for a charity or other good cause, and this might help friends to think that they are a 'good' person. The danger of this way of thinking, however, is that, if a person can gain merit by their own actions, what need is there for God? If the Pelagians were able to be so holy as to be sinless, did that mean that they were not tainted by Original Sin, which came from Adam and Eve in the Fall? If they were not in need of redemption, why would they need Christ?

Pelagius taught that:

- individual humans could achieve moral perfection in this life without any assistance from God.
- Adam's sin did not have a direct influence on humans coming after him. Instead, he was an example to humans. Humans are not sinful at birth: they make a choice either to do good or to do evil.
- newborn children do not have to be baptized.
- humans have free will and can choose to serve God, and live a virtuous life, as Jesus did, or they can choose freely to go against God, as Adam did.
- there is no **predestination**.
- there is no Original Sin.

These views were radical for Christians at the time, and were diametrically opposed to mainstream Christian views. As you will see in the following paragraph, Augustine argues forcefully that Pelagius was absolutely wrong in his teaching.

> **Predestination:** The idea that some people are chosen before their birth, by God, to be saved, and others not.

Augustine on Pelagius

According to the British theologian, Henry Chadwick, the dispute between Augustine and Pelagius developed only gradually. Chadwick argues that Augustine and Pelagius actually had more in common than might appear to be the case. They both believed that humans were born sinful. Where they differed was Pelagius' view that sin and evil were contingent, non-necessary facts, so humans could freely choose to live a holy life without sinning. Augustine strongly disagreed. He argued that Pelagius was wrong to say that sin and evil were only contingent (non-necessary) facts. Augustine's view was that, since the Fall, when Adam and Eve sinned against the will of God, all human nature is corrupt in its entirety, without exception. Further, he argued that Adam's sin is carried on through every generation. This is why, according to Augustine, all humans are born 'in sin' and this makes it impossible for them to make good, appropriate choices, and renders them incapable of following God's law. Redemption from their sins could only be brought about by the grace of God. In his argument with Pelagius, Augustine developed a hard-line view that was reminiscent of the Manichaean teaching that only a select few – **The Elect** – would be saved by God, not everyone.

> **The Elect**: In Augustine's view, the select few who would be saved by God

Frustratingly for Augustine, the Council of Diospolis in 415 upheld Pelagius' teachings as consistent with orthodox Christian views. Just three years later, however, in 418, at the Council of Carthage, Augustine's arguments persuaded the attending bishops to condemn Pelagius' teachings, and adopt Augustine's teaching on Original Sin and the need for God's grace for salvation. This condemnation of Pelagius was ratified, shortly after Augustine's death, at the Council of Ephesus in 431.

Augustine on human nature

Human relationships before and after the Fall

Augustine's writings on Genesis

Augustine's views on human nature begin with his study of the early chapters of Genesis. He believed that these chapters were absolutely central for Christians to understand God's will for human beings. Over a thirty-year period, he produced three separate and quite different commentaries on them, and a separate book focusing only on Genesis 1:

(i) *On Genesis: A refutation of the Manichees* (388–9). This is an allegorical interpretation, arguing against the Manichaean view of creation. He emphasizes the goodness of creation against the pessimistic Manichaean view of it.

(ii) *Unfinished literal commentary on Genesis* (393–5). He intended this to be a more straightforward interpretation of Genesis, for church members. It was left unfinished, probably because he worked on it while performing church duties in Hippo. He comments only on Genesis 1.

(iii) *Confessions, books 10–13* (c.397). Augustine was Bishop of Hippo by this stage, and produced a commentary on Genesis 1 only, incorporating both literal and allegorical elements. He discusses the themes of time, eternity, the work of God in Creation, and the days of Creation.

12 HUMAN NATURE

(iv) *The literal meaning of Genesis* (401–16). This was written during the period when Augustine was in conflict with the Donatists and Pelagians. His aim was to refute false views of Genesis and to uphold the 'proper literal meaning', unless to take it literally would be absurd.

Human will before the Fall

The traditional Christian view of the accounts of Creation in Genesis is that God deliberately planned and created the world and that humans have a unique place in it, being given a relationship with God, thus setting them apart from all other creatures. They are also given the special responsibility of ruling (exercising dominion) over the world and all the creatures in it. Gen. 1: 26–7 says:

> Then God said, 'Let us make humankind in our image, according to our likeness; and let them have dominion over the fish of the sea, and over the birds of the air, and over the cattle and over all the wild animals of the earth, and over every creeping thing that creeps upon the earth.' So God created humankind in his image, in the image of God he created them; male and female he created them.

Humans are given this unique position at the head of creation, but this role carries with it certain responsibilities – **stewardship**, abiding by God's rules, multiplying and living up to the privilege of being made in the image of God (***Imago Dei***). According to Augustine, this is the only time when the human body, will and reason are in complete harmony with each other. He thought that, at this time, humans lived together in loving friendship, in harmony with each other, other creatures and with God. In particular, he talks positively about the relationship between Adam and Eve. Eve's position in creation is secondary to that of Adam, but she is necessary to him for reproduction:

> If it were not the case that the woman was created to be Adam's helper, specifically for the production of children, then why would she have been created as a 'helper' (Gen. 2: 18)? If it is necessary for one of two people living together to rule and the other to obey so that an opposition of wills does not disturb their peaceful cohabitation, then nothing is missing from the order we see in Genesis directed to this restraint, for one person was created before, the other afterwards, and most significantly, the latter was created from the former, the woman from the man. I cannot think of any reason for woman's being made as man's helper, if we dismiss the reason of procreation.
> (Augustine, *The Literal Meaning of Genesis IX, 5*, in Elizabeth A. Clark, *Women in the Early Church*, Liturgical Press, 1983; rpt 2017, p. 12)

Stewardship: According to Augustine, God gives humans special responsibilities to look after the earth

Imago Dei: Latin for 'in the image of God'

Exercise

'I cannot think of any reason for woman's being made as man's helper, if we dismiss the reason of procreation.' Discuss this statement. What reasons might a fifth-century person give for agreeing or disagreeing with Augustine's statement?

Cupiditas: Latin word, used by Augustine, for self-love

Caritas: Latin word, used by Augustine, for generous love

Augustine talks of how the human will is heavily influenced by two concepts – ***cupiditas*** (love of self and selfish needs) and ***caritas*** (generous love of others). By *cupiditas*, Augustine meant having a selfish attitude, a love of possessions and things that a person desires for their own needs or wishes. A greedy, self-centred, lustful person is consumed by *cupiditas*. *Caritas*, on the other hand, says Augustine, is to live according to Jesus' example of **agape**, which is the concept that differentiates Christians from other people: a selfless and generous love for the wellbeing and good of others. He quotes Paul's statement in 2 Cor. 13:11: 'Mend your ways; take our appeal to heart; agree with one another; live in peace; and the God of love and peace will be with you.'

> **Agape:**
> Jesus taught that selfless love was the highest form of love

Both of these are necessary ideas to understand his thinking on the human will. He says that, for genuine love to exist between two people, each must first love themselves in order to love anyone else. When this happens, it leads to the love of God.

Augustine talks extensively about the importance of friendship in his own life. In the *City of God* (XIX,19), he warned his fellow monks that they should not be so devoted to prayer and study that they forgot the needs of their brothers. His vision of the monastic community was not one of asceticism and solitary meditation, but of a community of like-minded men who together searched for God. It is in this monastic context that Augustine felt that true friendships could be forged and maintained. He believed that friendships could help individuals to become better Christians. Friends can help each other learn about God, and each individual's relationship with God, in a way that engaging in a solitary search for God could not achieve.

> **Exercise**
> How would you define 'friendship'? How might it differ from 'love'?

Human will after the Fall

Augustine's teaching on the Fall is based on and influenced by his reading of Genesis 1–3. He bases his ideas on the Fall by treating the texts both as literally (historically) true and also as having symbolic meaning. In his view of human nature, Augustine began with what human life must have been like before Adam and Eve's fall from God's grace. At this stage, he thought that Adam and Eve lived in the Garden of Eden in close touch with God. God had created a fertile garden for Adam to work in and to enjoy its produce (2:16–17). God created Eve to be Adam's companion and they lived together in loving friendship, in harmony with the idyllic world of Eden. They enjoyed a sexual relationship, but this did not include any element of lust, because this was part of Eve's punishment after the expulsion from Eden (3: 16). Both Adam and Eve lived in the garden without clothes, perhaps a symbol of their innocence until they had to hide their nakedness from God with fig leaves.

The next element in the narrative is when Adam and Eve make a choice about knowing the difference between good and evil, when tempted by the serpent (Gen. 3: 1–7).

HUMAN NATURE

Original Sin

In his *City of God*, Augustine has a lengthy discussion of the Fall. His key question was to know why Adam and Eve broke away from their perfect relationship with God in the Garden of Eden. For Augustine, the reason was pride. Adam and Eve had been tempted by the serpent to eat the fruit of the tree of the knowledge of good and evil, and, having eaten it, they thought that they were equal with God, able to know (**Yada**) what only God knew, including the difference between good and evil. Their pride resulted in them becoming separated from the special harmonious relationship they had shared with God, and with each other. Their choice resulted in the first sin: Original Sin. Having committed this sin, they could not return to the perfect relationship with God. They condemned themselves to life – mortal life – outside the Garden of Eden. The consequences are spelled out in Genesis 3:14–19:

> And to the man he said, 'Because you have listened to the voice of your wife, and have eaten of the tree of which I commanded you, "You shall not eat of it", cursed is the ground because of you; in toil you shall eat of it all the days of your life; thorns and thistles it shall bring forth for you; and you shall eat the plants of the field. By the sweat of your face you shall eat bread until you shall return to the ground, for out of it you were taken; you are dust, and to dust you shall return.'

Augustine argued that all human beings were present in Adam's sin and therefore condemned by it. Because of Adam's sin, no human could be perfectly good. Augustine then argued that Adam is no longer able to control his libido and his bodily desires, particularly his lust for sexual intercourse. He calls this drive **concupiscence.** Augustine was careful to reject the Manichaean belief that the body is evil, and also the Neo-Platonist view that the body is imperfect. He says that the body cannot be evil because it was created by God, who is perfect, and everything created by God is good (Gen. 1: 31) Since the Fall, however, the human will is weak and allows concupiscence to dominate human life. This applies to all areas of daily human life, but especially to sexual intercourse. Adam and Eve chose the path of *cupiditas* – lust, selfishness and attachment to material possessions. Through sexual intercourse, and Adam's 'seed', every person is tainted with Original Sin and cannot live a morally pure life. Adam's Original Sin has corrupted the whole of humanity and no human is capable of getting out of their sin by their own efforts. Only God can save people by

Yada: A Hebrew word meaning 'able to know'

Concupiscence: Augustine's term for uncontrolled desires, including sexual lust

Adam and Eve are driven out of Paradise

Augustine's Teaching on Human Nature | 15

his grace through the salvation offered by Jesus Christ. Even those who live a religious life as a monk or nun (and therefore do not engage in sexual intercourse) are still tainted by Original Sin and cannot save themselves.

God's grace

> **Grace:** God's unconditional love and gifts to humanity. An important term for Augustine

Augustine, along with many other ancient theologians, was convinced that no human could ever be reconciled with God by their own efforts. Humans could not, on their own, choose how to help themselves. They could not even choose what was the right thing to do, never mind choosing to do it. For Augustine, the only way that the relationship between humans and God could be rectified was for God to take the initiative through his divine **grace**. Augustine said: 'This grace, which perfects strength in weakness, brings everyone who is predestined and called by God to supreme perfection and glory. This grace not only shows us what we ought to do, it makes us do it. It not only makes us believe what we ought to love, it makes us love it' (Augustine, *On the Grace of Christ*, 13).

Humans never deserved God's grace, but God was willing to offer it freely to any human who asked for it. The only way that this could happen was through the self-sacrifice of Jesus on the cross. By giving himself up to be killed, Jesus made himself a sacrificial offering for the sake of all humans. This was the only way that the price for the sin of Adam and Eve at the Fall could be paid.

Just as the power of Original Sin forces humans to do what is wrong, so the power of grace forces them to do what is right. Augustine taught that, after the Fall, the human soul became divided. Humans continued to know the difference between good and evil, but, because of their desires, often chose to do evil instead of good.

Augustine references Paul's teaching in Romans 7:14–20, where he refers to this state:

> We know that the law is spiritual; but I am not: I am unspiritual, sold as a slave to sin. I do not even acknowledge my own actions as mine, for what I do is not what I want to do, but what I detest. But if what I do is against my will, then clearly I agree with the law and hold it to be admirable. This means it is no longer I who am the agent, but sin that has its dwelling in me.

Key points in Augustine's doctrine of Grace

- GRACE
  - Attained only through Jesus' death
  - Overcomes human nature
  - Undeserved by humans
  - God's love and mercy

16 HUMAN NATURE

This idea goes back to an ancient Greek philosophical term used by Aristotle, ***akrasia*** (the weakness of will), though Augustine rejects Aristotle's interpretation of it. He also rejects Aristotle's use of the term ***sophrosyne***: the idea that humans can live well by using their self-control or by performing acts of charity.

For Augustine, grace was the gift of God to all humans who wished to accept it. His was a doctrine of **internal grace**, whereby God acts within the human will, forcing it to do what is good and avoid doing what is evil. This is the opposite of what Pelagius had taught – **external grace**, whereby God provides humans with the means to do what is right but leaves them to make the decision themselves.

Augustine taught that grace is the only means by which humans may be saved from eternal damnation and punishment because of their sinful nature. Salvation cannot be earned.

> **Akrasia**: Aristotle's word for weakness of the will, related to the moral life

> **Sophrosyne**: Aristotle's word for showing self-control, moderation and a deep sense of one's self, resulting in true happiness

Interpreting Augustine today

Introduction

The influence exercised by the life of St Augustine has been immense throughout the Western Church in the last 1,500 years. His doctrines of the Fall, of Sin and of Grace were unquestioned. Medieval theologians gave him the title 'The Doctor of Grace'. Most medieval thinkers, including **Thomas Aquinas** (1225–74), considered themselves to be Augustine's disciples. In some of the arguments between Protestants and Roman Catholics in the Reformation period, both sides appealed to Augustine's writings and judgements to support their views on contentious issues such as grace. On the other hand, as British theologian Jonathan Hill explains:

> Augustine came under heavy fire from the Orthodox Church, who disagreed with most of his characteristic doctrines – above all his doctrine of the Trinity. To this day, the Western belief that the Spirit proceeds from the Son as well as from the Father is a major barrier to ecumenical dialogue between East and West. Moreover, many Protestant theologians themselves deplore the hold that Augustine has exercised over their history, lambasting him for his pernicious views on sin, damnation and sex.
>
> (*The History of Christian Thought*, p. 88)

> **Internal grace**: Augustine's view that God works within the human soul, forcing it to do good and avoid evil

> **External grace**: Pelagius' idea that God provides the means to do what is right, but leaves people to make decisions themselves

The Fall and Original Sin

A key question for modern readers of Augustine – and, more generally, for Christian believers – is whether his teachings on the Fall and on Original Sin make sense in the twenty-first century. Many of his ideas on these issues come from his reading of chapters 1–3 of Genesis. Augustine read these chapters literally, as historical narratives, for the most part. In the intervening 1,500 years, however, most scholars and very many believers understand them in a very different way – as mythological accounts of how an ancient people struggled to understand the reason for their existence, to express their belief in God who created their world, and their belief that they had a relationship with that God. The majority of Christian believers do not think Genesis 1–3 are historical documents. For these believers, Adam and Eve are not historical figures and the Fall was not a historical event.

Augustine's Teaching on Human Nature

> **Exercise**
>
> Archbishop James Ussher (1581–1656) used all the dates in the Bible to calculate the age of the universe from its creation by God. In his book *The Annals of the World*, published in 1658 after his death, he worked out that the earth was created on 22 October 4004 BCE. Interestingly, this date was also calculated by Dr John Lightfoot (1602–75) some years earlier, in 1644. Lightfoot added that Creation occurred at 9.00 a.m.
>
> Find out more about Ussher and Lightfoot, particularly how they arrived at their conclusions about the date of the earth. Make a list of any difficulties their approach might raise for 21st-century readers. Discuss with your classmates.

Many Christians now believe that the authors/editors of Genesis have combined two different origin stories, one in 1:1–2:4a and the second in 2:4b–3:24. The first account emphasizes the order and regularity with which God created the universe. Everything that exists came into being as a direct result of the words and acts of God. The second account changes the order of creation, with man appearing first, then plants and animals, and woman appearing later. Man and woman are servants of God, whereas in the first story they are created together and raised to the dignity of God's agents in Creation.

There are several points of connection between the two stories.

> **Transcendence:** The idea that God is not part of the world and is independent from it

- In both, wholeness is a key aspect: in the first, God rests when Creation is complete; in the second, the creation of woman brings completion to God's work. It is particularly significant that humans are created 'in the image' of God, which gives humans immense value and dignity.
- Both stories reflect a monotheistic theology; one shows God's **transcendence**, the other his **immanence**.

> **Immanence:** The idea that God is present in the world and can interact with it and with humans

English theologian **Keith Ward** (1938–present) thinks that the two Creation accounts come from different tribal stories that have been placed side by side by the editor of Genesis. They express different and important symbolic truths. According to Ward, the editor was not worried about the fact that, if taken literally, they are incompatible. This is not a problem because different stories can depict different theological truths. Like metaphors, they cannot contradict each other – only literal accounts can be contradictory – but they can complement each other. The two Genesis origin stories offer important complementary truths and the editor did not wish to lose any of these truths, so included them both.

Ward, *Religion and Creation* (pp. 288–93), also points out several theological themes in each of the Creation accounts, which may be helpful to Christians now in trying to understand how Genesis 1–3 can be meaningful to them even though the texts are not historically true.

In the first account (which is highly structured, beginning from nothing up to the high point of the creation of humans):

- God creates a perfect world that has order and purpose – God is omniscient.
- God creates the world from nothing (*ex nihilo*) – God is creative and powerful.

18 HUMAN NATURE

- Humans are given the highest place in creation, as they are created last – God wishes to have a special relationship with humans.
- God rested on the seventh day – Christians (following Judaism) take this to mean that the Sabbath, God's holy day, is grounded in the act of Creation.

In the second account (which has a very different structure, telling the story of Adam who needs a companion, and the creation of a human community):

- Humans are created from the 'dust of the earth', enlivened by the 'breath of life'. Their lives depend entirely on God, who gives life and takes it away.
- The proper home for humans is a garden, a place of life and joy (Eden), in which all creatures can flourish in total dependence on God. At its centre is the tree of life.
- Humans are given the responsibility of looking after the garden. The other significant tree in the garden is the 'tree of the knowledge of good and evil'. When the serpent persuades Adam and Eve to eat the fruit of this tree, they became knowledgeable but sinful, and therefore had to leave paradise. Humans brought sin upon themselves and they lost the sense of the presence of God.
- God made the man a 'helper and partner'. This means that to be a human person is to be in a community. Adam gave names to all the animals, but a full moral and responsible relationship can only be between humans. With the creation of Eve, a special relationship is established between men and women so that they may live together in the deepest form of union.

Augustine and modern science

(i) Augustine understood the Fall to be the result of human disobedience in God's perfect world, (mis)using their free will. This view, however, depends upon a literal reading of the Creation stories, which, as we have seen above, is not tenable in the twenty-first century, given a scientific understanding of the world. While Christian Fundamentalists may attempt to read the Bible as the 'literal word of God', they must turn to a symbolic understanding of certain passages. For instance, in Judges 10:1–15, it is reported that God enabled Joshua to win a battle by making the sun stand still. No scientist will support the assertion that this could happen, so a nuanced view must be taken. English philosopher **John Hick** (1922–2012) argued that Augustine's view of the Fall is

---

John Hick (1922–2012) John Hick was an important English philosopher of religion and theologian, who was, for many years, Professor of Philosophy at Birmingham University. He is known particularly for his advocacy for religious pluralism (see chapter 8). He participated in several **multi-faith** groups and wrote several books on this, most notably *God and the Universe of Faiths* (1973). He edited and contributed to the controversial book *The Myth of God Incarnate* (1977) that raised many protests from evangelical Christians. His overarching project was to develop a global theology that would aid understanding between believers in the major world religions.

Multi-faith: A society in which members of different religious faiths live

Augustine's Teaching on Human Nature

implausible for people now because it depends on a literal view of the Bible, and on the existence of angels and demons, for which there is no plausible scientific evidence (Hick, *Evil and the God of Love*, Macmillan, 1966, pp. 169ff.).

(ii) Augustine's assertion that the world was created perfect and then became imperfect because of human sin may be convincingly refuted by both geological and biological findings. Evolutionary biology, as developed by Charles Darwin and others, states that human beings evolved from simpler creatures that did not have the kind of consciousness that would enable them to make sophisticated choices about rebelling from God. This means that a literal understanding of the story of the Fall would make no sense. Evolutionary biologist and prominent atheist **Richard Dawkins** (1941–present) has many times repeated that the Jewish/Christian idea of the Fall is absurd because it lacks any kind of scientific evidence. (See, for example, *The God Delusion*, 10th Anniversary edn, Black Swan, 2016.) Geological discoveries show that the physical world developed slowly over millennia, so that the idea in the Creation narrative that God created the world in six days (Genesis 1) has no physical foundation.

(iii) The existence of human evil in the world is undeniable. Evil may be attributed to humans when men and women commit atrocities against each other. Augustine explained that God created humans morally good, but also with free will. If free will is to be a meaningful concept, it must be truly free, i.e. not controlled by God. If God had created humans who always chose to do good, this would not be genuine free will. Humans must be capable of making the 'wrong' choice. For Augustine, 'evil' is not a thing or substance, so God did not create it; evil occurs when something goes wrong with something good. He uses the example of blindness: this happens when the eye stops working properly, where there is an absence of sight. He uses the word 'privation' to describe this state (a privation is an absence or lack of that thing). So, evil is an absence of good. The blind eye is failing to perform its correct function of seeing. Blindness is not an evil in itself; it is simply the absence of sight. For Augustine, evil is a falling short of the goodness of God and of God's intentions for humans. Augustine says, in the *Enchiridion*:

> What, after all, is what we call evil except the privation of good? In animal bodies, for instance, sickness and wounds are nothing but the privation of health. When a cure is effected, the evils that were present (i.e. the sickness and the wounds) do not retreat and go elsewhere. Rather, they simply do not exist any more. As God made only things that exist, and because 'evil' is not an existing thing, so God cannot be responsible for any evil or suffering in the world.
>
> (Augustine, *Enchiridion*, 11)

HUMAN NATURE

FURTHER READING

St Augustine, *Confessions: A New Translation by Henry Chadwick*. Oxford World's Classics. Oxford University Press, 2008

Kenneth Boa, *Augustine to Freud: What Theologians and Psychologists Tell Us About Human Nature*. Broadman & Holman Publishers, 2004

Henry Chadwick, *Augustine: A Very Short Introduction*. Oxford University Press, 2001

Jonathan Hill, *The History of Christian Thought*. Lion Publishing, 2003

Miles Hollingworth, *Saint Augustine of Hippo: An Intellectual Biography*. Bloomsbury, 2013

Judith Chelius Stark (ed.), *Feminist Interpretations of Augustine*. Penn State Press, 2007

Keith Ward, *Religion and Creation*. Oxford University Press, 1996

Thought Points

1. To what extent did Augustine's life experiences shape his views on human nature?

2. Do you agree that Augustine's view of human nature was pessimistic?

3. Do you think that there is a 'human nature'? If so, how would you define it? If not, why not?

4. Does any person have 'free will'? Does God have 'free will'?

5. List the strengths and weaknesses of Augustine's teaching on the Fall, then discuss your findings with your fellow students.

6. Read the following quote from Richard Dawkins, then give your assessment of it: 'What kind of ethical philosophy is it that it condemns every child even before it is born, to inherit the sin of a remote ancestor.... But now the sadomasochism. God incarnated himself as a man, Jesus, in order that he should be tortured and executed in atonement for the hereditary sin of Adam' (Dawkins, *The God Delusion*, p. 287).

7. 'Good and evil are present in both good and evil people' (**Reinhold Niebuhr**). Discuss.

CHAPTER 2

Death and the Afterlife

LEARNING OUTCOMES

In this chapter, you will be learning about different Christian interpretations and teachings on

- heaven, hell and purgatory
  - whether heaven, hell and purgatory are actual places, or spiritual states, or symbols of a person's spiritual or moral life on earth
- election
  - different Christian views on who will be saved
    - limited (only a few will be saved)
    - unlimited (all are called to salvation but not all will be saved)
    - universalist (all people will be saved)

Introduction

One of the most fundamental questions religions attempt to answer is 'What happens when we die?' When we lose somebody we love, then this question becomes especially poignant – is this the end or will we see them again? If so, in what form? Do we have any hope of an afterlife?

When the new United States Constitution was being established in 1789, President Benjamin Franklin is famously quoted as saying 'In this world, nothing can be said to be certain, except death and taxes.' So, for something that is so inevitable, the question of what happens after we die is one that is as yet unsolved. There are, however, a number of responses.

Many philosophers, including Socrates, Plato and the Stoics, offer to ease the 'sting' of death by reducing our attachment to life, by offering an eternal alternative, such as moral virtue or eternal perfection. The fear of death can have a negative effect on the living, in response to which Epicurus makes the following claim in his *Letter to Menoeceus*: 'Therefore, the most frightful of evils, death, is nothing to us, seeing that when we exist, death is not present, and when death is present, we do not exist. Thus

HUMAN NATURE

it is nothing either to the living or the dead, seeing that the former do not have it, and the latter no longer exist' (in Ben Bradley, Fred Feldman and Jens Johannson (eds.), *The Oxford Handbook of Philosophy of Death*, Oxford Handbooks, Oxford University Press, 2015, p. 207).

Epicurus offered this as a remedy to the fear of death – if death is 'nothing to us', then surely we should not fear it? However, this claim has been open to criticism, in that, although death in itself may be nothing to us, the anticipation of our own death (or that of those whom we love) is indeed important as it signifies the end of all we know. This uncertainty is the root of Christianity's attempt to answer the ultimate question of 'What happens when we die?'

Christianity teaches that humankind have souls which are capable of surviving bodily death. The belief is that, after death, people are resurrected and they continue on to a new and different dimension – some to spend eternity with God. These beliefs still raise some philosophical difficulties – what are 'heaven' and 'hell'? Indeed, with no empirical evidence, how can one prove they (or, indeed, the soul) exist? Although the Bible does provide teaching on life after death, this is open to interpretation and needs to be understood with reference to other Christian beliefs. For example, the notion of eternal reward and punishment could be seen to be incompatible with the concept of the God of classical theism (his **omnibenevolence**, **omnipotence**, **omniscience**). If God is indeed all-loving, then surely condemning his own creation to an eternity of suffering contradicts this theory? Equally, the question of omniscience needs careful consideration. If God truly is all-knowing, then He would know which of his creation would fall and which would be raised into an eternity with him. Would this render the notion of reward and punishment irrelevant, given that it could be argued that our lives are mapped out before we are born?

English philosopher John Hick developed Irenaeus' **theodicy** to argue in favour of universal salvation – whereby all people will achieve moral perfection upon death and all will enter the kingdom of heaven (Hick, *Evil and the God of Love*). Again, this raises the question of leading a good, Christian life. What would be the point in leading a good, prayerful life without sin when you would ultimately spend eternity after death in heaven regardless? These questions are addressed in many different ways by Christian thinkers and philosophers, and as a result there are diverse views and beliefs about life after death within the Christian tradition.

Omnibenevolence: God's central characteristic of being all-loving

Omnipotence: God's central characteristic of being all-powerful

Omniscience: God's central characteristic of being all-knowing

Theodicy:
A justification of the righteousness of God, given the existence of evil

Influences on Christian teaching on the afterlife

In the Old Testament, the theme of life after death was not a prominent subject. There is, for instance, nothing explicit about the afterlife in the **Torah**, the most important section of the Jewish Bible.

Torah: The first five books of the Old Testament

However, there are a few references to the possibility that death was not the end – for example, the death of Abraham: 'Then Abraham breathed his last and died at a good old age, an old man and full of years; and he was gathered to his people' (Genesis 25:8 – New International Version (NIV)).

Abraham accepting God's call

The question here is what 'gathered to his people' meant. Historically, at death, people were buried far away from their family base, so it could not be suggested that Abraham's body was returning to his homeland, Ur of the Chaldeans (Genesis 11:31). There is a distinct implication, however, that, after his death, Abraham would still exist in some recognizable form and return to a place where people would be familiar with him.

'Gathered to his people' is a phrase used repeatedly throughout the Old Testament – for instance:

- 'Isaac breathed his last and was gathered to his people, an old man of ripe age' (Genesis 35:29)
- 'When Jacob finished charging his sons, he drew his feet into the bed and breathed his last, and was gathered to his people' (Genesis 49:33)
- 'So Aaron will be gathered to his people, and will die there' (Numbers 20:26)
- 'Then die on the mountain where you ascend, and be gathered to your people, as Aaron your brother died on Mount Hor and was gathered to his people' (Deuteronomy 32:50)
- 'Therefore behold, I will gather you to your fathers, and you will be gathered to your grave in peace' (2 Kings 22:20)

So, although there is no direct reference to the afterlife, there are certainly suggestions throughout the Old Testament that death may not be the end and there could be a life beyond bodily death.

Exercise
Look carefully at the quotations above and decide whether you agree that these may provide evidence for a belief in life after death.

One other reference to life after death in the Old Testament is found in Daniel 12:2, which states 'Multitudes who sleep in the dust of the earth will awake: some to everlasting life, others to shame and everlasting contempt.' The book of Daniel was written to encourage Jewish people who had been or were being persecuted for their faith, so it could be suggested that the promise of eternal life would encourage them to continue with their faith. This was due to the fact that many who turned against Judaism and abandoned it often escaped persecution. For Jews at the time, it might be suggested that this encouraged their faith in God – for, although life might not be fair, it is short and they would be rewarded by eternal life without suffering, pain and contempt. This may also assist the justification of the God of Classical Theism – he can indeed be all-loving, as a physical life of pain and suffering is nothing compared to the eternal reward in heaven.

The Jewish population in pre-Christian Palestine (around the time of Jesus) were divided in their beliefs about life after death. As D'Souza states:

> The Jewish consensus about what happens after death emerged as a consequence of a debate between the Sadducees and the Pharisees. The Sadducees were biblical literalists who based their rejection of immortality on what is said, and not said, in the Torah. The Pharisees were intellectuals who made arguments that went beyond literal text. They insisted, for example, that since we are created in the image of God, we share in God's immortality. The debate lasted two centuries and was only settled in favor of the Pharisees around the first century BC. Now, according to historian Jacob Neusner, the belief in life after death is 'authoritative' in Judaism.
>
> (Dinesh D'Souza, *Life After Death: The Evidence*, p. 45)

Later in Judaism, the concept of life after death developed. They came to believe that the dead would be resurrected to begin a new kind of life, but only once the Messiah returned to liberate souls from death, at a time of God's choosing. This development in thought, alongside Ancient Greek influences (such as Plato's dualism) led to the beliefs that Christians hold about life after death today.

Resurrection

There is no belief in reincarnation in Christianity – Christians reject the thought that souls move from one body to another, and instead believe that the soul will be given a new physical body in which to continue to live after death. This is known as **resurrection** – a physical, embodied existence after death. Jesus had a bodily resurrection and spoke of a physical life after death in which there would be reward and punishment for deeds done. **The Book of Common Prayer** (Church of England) states 'I believe in the resurrection of the body ... and the life everlasting', thus rejecting Platonic ideas that the soul leaves the body and continues a disembodied existence in another realm.

The resurrection of Jesus offers some insight into these beliefs – the resurrection offered hope in a time of despair, in which Christians may still find comfort during the loss of a loved one: the hope that there is something beyond earthly existence and a chance that they will be reunited in heaven. The death of Jesus was also a

> **Resurrection:** Being brought back from death

> **Book of Common Prayer:** Church of England's collection of orders of service and prayers, first published in 1549

Death and the Afterlife

> **Epistemic distance**: The idea that there is a gap between God's knowledge and human knowledge

sacrifice for the sins of humankind – his punishment and death paid the price for all sinners and paved the way for the establishment of a new kingdom. Jesus had bridged the gap of sin between humans and God (**epistemic distance**) and humans no longer needed punishment – they could then repent, receive God's forgiveness and enter the **Kingdom of God** after death, their sins having been atoned for by Jesus.

The Gospels state that, after Jesus was crucified, his body was placed in a tomb and a huge stone rolled in front of the entrance. However, three days later, the stone had been moved and the tomb was empty – Jesus was then seen and heard by his followers as a man in a physical body. This is where the Christian belief in continued embodied existence stems from – the resurrection of Jesus shows Christians that they too will be resurrected.

> **Kingdom of God**: Jesus' teaching that people, following their repentance, would enter God's kingdom

In his letters to the Corinthians, written in the 50s CE, only about 20–25 years after the actual events, St Paul provides the first explanation of the importance of the resurrection. He writes about life after death using metaphors to explain his beliefs in the bodily resurrection.

(i) In 1 Corinthians, he compares life after death to a seed transforming into a plant – showing how the earthly body is like a seed which, upon death, will bloom into flower and fulfil its potential without the constraints of the grain (15:35–8).

(ii) In 2 Corinthians, he compares earthly and resurrection life to a tent being replaced by a solid house – showing that life in this world is temporary and will be replaced by solid foundations in the afterlife (5:1).

(iii) Also in 2 Corinthians, he compares being naked in this life to being clothed in the afterlife, showing that Christians will not need to feel ashamed or cover themselves up in the afterlife (5:3).

> ***Parousia***: The Christian belief that Jesus will return to earth to judge every human who has ever lived, selecting those who are worthy to live with God forever

Several passages in the NT imply that some early Christians thought that the 'new era' was imminent. ***Parousia*** is the Greek term that means 'being present' or 'arrival'. It is used in the NT for the return of Christ after his resurrection to place ultimate judgement on the world and select the worthy to live eternally in the 'new' world that would be restored by God. The fullest description of this 'new world' can be found in the book of Revelation:

> Then I saw a new heaven and a new earth; for the first heaven and the first earth had passed away, and the sea was no more. And I saw the holy city, the new Jerusalem, coming down out of heaven from God, prepared as a bride adorned for her husband. And I heard a loud voice from the throne saying, 'See, the home of God is among mortals. He will dwell with them; they will be his peoples, and God himself will be with them; He will wipe every tear from their eyes. Death shall be no more; Mourning and crying and pain will be no more, For the first things have passed away.'
>
> (Revelation 21:1–4)

The author depicts the *Parousia* as a state of sheer bliss – the end of all pain and suffering, and the beginning of a brand-new creation with God dwelling among his people.

Heaven

American nun Mother Mary Angelica (1923–2016) said the following about **heaven**:

> To most of us, heaven is rather abstract. It's a kind of fuzzy thing. Often in life, we look forward to events – graduations, doctorates, marriage, and so on. But when our anticipation is great, the event, when it occurs, seems to lose something. That's why, I believe, we don't like to talk about heaven. We are so afraid it won't be anything like what we are expecting, and so we begin to doubt.
> (Mother Angelica, *What is Heaven?* EWTN Publishing, 2019, p. 1)

> **Heaven:**
> In Christianity, the 'place' where those saved by God would reside for ever

St Paul said, 'No eye has seen, no ear has heard, no mind has conceived what God has prepared for those who love him' (1 Cor. 2:9). This shows that the eternal reward for those who love God and live a moral, just life is inconceivable to the human mind.

The NT speaks of heaven as being an eternal reward for leading a good, moral life and following the example of Jesus. If a person is to accept Jesus Christ as the **Son of God** and repent of their sins and wrongdoings, then their reward is in the afterlife. According to Paul, upon death a person's body will be transformed into a spiritual being, and it will move from the plane of physical existence to a spiritual realm. People will have a new life in a new kind of existence. After death, they will be who they are now, but transformed and renewed by an act of God. This transformation will restore not only the God–human relationship, but the relationship with the whole of creation. This will be a state in which humans come to see God 'face to face' – a place of pure knowledge where sin has been destroyed and the soul experiences joy in its purity.

> **Son of God:**
> One of the Christological titles for Jesus

Aquinas speaks of heaven as a '**Beatific Vision**', which he describes as a human's final end, a state in which a human being attains perfect happiness. This, he argues, can occur only when every desire has been satisfied and when it is not possible to be happier: 'Man is not perfectly happy, as long as something remains for him to desire and seek' (*Summa Theol.* 1–11, q3, a.8). For Aquinas, this will be the final and perfect state of everlasting happiness with God, achieved after death, in heaven. In *The Ethics of Aquinas*, Stephen J. Pope explains this:

> **Beatific Vision:**
> Aquinas' view of heaven as a place of perfect happiness

> The human intellect is orientated to sense understanding for its activities, so temporal happiness depends somewhat on the body and its organs. Naturally, this does not apply to the beatific vision, which excludes all sense mediation.
>   The essence of complete human happiness does not require the body . . . yet the integral, natural relationship between body and soul is not abolished; rather, it is completed by the beatific vision. The soul's desire thus rests completely only when this essential relationship is reestablished, and in this the body participates in its own way in the fullness of divine wealth.
> (Stephen J. Pope (ed.), *The Ethics of Aquinas*, Moral Traditions Series, Georgetown University Press, 2014, p. 64)

Exercise

Upon being asked what heaven would be like, an 8-year-old boy replied, 'Heaven would be being allowed to play Minecraft all day long.' This may differ from typical Christian beliefs about heaven. What would your ideal 'heaven' be, and why? Do all Christians have the same view of heaven?

What is suggested here is that, throughout life, our human intellect is wired to seek happiness and pleasure. Whatever happiness or pleasure we are able to find, however, is not enough and we still seek more. This can be on a small or large scale – for example:

(i)   I will be happy when I have received my provisional licence . . .
(ii)   I will be happy when I have passed my theory test . . .
(iii)   I will be happy when I have passed my practical test . . .
(iv)   I will be happy when I own my own car . . .
(v)   I will be happy when I can afford a better car . . .
(vi)   I will be happy when I get a job . . .
(vii) I will be happy when I have a house of my own . . .

According to Aquinas, the only time we can be truly fulfilled is at death, when we are at one with God. At that point, and that point alone, do we stop seeking happiness and fulfilment and can revel in what he calls 'divine wealth'.

Most Christians believe that life after death will involve some kind of judgement and that, after death, the faithful will go to heaven. As heaven is an abstract concept, metaphors and symbols are needed to enhance a Christian's understanding of heaven whilst still appreciating that the afterlife is a mystery. Biblically, God is referred to as the Father to whom the faithful will return upon death. Symbolically, this could imply that, upon death, individuals 'return home' to be with their Father. John (14:2) states 'My father's house has many rooms; if that were not so, I would have told you; I am going there to prepare a place for you.' This suggests that heaven is a homely, comfortable place. In Revelation (21:21), it is stated that the streets of the 'city' of heaven were made of gold, implying that there is more than enough wealth so there will be no-one who will have to go without.

These ideas of the perfection of heaven have raised significant issues with some philosophers. The moral philosopher Bernard Williams states:

> The Don Juan in hell joke, that heaven's prospects are tedious, and the devil has the best tunes, though a tired fancy in itself, at least serves to show up a real and (I suspect) a profound difficulty, of providing any model of an unending, supposedly satisfying, state or activity that would not rightly prove boring to anyone who remained conscious of himself and who had acquired a character, interests, tastes, and impatiences in the course of living, already, a finite life.
> (B. Williams, in John Martin Fischer (ed.), *The Metaphysics of Death*, Stanford University Press, 1993, p. 87)

Williams goes on to imply that, as long as a person has character, then, however amazing and pleasurable heaven was at the beginning, surely the repetitive nature and the lack of freedom of choice would soon become boring, unless God was to strip the character and essential nature from people (at which point, the want/need for an afterlife could arguably become redundant). He argues that life has meaning and purpose because of the limited time we have to achieve what we want to achieve – whether that be getting a degree, having children, travelling into space, or something else. Once we have achieved what we set out to, then we have a sense of pride and value. If it was just handed to us on a plate, we would eventually become bored and unappreciative.

Some respond to this objection with the argument that, given God is omnipotent, He would be able to produce a heaven in which this did not happen. Yet, would this not involve the sacrifice of our free will? And if the ultimate eschatological aim in life is to achieve eternity in heaven (with no free will to choose to do wrong / turn away from God), then that may beg the question as to whether God should have given humans free will at the moment of creation at all.

Hell

The book of Revelation (19:20; 20:10, 14, 15; 21:8) describes **hell** as being a 'burning lake of fiery sulphur'. Other passages in the NT (such as the tale of Lazarus and the Rich Man: Lk. 16:19–31) suggest that hell is a place of no escape. Traditional images of hell depict a pit of fiery misery from which there is no release. **Dante Alighieri** (1265–1321), in the *Inferno*, offers the following description, which he says may be found on the gates of hell:

> Thro' me the way into the realm of dole;
> Thro' me the way of endless anguish prove;
> Thro' me the way to ev'ry damned soul.
> Justice did first my lofty builder move;
> I by the Might Divine was built of yore,
> By highest Wisdom, by perennial Love.
> No thing had been created theretofore,
> If not eternal – I eternal too;
> Ye who pass thro' leave hope for evermore.
> (Trans. Thomas Brooksbank, John W. Parker, 1854, p. 17)

> [Paraphrase] Dante paints a graphic image of the pilgrim's sight of the gates of Hell which are inscribed with a frightening description of what he would see and experience when he passed through. There would be grief, everlasting pain and many lost souls. Death would be eternal and there could be no return. The pilgrim should prepare to surrender any hope of salvation.

Hell:
The 'place' where the damned will spend eternity, traditionally described as punishment and extreme suffering

Dante describes hell as being an utterly dysfunctional state in which inmates lack faith in God and live eternally without any hope. There are nine circles of hell (Limbo, Lust, Gluttony, Greed, Anger, Heresy, Violence, Fraud and Treachery). Betrayers of special relationships (including Lucifer) are seated in the centre of the circles because of their fraud and treachery (in Lucifer's case, being a fallen angel and turning away from God). Dante describes hell in the following way:

> Sighing and wailing echoed through pitch darkness, while the dead argued with each other, raging and wailing against their eternal fate. Their sounds stirred up a swirling storm in which sand was swept around by the wind. This is the situation, not only for those humans who showed contempt for God, but also some angels who existed for themselves, not for God.
> (*ibid.*, p. 49)

In Dante's hell, there is no escape and no redemption, because all who are there have alienated themselves from God's love and grace by their own choice.

The language of hell also needs consideration. In ancient times, there was a belief that hell was located at earth's core, and heaven was above the earth in the skies.

Modern cosmology puts paid to that belief – however, the symbolism of polar opposites may be of some help when attempting to understand the concepts of heaven and hell. 'Hell-type' language may be useful if taken metaphorically and used as an example of spiritual and psychological alienation from God. For Lutheran theologian and philosopher **Paul Tillich** (1886–1965), 'heaven and hell must be taken seriously as metaphors for the polar ultimates in the experience of the divine' (Tillich, *Systematic Theology III*, p. 446). In referring to heaven and hell as polar opposites (whether it be in earth's core as opposed to the sky, or with God versus without God), this language has its use in maintaining the psychological point that hell is not only an eternity without God, but an eternity entirely removed from, and at the polar opposite of, good.

A detail from Hell, by the medieval Dutch painter Hieronymus Bosch

> **Paul Tillich (1886–1965)** Paul Tillich was a German-American Protestant theologian and philosopher. Born in Prussia, he served in World War I as an army chaplain. He became a professor of theology at Frankfurt University but was expelled by the Nazis in 1933, when he moved to the USA. He was important in making links between traditional Christian belief and modern secular culture. He showed that every culture and age has to use its own thought forms to try to understand the nature of God. His most important work was the three-volume *Systematic Theology* (1951–64).

Purgatory: A post-biblical idea referring to a state of cleansing after death, before entering heaven

Purgatory

Although the word '**purgatory**' is not mentioned in the NT, it was later used to refer to a state of cleansing that may be required after death, before a person can enter heaven. To explain further, one could argue that heaven is necessarily morally perfect – so the inhabitants of heaven must also be morally perfect. God is seen to be total moral perfection – he does not sin, because he chooses not to. Indeed, the essential nature of God is holy. As Walls states:

> If heaven is essentially morally perfect, it must be the case that the creaturely occupants of heaven are also incapable of sin. This is not to say that they are essentially good in the same sense that God is in his very nature, but to say that those in heaven must have at least acquired a new nature, or had their nature so transformed that it is impossible for them to sin. In traditional terminology, they must become impeccable, or immutable. They must have a settled character that is good through and through, one that is no longer vulnerable to sin.
> (Jerry L. Walls, *Purgatory: The Logic of Total Transformation*, Oxford University Press USA, 2011, p. 4)

It is the predominantly Roman Catholic belief that, although most people are 'good' upon their death, they are not yet sufficiently worthy to meet God in their current state, yet equally not sufficiently bad for hell. The **Catechism of the Catholic Church** (ed. Geoffrey Chapman, 1994, ch. 3) states: 'All who die in God's grace and friendship, but are still imperfectly purified, are indeed assured of their eternal salvation; but after death they undergo purification, so as to achieve the holiness necessary to enter the kingdom of heaven.' Hence, there must be a period of moral cleansing and purification after death, but before entering heaven. Roman Catholics also teach that the process of purgatory can begin within their earthly existence – by attending confession and repenting for the sins they have committed, and also by attempting to put right what they have done wrong (by doing good deeds for those in need).

The concept of purgatory was present throughout the early church. The fourth-century theologian, **Gregory of Nyssa** (c.335–94), stated: 'When the process of purification has been completed, the better attributes of the soul appear – imperishability, life, honour, grace, glory, power, and, in short, all that belongs to human nature as the image of Deity' (Gregory of Nyssa, *On Soul and the Resurrection*, Aeterna Press, 2016, p. 7). He uses this to form part of the argument that, allowing a state of spiritual cleansing would fit with the concept of an omnibenevolent God who wants to allow as many people into the kingdom of heaven as possible, as opposed to immediately banishing to hell those who are not morally perfect immediately upon death.

Roman Catholic theologian **Karl Rahner** (1904–84) developed the concept of purgatory in a way which many would argue is a more attractive concept than the one of fire and brimstone. Instead of purgatory being a horrific place of pain, Rahner views it as more of a state of higher awareness of the consequences of a person's own sin. William V. Dych explains it the following way:

> **Karl Rahner (1904–1984)** Rahner was a German Roman Catholic, who trained in the Jesuit order. He was heavily involved with the **Second Vatican Council** (Vatican II). He presented Thomistic theology (i.e. that of St Thomas Aquinas) using Heidegger's terminology, in order to avoid the criticisms of Aquinas made by Kant. He wrote many books, notably his *Theological Investigations* (23 vols., 1954–84).

Catechism of the Catholic Church: A book listing all the beliefs of the Roman Catholic church. The most recent edition was produced by Pope John Paul II in 1992

Second Vatican Council (Vatican II): An important and influential council of the Roman Catholic church that met in Rome between 1962 and 1965. Its aim was to energize and modernize the Church

Rahner asks whether the notion of purgatory can be brought into closer proximity with the pain and darkness of death and the whole process of dying in its many phases. Or can purgatory be seen in the light of a modified theory of the 'transmigration of souls', which might also be useful in cases such as those of infants who die without the opportunity of freely choosing God?

(William V. Dych, *Karl Rahner*, Outstanding Thinkers Series, Continuum Press, 2000, p. 144)

This offers the entirely different concept of purgatory being a place of hope – even if a person has not had the opportunity to develop spiritually or morally, then in purgatory their souls can be saved and they will not be subject to an eternity separated from a God they never had the opportunity to choose freely. For others, it would offer a form of 'self-inflicted' pain, whereby they are able to appreciate fully the pain they have inflicted upon others through their own personal sinfulness, and come to a complete understanding of the meaning of God's grace and repentance.

Another theologian who saw value in the concept of purgatory was John Hick.

In his book, *Death and Eternal Life*, he suggested that all must have an opportunity after death to be purified, as hell could not possibly be part of an omnibenevolent God's plan. He offers the following explanation:

A rehabilitation of the notion [of purgatory] was much to be desired; for the basic concept of purgatory as that of the period between this life and man's ultimate state seems unavoidable. The gap between the individual's imperfection at the end of this life and the perfect heavenly state in which he is to participate has to be bridged; and purgatory is simply the name in Roman theology to this bridge.

(Hick, *Death and Eternal Life*, p. 202)

Hick sees it as simply an 'in-between' state after the world we are aware of in life, and a state of preparation of the perfection to come. It is quite simply a continuation of the 'soul-making' theodicy, and allows more time for the souls of the departed to come into line with that of God.

Although there is no direct biblical reference to purgatory, Roman Catholics often cite biblical passages such as 1 Corinthians 3, which discusses the idea that, upon death, people are still 'worldly', and that, after death, there will be a form of cleansing by fire of the work that each person has done throughout their life. If what the person has built survives, then he or she will receive a reward. However, if it perishes, then the builder will suffer loss, though be saved – although only out of the flames. Their reward will not be in heaven.

Other passages Roman Catholics refer to include:

- 2 Maccabees 12: This passage implies that the idea of purgatory was an ancient tradition, rather than a concept introduced centuries after the time of the NT. In the passage, the Jewish leader Judas Maccabeus leads his army into battle. God grants the army victory, although many men had been killed by this point. When preparing the bodies for burial, it was found that many were secret idolaters, wearing concealed amulets of devotion to pagan gods under their clothes. Chapters 40–2 state:

    Then under the tunic of each one of the dead, they found sacred tokens of the idols of Jamnia, which the law forbids the Jews to wear. And it became clear to all that this was the reason these men had fallen. So they all blessed the ways of the Lord, the righteous Judge, who reveals the things that are hidden; and they turned to supplication, praying that the sin that had been committed might be wholly blotted out.

This seems to be implying that people should pray for the dead as this can make a difference to the outcome of judgement for the person who has died.

- Matthew 12:32 states: 'Anyone who speaks a word against the son of man will be forgiven, but anyone who speaks against the Holy Spirit will not be forgiven, either in this age or the age to come.' This suggests that some sins can be forgiven in the 'age to come' (arguably after death)

There are a number of arguments against purgatory that need some consideration.

- From a Protestant point of view, the concept of purgatory is incorrect. If there was a need for repentance and punishment after death, then arguably Jesus did not complete the ultimate sacrifice on the cross in order to atone for the sins of all people. Jesus suffered on the cross to take the sins of the world away so that humans and God could be at one – i.e. there would be no separation. The concept of purgatory implies that this act of sacrifice and atonement was not enough, and that sin continues to be held as a divide between humans and God that still needs punishment.
- The concepts of heaven and hell are eternal places – if this is the case, how could it be considered possible that there is a place a person has to enter for a specific amount of time? Surely this would make the idea of eternal salvation or damnation questionable?

Election

Election (sometimes referred to as predestination) is closely associated with the work of sixteenth-century theologian **John Calvin** (1509–64), and is the belief that God chooses the eternal destiny of heaven or hell for each person. Being omniscient, God is aware of their destination before they are even born – which makes theological, if not logical, sense.

> **John Calvin (1509–1564)** Calvin was a hugely influential French Protestant reformer who came to religion via Classics. At the age of 25, he published his most famous book, the *Institutes of the Christian Religion*, which was an introduction to Protestant theology. He preached and taught around northern Europe and became widely known for his views on **Double Predestination** and Election. He had a profound influence on Protestantism and is a seminal figure in the development of European culture.

Election: The state of being chosen by God, mostly associated with John Calvin's theology. It means the same as predestination

Double Predestination: The view that God chooses only a certain number of people to achieve salvation

Limited Election

Westminster Confession of Faith:
A compilation of the beliefs of Calvinistic Protestant churches

The **Westminster Confession of Faith** states: 'By the decree of God, for the manifestation of his glory, some men and angels are predestined unto everlasting life; and others foreordained to everlasting death.' This provides the basis for belief in limited Election: that all are predestined to heaven or hell by God before they even exist on the earth. Limited Election may refer to Matthew 22:14 which states 'Many are invited but few are chosen.' Augustine argued that God's grace is required for the salvation of man, as Original Sin has such a hold over the world that it can only be grace given by God that can bring about salvation. Humanity has been so weakened by Original Sin that even the sacrifice of Christ cannot atone for it – humans lack any capacity to achieve merit for grace, so that the only possible way of achieving this is the result of God's mercy alone. Augustine states, 'So that the purpose of God does not stand according to election, but election is the result of the purpose of God' (Augustine, *Earlier Writings*, ed. J. H. S. Burleigh, John Knox Press, 1953, p. 390). If grace must be given by God, then God is in control of who receives this grace. God's grace is key to Augustine's doctrine of Predestination. If eternal salvation/damnation were as a result of the moral behaviour of humanity, then God would be in a place in which he had to act in a certain way – to allocate reward or punishment. This would bring into question the omniscience, omnibenevolence and omnipotence of God – he would be acting as a result of the behaviour of humanity and would therefore not be immutable, thus not be God. As a result of this, although God has called all people to salvation, from the beginning of time, He knew that only a few would receive a place in heaven and these people are the 'elect'. Equally, those who are not the Elect are therefore incapable of receiving grace and are predestined to **perdition**. John Calvin is in broad agreement with Augustine's view on limited Election. He believes that the will of God is hidden (*voluntas abscondita*) and we should not even attempt to question God's will as God has the ultimate foreknowledge of what will happen. Calvin states:

Perdition:
A Calvinist word for hell

> Since God illuminates the minds of his own with the spirit of understanding, so that they may grasp these mysteries which he has designed to lay open by his Word, now no abyss is there, but a way in which we are to walk in safety and a lamp to guide our feet, the light of life and the school of certain and manifest truth. Yet, his wonderful way of governing the world is justly called an 'abyss' because, while hidden from us, it ought reverently to be adored.
>
> (B. A. Gerrish, *The Old Protestantism and the New: Essays on the Reformation Heritage*, T&T Clark, 2004, p. 143)

Unlimited Election:
Calvin's view that all people are called to salvation, but not all will be chosen

Here, we are able to see that what is revealed to humans is what they have the ability to understand – God takes into account their limited knowledge. Although this may be the case, Calvin argues that people have a duty to act morally, as if there was **unlimited Election**, as we cannot know who are the Elect and who are not. Morality would also reaffirm a position in the next life, and the Elect, although they are sinners, will be able to see God's grace given to them.

Unlimited Election

In comparison to limited Election, the idea of 'unlimited Election' is the belief that, although heaven is available for all, not all will be saved. This idea stems from theologian **Karl Barth** (1886–1968), who argues that, because Jesus was God Incarnate, He was the elected and it is He who will elect humans. Therefore, as a result of Christ's death and resurrection, all can be saved, because Jesus took on human form and removed the divide between the whole of humanity and God. The 'choice' that God has in the matter is sending his son to earth, which he did, so that all could be saved. Barth states, 'There is no condemnation – literally none – for those that are in Jesus Christ' (*Church Dogmatics: Study Edition 22:IV.1: The Doctrine of Reconciliation*, T&T Clark, 1969, p. 6).

> **Karl Barth (1886–1968)** Barth was a Swiss Reformed theologian. He studied at Berlin, Tubingen and Marburg universities and made his name with his *Commentary on Romans* (1919). He refused to take an oath in support of Hitler and was dismissed from his professorship at Bonn, but was quickly employed at Basel University, where he stayed till 1962. His main theological themes were the frailty of human beings and the unfailing love of God, shown through the life of Jesus Christ.

Universalism: Roman Catholic view that universal salvation must be achieved within the Church, because they believe that there is no salvation outside it (*extra ecclesiam nulla salus*)

Universalism

Universalism (*apokatastasis*) is the notion that all people will be saved. John Hick believed that it was necessary for all people to achieve perfection in heaven, as that is the only opportunity for humanity to complete the process of 'soul making' (as referenced in his theodicy). Hick believed that the only way a truly omnibenevolent God could exist was with universal salvation – that it was not logically possible for an *all*-loving God to condemn any person to an eternity of suffering in hell, therefore all souls must reach perfection in heaven. This might make people question the relevance of living a moral life, as, if all can enter the Kingdom of God, however they have lived, then does that remove the need for goodness and morality? Indeed, can one reject God altogether in life and still achieve moral perfection next to him after death?

Gustave Doré's illustration of heaven in medieval Florentine poet Dante's Divine Comedy

Death and the Afterlife

> **Exercise**
> Do you agree with Hick's point? Why should people be moral if they will go to heaven anyway?

The Parable of the Sheep and Goats (Matthew 25)

In this parable, it is stated that, at the end of time, God will separate people from one another just as a shepherd separates his sheep and goats, thus separating and dividing those who actively seek justice from those who do not. As we are made *Imago Dei* (in the image of God), any human who has helped another has therefore helped God. Anyone who chose to ignore a person in need, therefore, has chosen to ignore God and turn away from him, so will be judged and punished. Verse 40 states: 'Truly I tell you, whatever you did for one of the least of these brothers and sisters of mine, you did for me.'

The parable sums up the following beliefs about life after death:

(i) Judgement – all will be judged at the end of time
(ii) Physicality – heaven and hell are both separate, physical places
(iii) Reward – people in heaven have rightly earned their place there through their good deeds in life, which mirror those of Jesus – helping the poor and the sick. It will not just be Christians who are saved; anyone who has lived a just life will gain entry to heaven.
(iv) Help – when you act to help others, then in turn you are acting to help Jesus/God
(v) Purgatory – there is no mention of purgatory in this passage
(vi) Action – salvation comes from action, not belief alone. If you actively pursue justice for the marginalized, then you will enter the kingdom of heaven.

The Kingdom of God

Jesus' teaching on the Kingdom of God is hugely influential regarding Christian beliefs about death and the afterlife, but is open to varying interpretation. It describes God's reign and the fact that the kingdom could be one of three things: an actual place, a spiritual state or a symbol of moral life. These different interpretations may determine whether heaven, hell or purgatory are real places or states of mind.

> **Inaugurated eschatology**: The NT idea that the Kingdom of God has already begun during Jesus' lifetime

- The Kingdom as a present, actual place
  Jesus' teachings and parables explain the 'newness' of the Kingdom of God and exemplify the need to overcome prejudices and evils on earth. In many of Jesus' teachings, it is apparent that the Kingdom of God has already begun. This has become widely known as '**inaugurated eschatology**', which Gladd and Harmon refer to as 'Reflecting the observation that while the latter-day new-creational

kingdom has begun with the work of Jesus, it has not yet been consummated in all its fullness. Another way to refer to this phenomenon is "already-not yet"' (Gladd and Harmon, *Making All Things New: Inaugurated Eschatology for the Life of the Church*, p. iv).

In other words, the Kingdom of God has already found its fulfilment through Jesus Christ, the pouring of God's spirit and the founding of the Christian movement, but it has not yet achieved its full potential. The promises of the Kingdom of God have been initially fulfilled by Jesus Christ; however, they are awaiting their complete and final consummation.

For many Christians, the teachings of Jesus and his example on earth illustrate the 'nowness' of the Kingdom of God – the radical change from the failings of the past, and the new teaching of love and compassion. Through Jesus, Christians are called to bring the Kingdom of God to earth, for example in The Lord's Prayer, which states: 'Thy Kingdom come, thy will be done on earth as it is in Heaven' (Matt. 6:10). Again, this reflects the Kingdom of God to be a current, present, actual place.

- The Kingdom as a spiritual state
Other teachings talk of the Kingdom as a state where the righteous live in perfect harmony with God in a redeemed world, separate from our current state of being. St Paul says that the resurrection of Jesus is the first sign that the fallen world will be restored to its original perfection once again, and humans will finally be able to see and know God in this new Kingdom (1 Cor. 13:12). Before the resurrection, humans could only see this state through a 'dark glass'. Revelation 21:1–4 refers to the concept that the sacrifice of Jesus' death has washed away the sin of humankind so that the righteous may live eternally and experience the joy of God's presence. New Testament writers use a wide range of images to express the future Kingdom as a time of perfection – and that the human/God relationship is not yet completed, but it will be in time to come.

- The Kingdom as a symbol of moral life
The questions of punishment and justice are often presented in the Old Testament. The Prophet Jeremiah states:

Righteous are you, Adonai,
When I plead my case with you.
Yet I speak with you about justice.
Why does the way of the wicked prosper?
Why do all the treacherous thrive?

(Jeremiah 12:1)

The wicked often seem to prosper and the good suffer on earth – however, in the Kingdom of God, the good will get their reward and the evil will suffer through being excluded from the Kingdom.

One example of this is the parable of the Rich Man and Lazarus (Luke 16:19–31). A common belief at the time was that, if you were wealthy, it was because God had blessed you. Lazarus was a poor, ill man who sat at the gate of the rich man and watched him wear the finest clothes and eat the finest foods. The rich man ignored Lazarus' suffering and did nothing to help. Both Lazarus and the rich man died on the

Hades:
Latin name for hell

same day. As opposed to the earthly trials Lazarus had faced, he found himself sitting with the righteous in heaven, whilst the rich man was sent to **Hades** (another word for hell, but a place of half-existence for human spirits awaiting judgement – a place of torment and suffering for the wicked).

It could be said that this would answer the question posed by Jeremiah about why the wicked prosper. For Jesus, although the rich man prospered for his short life on earth, ignoring the suffering of the needy and apparently thriving as a result of his greed and ignorance, he will then spend his eternal afterlife in a torturous place, whereas the righteous will prosper in the Kingdom of God. So, it could be suggested that the Kingdom of God is a place of reward for those who live a moral, just life. This can also be linked to the first point, of the Kingdom of God being an actual, physical place.

FURTHER READING

Dinesh D'Souza, *Life After Death: The Evidence*. Regnery Faith, 2015

Benjamin L. Gladd and Matthew S. Harmon, *Making All Things New: Inaugurated Eschatology for the Life of the Church*. Baker Publishing Group, 2016

John H. Hick, *Death and Eternal Life*. Macmillan, 1966

P. Johnston, *Shades of Sheol: Death and Afterlife in the Old Testament*. IVP Press, 2002

Terence Nichols, *Death and Afterlife: A Theological Introduction*. Brazos Press, 2010

Richard Swinburne, *Evolution of the Soul*, rev. edn. Oxford University Press, 1997

N. T. Wright, *The Resurrection of the Son of God*, SPCK Publishing, 2017

Thought Points

1. If 'death' is the cessation of life, how can there be 'life after death'? Discuss.

2. Why should Christians worship God if God enforces punishment on them in purgatory after they die?

3. What is the teaching of the parable of the Rich Man and Lazarus? Does it mean that Christians must not be rich?

4. 'Christians only believe in God because of the promise of everlasting life.' Discuss.

5. Explain the theory of 'Election' to someone who is not Christian.

6. 'The concepts of "heaven" and "hell" come from a very ancient society that is totally different from ours in the twenty-first century. Therefore, we should not believe in heaven or hell.' Discuss this statement.

7. Discuss the proposition that a God who inflicts *eternal* punishment on humans is not worth worshipping.

SECTION II

FOUNDATIONS: THE KNOWLEDGE OF GOD

CHAPTER 3
Knowledge of God's Existence

LEARNING OUTCOMES

In this chapter, you will be learning about the knowledge of God's existence
- Natural knowledge of God
  - An innate sense of the divine
  - Seen in the order of creation
- Revealed knowledge of God
  - Through faith and God's grace
  - Revealed knowledge of God in Jesus Christ

Introduction

What can we know for certain? If I were to ask the question 'What is 2 + 2?', then quite clearly the answer is '4'. We know this as a result of logical, *a priori* knowledge. We do not need experience of this in order to understand that if we have two biscuits, then are given two more, we would end up with four biscuits.

If I state that I know that the capital of England is London, I know that this is a fact because I use first-hand reports or experience – *a posteriori* knowledge. I can 'know of' a person, in the sense I know that Barack Obama exists (I am aware of him and his characteristics, but do not have a personal relationship with him). Yet, I can also 'know' a person, such as my friend Tilly, and have a personal relationship – knowing that she does not eat meat, she likes white wine and her favourite singer is Seth McFarlane.

All of the above forms of knowledge are quite ambiguous, in that they are subject to interpretation. I 'know' all four things, but the basis of my knowledge is different for each of them. This poses the question of what constitutes true knowledge? True knowledge could be identified as hard, incorrigible facts (such as scientific knowledge) – however, is this limiting what we can 'know'? One thing I know to be true more than anything else is that I love my son, yet this cannot be measured in scientific terms. If we only base knowledge on scientific fact, then our understanding of life and what makes it worthwhile is removed.

A second form of knowledge, developed in ancient times, is referred to as 'wisdom', and this was the original aim of Philosophy: the love of wisdom, from the Greek words *philos* (love) and *sophos* (wisdom). This provided knowledge that came separately from sense experience and was meant as an understanding of one's place in society and how a person should live their life.

Knowledge of God

As God is not a physical being, he is not available to us empirically as we cannot gain access to this knowledge through our senses. Hence, if one believes real knowledge can only be gained through the senses (empirical experience), then it could be said that God cannot be known to us at all. God is also said to be beyond the realm of rationality and therefore beyond the understanding of the rational, human mind. This, therefore, shows that God cannot be known through logical reasoning. As a result of this, A. J. Ayer concluded that God-talk was essentially meaningless. Norman Geisler explains:

> 'All God-talk is nonsense or empty.' The result of Ayer's logical positivism is as devastating to theism as its traditional agnosticism. God is unknowable and inexpressible. It is even meaningless to use the term 'God'. Hence, even traditional agnosticism is untenable, since the agnostic assumes that it is meaningful to ask the question whether God exists. For Ayer, the word God, or any transcendent equivalent, has no meaning. The term God is neither analytic nor synthetic; that is, it is neither offered by theists as an empty, contentless definition corresponding to nothing in reality, nor filled with empirical content, since 'God' is allegedly a supra-empirical being. Hence, it is literally nonsense to talk about God.
> (Geisler, *Christian Apologetics*, p. 5)

St Bonaventure (1221–74) believed that the human mind has three different ways of seeing:

(i) The eye of the flesh
(ii) The eye of reason
(iii) The eye of contemplation

'The eye of the flesh that he might see the world and the things contained in the world; the eye of reason that he may see the soul and the things contained in the soul; and the eye of contemplation that he might see God and the things contained in God' (Bonaventure, *The Journey of the Mind to God*, p. 60).

He amalgamates three forms of knowledge to come to a 'complete' understanding of the human psyche and understanding: empirical/scientific knowledge, use of logic, and faith. English theologian John Polkinghorne (1930–present) develops this

Knowledge of God's Existence

> **Natural Theology**: God may be known through reason and the observation of the natural world

> **Revealed Theology**: God may only be known when he allows himself to be known – e.g., through the Bible. Also known as 'special revelation'

metaphor and uses the example of binoculars: one eye sees science, the other sees spiritual truths about God, yet both eyes are required to work together in order to give a complete understanding (picture) of the world. American theologian James Emery White (1961–present) argues that people who say that science is about facts while religion is about mere opinions make an error in assuming that scientific facts are not open to interpretation. To say that religion is a foolish attempt to believe impossible things is absurd. Science and religion are asking different questions about what the world is really like. He says that science and religion are both valid ways of looking at the world – science asks 'how' questions, while religion asks 'why' questions. Science and religion are not necessarily in opposition.

Scientist **Albert Einstein** (1879–1955) famously said: 'Science without religion is lame. Religion without science is blind' (John F. Haught, *Science and Religion: From Conflict to Conversation*, Paulist Press, 1995, p. 30). Knowing that somebody exists in reality is very different from knowing somebody personally. Christians believe that God can not only be known in a sense of his attributes (omniscience, omnibenevolence, omnipotence), but also be known in a personal relationship. They believe this knowledge comes from both **Natural Theology** and **Revealed Theology**.

> **Exercise**
> Read this quote and explain how it might relate to the discussion on human knowledge:
> 'Trust in the LORD with all your heart and do not lean on your own understanding.'
> (Proverbs 3:5).

Natural/Revealed Theology introduction

Natural Theology considers that God may be known through reason and observation of the natural world. Whilst it may offer a reasonable and rational justification for the existence of God, you have to admit that the definition of God as an infinite being would lie beyond the realms of human reasoning. A similar argument can be used in terms of **Revealed Theology**, which states that God can only be known when he allows himself to be known, whether through scriptures, Prophets or prayers, etc. Whilst this states that God can only be known through revelation, it is much more difficult to offer rational justification of why these revelations should be taken as truth statements. This could lead people to think that revelation alone could be deemed to be irrational.

Natural Theology

In his work *Critique of Practical Reason* (1788), **Immanuel Kant** (1724–1804) stated: 'Two things fill the mind with ever increasing wonder and awe, the more often and the more intensely the mind is drawn to them: the starry heavens above and the moral law within me.' This points to the concept of Natural Theology – the theology in which the thinker attempts to understand the nature of God through reason and experience of the natural world. In Acts 17: 22–23, Paul's speech to the Athenians convinces the people that they are worshipping the true God even though they are not sure he exists, as they can know God simply by understanding what his creation tells them about his nature. This desire to know the 'unknown God' has been a universal quest of ancient philosophers, with Cicero finding the **Universal Consent argument** most plausible. He thought that all humans, whether civilized or not, have a natural instinct to believe in God, and that people learn more about God by using their reason. Similarly, belief in the immortality of the soul is universally agreed, though reason is necessary to understand the nature of the soul and how it can survive (Cicero, *The Nature of the Gods*, 1.123, quoted in Richard O. Brooks, *Cicero and Modern Law*, Routledge, 2000, p. 44).

Cicero's argument is based on the premise that, if so many people believe in God, then not only is it reasonable to argue for his existence, but also he simply *must* exist. His argument was influential for the thought of Augustine and Thomas Aquinas.

The Catechism of the Catholic Church states: 'The desire for God is written in the human heart, because man is made by God and for God; and God never ceases to draw man to himself' (Pt 1 Sec. 1:27). It also concludes that the practices of prayer, ritual and sacrifice are so widespread that, 'despite ambiguities', one may well call humankind 'religious beings' (Pt 1 Sec. 1:28). This suggests that within each person there is an innate sense of the divine that offers the capacity to be drawn to, know and understand God.

Protestant reformer John Calvin agreed with this, suggesting that all people have an innate '***sensus divinitatis***', or a divine sense, which draws humankind to God. He also discusses 'the seed of religion' (***semen religionis***) which, although it is found within all people, some are unaware of as a result of sin. It is sin that removes humanity from God and makes the epistemic distance much more prominent. According to Calvin, there are three areas in which one can experience the '*sensus divinitatis*':

(i) the conscience
(ii) appreciation of aesthetics
(iii) intellectual capacity

The conscience refers to the internal feeling of guilt that a person has when doing something they know to be wrong, and it is this innate sense of morality which, one could argue, demonstrates how humans understand God's goodness. Calvin suggests that our conscience is given by God and is part of the human response to God's goodness. Humans are also the only creatures who take pleasure in aesthetics, and can appreciate the beauty of the natural world. We may see a beautiful sunset or hear a bird's morning song and this may lead us to believe that God is at work within the natural world. We can reason towards the existence of God through nature. This ability to reason leads on to the third point – the intellectual capacity of humanity. The ability to reason can help us to see the intrinsic detail of the natural world, natural laws and the finely tuned design of the world. This helps humans to reason towards the apparent intelligent design and thereby recognize God's existence as that designer.

Universal Consent argument: Cicero's argument that humans have a natural instinct to believe in God

Sensus divinitatis: Calvin's view that all humans have an innate sense of God, drawing them towards God

Semen religionis: Seed of religion – Calvin's view that all humans have a sense of God, though some are unaware of it because of sin

American theologian James Beilby agrees that the ability to recognize God is innate and automatic: 'I may see God's majesty while observing the night sky while you receive a sense of God's presence while listening to a Mozart symphony' (Bellby, *Epistemology as Theology*, p. 181).

One may suggest that the natural world provides a point of contact between God and humans. The Creation stories in Genesis state both that 'God created man in his image . . . male and female he created them' (Genesis 1:27) and 'God breathed the breath of life into Adam' (Genesis 2:7). This suggests that there is a spark of the divine in each person, which in turn could suggest that, if each person has the essence of God within them, then we may be innately inclined to seek and respond to God throughout life. The idea that we are made in the image of God has led supporters of natural theology to a view that mirrors the thinking of Calvin. We are created in such a way that we have the ability to appreciate goodness and beauty in the world and in other people, and can recognize this as a manifestation of the creativity and goodness of God. Supporters of this argument, such as C. S. Lewis, Joseph Butler and Cardinal Newman, also suggest that we have an innate sense of morality that makes individuals take this inner conscience as the 'voice of God' and they use this as evidence to point to the fact that God does indeed exist and makes moral demands of his people.

> **Exercise**
>
> Do you agree with the suggestion that humans have an innate sense of God? Conduct a debate with your classmates/friends.

Biblical teaching also points towards the concept that the natural world demonstrates truths about God. Psalm 8:1–4 states:

> Lord, our Lord, how majestic is your name in all the earth!
> You have set your glory in the heavens, the work of your fingers,
> The moon and stars, which you have set in place,
> What is mankind that you are mindful of them,
> Human beings that you care for them?

In his letter to the Romans, Paul also expressed the view that human reason and experience can lead humanity towards knowledge of God. Indeed, he says, people have angered God because they have ignored the obvious fact of his existence and lead immoral, godless lives instead. He tells the Roman Christians that God is angry with people who reject his existence and power, because God has provided evidence that he exists. Because of this, 'their thinking became futile and their foolish hearts were darkened' (Romans 1:21).

Aquinas, Calvin and **William Paley** (1743–1805) all point to the apparent order and design of the world, which one can use to reason towards the existence of God. It is argued that it is *reasonable* to infer that there is a God, given the clear signs of purpose and organization in the world.

Aquinas, in his **Five Ways**, argued for purpose (*telos*, hence 'teleological' argument). Teleological thinking is a way of understanding things in terms of their

Five Ways: Aquinas' five arguments for the existence of God

purpose – for example, the adult is the *telos* of the child, or the oak tree is the *telos* of the acorn. When archaeologists discover an artefact unlike anything they have ever seen before, they recognize that it was made to achieve a purpose, even if they do not know what that purpose was – i.e., they infer the existence of a designer who shaped the object, because, according to Aquinas' argument, order implies purpose, or an intelligent plan. Aquinas goes further and argues that inanimate things have some purpose. For instance, a plant seed does not behave randomly but acts for a purpose – to grow into a plant or fruit. He also argues that things like cells act towards their proper purpose instinctively, without knowledge or intelligence. They cannot know or choose what kind of cells they will develop into. Aquinas states that things without knowledge must be directed towards their end. The 'director' is, according to Aquinas, God.

William Paley also argued for design, using his famous watch analogy, stating: 'Arrangements, disposition of parts, subservience of means to an end, relation of instruments to a use, imply the presence of intelligence and mind' (Paley, *Natural Theology: or, Evidences of the Existence and Attributes of the Deity, Collected from the Appearances of Nature* [1802], ed. M. Eddy and D. Knight, Oxford University Press, 2006, p. 12).

(See Brown and Greggs, *Philosophy of Religion for OCR*, ch. 4, for further detail regarding the above arguments.)

> **Exercise**
>
> 'This skilful ordering of the universe is for us a sort of mirror in which we can contemplate God, who is otherwise invisible' (Calvin, *Institutes of the Christian Religion*, p. 151).
>
> Using this quote and the discussion above, write a short report, comparing and contrasting the views on natural theology found in this section.

Revealed Theology

Christians believe that God gives them the fundamental, distinctive teachings of their faith as a revelation. The English word 'revelation' comes from the Latin word *revelatio*, a translation of the Greek word for the NT, *apocalypsis*, meaning unveiling or uncovering. Revealed theology (or **special revelation**) considers that God can only be known when he allows himself to be known, through the medium of Prophets (direct), scripture or prayer (indirect). These direct and indirect revelations are referred to as '**Immediate revelation**' and '**Mediate revelation**' and the differences are shown below:

Most Christians think of the Bible as a mediate revelation, in which the words of those who had immediate revelations are preserved and can be referenced and interpreted by people today. Others, however, view the Bible as an immediate revelation in which every word has come directly from God and should therefore be followed as such.

Special revelation: Another name for Revealed theology

Immediate revelation: God makes himself known to humans directly

Mediate revelation: People learn about God indirectly

Immediate revelation	Mediate revelation
God makes himself directly known to people, for example:	People learn about God and gain knowledge about him in an indirect manner, for example:
The Prophets: had an immediate revelation when God spoke directly to them and gave them the exact words to share	Those who trusted Moses to take them out of slavery and into the Promised Land
Adam and Eve: God walked through the Garden of Eden and gave them direct instructions	Those who heard the words of the Prophets and acted accordingly
Abraham: God told him to sacrifice Isaac and promised him land for his descendants	Those who learned about Jesus from others who had met him
Moses: God spoke directly to him in the burning bush	
Anybody who met Jesus is said to have had a special revelation, and this is what gave the apostles authority after Jesus' death	

Revealed theology is also referred to as 'special revelation' because it did not (indeed, it does not) rely on people having particularly strong intellectual gifts, but is readily available to all, through faith. It confirmed the findings of natural theology, yet also uncovered further truths (such as laws, the doctrine of the Trinity, beliefs regarding life after death) which could not be found through reason alone. These truths could only ever be known because God chose to reveal them.

Revelation through faith

It can be argued that, whereas some knowledge of God is possible to achieve through knowledge and reason, as human beings have simple, finite minds, this is not sufficient to gain a full understanding. Faith in God's power and benevolence is necessary to understand his revelation to humans.

For Calvin, humans could have a relationship with God based on natural theology (creation, consciousness and so on); however, this overlooks the key factor of the Fall. The phrase Calvin uses: 'si integer stetisset Adam' (if Adam had remained upright) is key to this theology. If the Fall had not occurred, then all people would have known God directly and lived in a state of perfection. This was not the case, however, because humans are fallen and need to experience God's loving care, especially through the salvation offered by God through Christ the mediator. If individuals accept God's offer of salvation, then they may be saved (Calvin, *Institutes of the Christian Religion*, 1:1).

For Calvin, the only true knowledge of God is in salvation, which has to be mediated by Christ. Because humankind separated itself from God in the Fall, this revelation is necessary to achieve a full and complete relationship with God – natural theology is not sufficient alone.

The Roman Catholic position follows on from Calvin, stating that, although the Fall did not separate God and humanity completely, it did cause an epistemic chasm which may block or obstruct the natural desire for God as revealed through nature. It says that the effects of sin are seen in 'religious ignorance or indifference; the cares and riches of this world; the scandal of bad example on the part of believers; currents of thought hostile to religion; finally that attitude of sinful man which makes him hide from God out of fear and flee his call' (Catechism, para. 29). Yet, to overcome this, it states that 'There is another order of knowledge, one which man cannot possibly arrive at by his own powers; the order of divine revelation' (para. 50). As a result of the Fall, the natural world may indeed point towards God, yet it also points to many secular distractions. It is only through revelation that God is able to reveal his plan and aid humanity on the path towards righteousness.

Revelation Through Grace

In both Roman Catholic and Protestant theology, although faith may rely on the assent of the mind and spirit, God's grace (his unconditional giving to humanity) is required to complete the relationship. God's grace is required to strengthen the faith of humanity through the Holy Spirit. Aquinas offers one argument for this. Jean Porter explains it in the following way:

> The theological virtues of faith, hope and charity are regarded as operative principles stemming from grace (much as the acquired virtues stem from human nature), through which we act in ways directed toward attaining our final end of direct union with God. In addition, Aquinas holds that the transforming effects of grace go all the way down, transforming each of the operative capacities and powers of the human person.
> (Porter, *Nature as Reason: A Thomistic Theory of the Natural Law*, p. 389)

For Aquinas, the presence of the Holy Spirit is required to affirm faith fully, as the virtues of faith, without God's grace, can be regarded simply as human virtues.

Salvation through grace is also a necessary point to consider. Salvation is given freely to all by God through faith in Jesus as the Son of God. It is not a gift to be earned, yet it is a reward for the faithful. Christians believe that they continue to receive the grace of God through the Holy Spirit, who enables the understanding of God as Trinity:

(i) Father: who created and sustains the world
(ii) Son: the person of Jesus who was the sacrifice for the sins of humanity
(iii) Holy Spirit: activity of God in the world

If Christians continue to receive God's grace through the Holy Spirit, then they believe they will be able to demonstrate agape love just as Jesus taught. For Christians, the Holy Spirit is believed to:

- guide writers of the scriptures so they are able to produce the word of God with authority
- give people wisdom to understand God's revelations and what they mean
- support people in their faith and understanding of God

- give people the confidence to share their Christian faith
- strengthen the Church as a community of believers
- bring people to revelation

Christians believe that God's grace is revealed continually through the Holy Spirit, and it is this revelation that brings them to a deeper understanding of, and relationship with, God.

Revelation Through the Bible

Throughout Christian history, God is understood to reveal himself through religious experiences, via angels transmitting the voice of God (e.g. the Angel Gabriel and Mary), visions/voices (God declaring Jesus as his son at Jesus' baptism), dreams that proclaim messages or warnings (Jacob's dream), and conversion experiences (Saul to Paul). The biblical Prophets were very clear about the fact that they were not merely offering their own view with regards to the moral behaviour of people and their future judgement, but speaking the words of the Lord. Isaiah 6:6–8 describes how, after seeing a vision of God seated on the throne in the Temple, Isaiah was called to be a messenger from God and had a duty to reveal God's word:

> Then one of the seraphim flew to me with a live coal in his hand, which he had taken with tongs from the altar. With it he touched my mouth and said, 'See, this has touched your lips; your guilt is taken away and your sin atoned for.' Then I heard the voice of the Lord saying, 'Whom shall I send? And who will go for us?' And I said, 'Here am I. Send me!'

In Paul's letter to the Romans, it is clear that the Bible takes it for granted that the natural laws which we can easily experience point to the existence of God. God's existence is obvious in everything he has made.

A study of Acts 17:16–34

Acts 17:16–34

[16] While Paul was waiting for them in Athens, he was greatly distressed to see that the city was full of idols. [17] So he reasoned in the synagogue with both Jews and God-fearing Greeks, as well as in the marketplace day by day with those who happened to be there. [18] A group of Epicurean and Stoic philosophers began to debate with him. Some of them asked, 'What is this babbler trying to say?' Others remarked, 'He seems to be advocating foreign gods.' They said this because Paul was preaching the good news about Jesus and the resurrection. [19] Then they took him and brought him to a meeting of the Areopagus, where they said to him, 'May we know what this new teaching is that you are presenting? [20] You are bringing some strange ideas to our ears, and we would like to know what they mean.' [21] (All the Athenians and the foreigners who lived there spent their time doing nothing but talking about and listening to the latest ideas.)

[22] Paul then stood up in the meeting of the Areopagus and said: 'People of Athens! I see that in every way you are very religious. [23] For as I walked around and looked carefully at your objects of worship, I even found an altar with this inscription: to

> an unknown god. So you are ignorant of the very thing you worship – and this is what I am going to proclaim to you.
> [24] The God who made the world and everything in it is the Lord of heaven and earth and does not live in temples built by human hands. [25] And he is not served by human hands, as if he needed anything. Rather, he himself gives everyone life and breath and everything else. [26] From one man he made all the nations, that they should inhabit the whole earth; and he marked out their appointed times in history and the boundaries of their lands. [27] God did this so that they would seek him and perhaps reach out for him and find him, though he is not far from any one of us. [28] "For in him we live and move and have our being." As some of your own poets have said, "We are his offspring."
> [29] Therefore since we are God's offspring, we should not think that the divine being is like gold or silver or stone – an image made by human design and skill. [30] In the past God overlooked such ignorance, but now he commands all people everywhere to repent. [31] For he has set a day when he will judge the world with justice by the man he has appointed. He has given proof of this to everyone by raising him from the dead.
> [32] When they heard about the resurrection of the dead, some of them sneered, but others said, "We want to hear you again on this subject." [33] At that, Paul left the Council. [34] Some of the people became followers of Paul and believed. Among them was Dionysius, a member of the Areopagus, also a woman named Damaris, and a number of others.'

The Acts of the Apostles tells the story of how Jesus' first followers worked to spread the message about the death and resurrection of Jesus, and also describes the difficulties they encountered. It is also a message of hope for Christians today as it goes on to state how they were able to overcome these challenges and bring people to faith, establishing one of the earliest known Christian communities.

This passage combines elements of both natural and revealed theology. Paul has travelled to Athens which was the capital of culture and education, and where the citizens worshipped many gods through idols. Although Paul was used to sharing the news of Christ, this was a new challenge as it was the first time he had attempted to discuss and debate this with an audience from a philosophical background, who were well rehearsed in discussion and debate. He uses their statues of 'unknown gods' to share how the one true God can be known and understood through revelation, as opposed to superstition – worshipping an idol they do not know is worthy of worship, and building temples out of fear rather than through revealed knowledge of the divine. Paul argues that it is clear that everyone has a natural disposition to believe in God, and although natural theology can take us so far in our comprehension, revelation through Christ is necessary in order to achieve a complete understanding.

Alvin Plantinga (1932–) relates this position to views found in the work of John Calvin, saying:

> According to Calvin, everyone, whether in the faith or not, has a tendency or nisus, in certain situations, to apprehend God's existence and to grasp something of his nature and

actions. This natural knowledge can be and is supressed by sin, but the fact remains that a capacity to apprehend God's existence is as much a part of our natural noetic equipment as is the capacity to apprehend perceptual truths, truths about the past and truths about other minds. Belief in the existence of God is in the same boat as belief in other minds, the past and perceptual objects; in each case God has so constructed us that in the right circumstances we form the belief in question.

(Plantinga, *Faith and Rationality: Reason and Belief in God*, pp. 89–90)

Calvin refers to the passage from Acts in his *Institutes of the Christian Religion*, where he uses it to explain that, although everybody has the capacity and disposition to believe in God, not everybody will recognize the Christian God or choose Christianity. Calvin also points out that the sheer number of people who believe in God suggests an innate awareness of God and religion as a natural part of the human condition.

Faith and reason

In Christianity, faith is seen as a virtue. It does not see faith and reason as contrary to one another, yet teaches that reasoning will take you so far, but faith is needed in order to overcome the epistemic distance between humans and God.

Thomas Aquinas distinguished between **unformed faith** and **formed faith**. The former is where a person can intellectually accept another person's belief in God, but cannot accept it as being true for themselves. The latter is a faith in which a person accepts what they can believe rationally through the intellect, concluding that it is true. So, one is reason alone (no faith and therefore no belief), and the other is reason and faith together. Aquinas says of this:

Unformed faith: Aquinas' term for the belief of a person who can intellectually accept another person's faith in God, but cannot accept it as true for themselves

Formed faith: Aquinas' term for faith that a person accepts rationally, and accepts as true for themselves

It seems that unformed faith cannot become formed, nor formed faith unformed. It is said in 1 Corinthians 13:10 'when that which is perfect is come, then that which is in part shall be done away'. Now, in comparison with formed faith, unformed faith is imperfect. It will therefore be done away with when formed faith is come. It follows that it cannot be numerically one habit with formed faith.

(Aquinas, *Nature and Grace: Selections from the Summa Theologica of Thomas Aquinas*, ed. A. M. Fairweather and P. A. De Boer Snr, CreateSpace Independent Publishing Platform, 2014, p. 269)

Thomas Aquinas by Gentile da Fabriano, circa 1400

FOUNDATIONS: THE KNOWLEDGE OF GOD

For Aquinas, one needs both faith *and* reason working together in harmony in order to achieve a full knowledge of God. Reason can take us so far, but faith is volitional and gives us a stronger connection to God. English philosopher John Locke agreed with Aquinas that faith *is* reason. Locke believed that faith was a form of assent, so reason was required to regulate this, yet faith is simply rational belief in God, put into action.

Martin Luther goes one step further and rejects reason altogether, arguing that reason, common-sense arguments and mathematical proofs are of no value. Christians have the Bible, and that contains all the necessary proof they need (Luther, as summarized in John Shaw Banks, *Martin Luther: The Prophet of Germany*, Nabu Press, 2011, p. 100)

He argues that, if we use our limited human reason to access a divine being, then this reduces that being's status and capacity. He believes that, as we cannot comprehend God, let alone intellectually reason towards him, then we must use the Bible and faith alone.

On the other side of this debate are Richard Dawkins and Danish philosopher **Søren Kierkegaard** (1813–55). Kierkegaard stated that reason cannot grasp the essence of God, it can only undermine faith. For Kierkegaard, God will seem absurd from the position of reason. For him, faith and reason are in natural opposition to one another.

British evolutionary biologist and atheist Richard Dawkins is famously quoted as saying: 'Faith is the great cop-out, the great excuse to evade the need to think and evaluate evidence. Faith is belief in spite of, even perhaps because of, the lack of evidence' (Dawkins, *The God Delusion*, p. 12).

Given that one cannot scientifically test faith, it is impossible to argue against, hence it is the ultimate cop-out as there can be no further discussion. Once a person refers to faith, then all reason is defunct and intelligent discourse is over.

Barth/Brunner debate

At the heart of Calvin's theology runs a debate been natural and revealed theology, and this became the focus of a debate between two Reformed theologians – **Emil Brunner** and Karl Barth – in 1934. The debate centres around the questions of how, if humans are in a state of sin, they can know God and achieve God's grace, unless

> **Emil Brunner (1889–1966)** Brunner was a Swiss theologian from the Protestant Reformed tradition. He studied theology at Zurich and Berlin, was ordained, and ministered at a church in Obstalden for eight years before becoming Professor of Theology at Zurich in 1924, where he stayed until 1953. He was, for a time, a supporter of Karl Barth in opposing **liberalism** in theology, but they later became firm opponents because of a disagreement about the theology of Creation. Brunner is widely known for two influential books: *The Mediator* (1927) and *The Divine Imperative* (1932).

Liberalism: Individuals can believe whatever they like and their views should be tolerated by everyone, as long as they do not threaten society

Knowledge of God's Existence

there is general revelation through nature? On the other hand, grace is not something we can ask for and we only know of this due to the fact that God chose to reveal himself through Christ and in the Bible.

Brunner considered that humanity has some connection with God – however vague – as a result of 'sparks of glory' within nature. Barth was in complete disagreement. He argued that the teaching of Calvin regarding the Fall pointed to the fact that the Fall had so distorted the nature of humanity and its relationship with God that there could be no possible point of contact between God and humanity.

Brunner's arguments were as follows:

***Imago Dei*:** Brunner argued that the image of God in humans after the Fall had been destroyed, but only at the material level. The spiritual level of the *Imago Dei* has to exist as uncorrupted, so that humans can be addressed by God (which distinguishes them from animals). The material image has been almost totally corrupted from the image of God, however.

General revelation: Because of sin, humanity is almost blind to the special revelation of grace. Therefore, God must communicate *of* his nature *through* his nature. Nature is the only thing that provides a point of contact between God and humanity.

Conscience: God's law is apparent through the conscience of humanity.

True Knowledge: Revelation through Christ and faith is more helpful in achieving true knowledge than nature ever will be.

> We shall not be able to avoid speaking of a double revelation: of one in creation which only he can recognise in all its magnitude, whose eyes have been opened by Christ; and of a second in Jesus Christ in whose bright light he can clearly perceive the former. This latter revelation far surpasses that which the former was able to show him.
> (Brunner, *Nature and Grace*, Wipf and Stock Publishers, 2002, pp. 26–7)

Barth responded with three reasons explaining why he disagreed with Brunner's interpretation of Calvin:

The formal self cannot inform the material self of God's existence: The Fall has removed humanity from God so intrinsically that the formal, spiritual self has no way of informing the material self of any knowledge of God's existence. The material self is so corrupted that there is an absolute void between the spiritual and physical that cannot be removed – certainly not by nature.

No points of contact: Barth again disagrees with Brunner by stating that guilt and conscience can only be activated once a person has experienced the grace of God, and not before. These virtues do not *point* to God, they are as a *result* of God's mercy and grace.

Order of creation: Barth argues that humanity only sees order in creation after it has been revealed to people, and it does not cause any form of natural revelation pointing towards the existence of God. The natural world cannot provide any basis to salvation or the grace of God. Barth believes Brunner has placed far too much importance on human reason and this has undermined the uniqueness of faith.

Conscience: The moral response to the apprehension of God's existence

> **FURTHER READING**
>
> James Beilby, *Epistemology as Theology: An Evaluation of Alvin Plantinga's Religious Epistemology*. Routledge, 2006
>
> Richard Dawkins, *The God Delusion*, 10th anniversary edition. Black Swan, 2016
>
> Norman Geisler, *The Big Book of Christian Apologetics*. Baker Books, 2012
>
> Alister McGrath, *The Dawkins Delusion*. SPCK, 2007
>
> Alister McGrath, *Emil Brunner – A Reappraisal*. Wiley-Blackwell, 2016
>
> Alvin Plantinga, *Faith and Rationality: Reason and Belief in God*. University of Notre Dame Press, 1984
>
> Jean Porter, *Nature as Reason: A Thomistic Theory of the Natural Law*. Wm B. Eerdmans Publishing, 2005

Thought Points

1. How would you define 'knowledge'?

2. Explain the similarities and differences between natural theology and revealed theology.

3. Does the Bible come from God, from humans or from some combination of both? Explain your reasons.

4. 'I believe that God exists.' Does this statement mean that God exists?

5. 'I believe in unicorns and the tooth fairy.' Does this mean that unicorns and the tooth fairy exist?

6. 'Belief and faith are different things.' Discuss.

7. To what extent is faith in God rational?

CHAPTER 4
The Person of Jesus Christ

LEARNING OUTCOMES

In this chapter, you will be learning about Jesus' authority as
- the Son of God
  - Jesus' divinity as expressed in his knowledge of God, his miracles and his resurrection
- a teacher of wisdom
  - Jesus' moral teaching on repentance and forgiveness, inner purity and moral motivation
- a liberator
  - Jesus' role as liberator of the marginalized and the poor, as expressed in his challenge to political and religious authority

Introduction

Apostles' Creed: One of the most important Christian statements of belief, the current version dates from the eighth century

In this chapter, you will be learning about Jesus of Nazareth, a carpenter from a small village in a remote part of Roman-occupied Israel in the first century of what has become known as the 'Christian era'. Jesus was the so-called founder of the religion that was named after him, Christianity, which grew to be the largest religion in the world. As you will learn, there are many facets to Jesus – teacher of wisdom, Son of God, liberator of the oppressed, authoritative figure. Perhaps the best place to start is the official Church statement, the **Apostles' Creed**, which is a summary of what Christians should believe.

FOUNDATIONS: THE KNOWLEDGE OF GOD

The Apostles' Creed

I believe in God, the Father almighty,
Creator of heaven and earth.
I believe in Jesus Christ, his only Son, our Lord,
who was conceived by the Holy Spirit,
born of the Virgin Mary,
suffered under Pontius Pilate,
was crucified, died, and was buried;
he descended to the dead.
On the third day he rose again;
he ascended into heaven;
he is seated at the right hand of the Father,
and he will come to judge the living and the dead.
I believe in the Holy Spirit, the holy catholic Church, the communion of saints, the forgiveness of sins,
the resurrection of the body,
and the life everlasting.
Amen.

As you can see, the creed is set out in three distinct sections, one for each of the three persons of the Trinity. What is noticeable, however, is that the section about Jesus is much more detailed than those about God the Father and the Holy Spirit. This is because, in the early centuries of Christianity, there was much more discussion – and argument – about the nature of Jesus, than about the other two persons of the Trinity. The current version of the Apostles' Creed comes from the eighth century, and is an expansion of the **Old Roman Creed** that was in use from the middle of the second century (J. N. D. Kelly, *Early Christian Creeds*, A & C Black, 1970, p. 104).

In the Apostles' Creed, there are a number of positive statements concerning the importance of Jesus. The reasons why this creed has so many statements about Jesus is because, in the first centuries of Christianity, as it was emerging as a major religion, a number of splinter groups arose, whose members believed something different from the 'official' beliefs. Groups like the Ebionites, Docetists, Arians, over-emphasized various aspects of Jesus' personality, his

Old Roman Creed: An early Christian creed from the middle of the second century

An ancient icon of Jesus and the Virgin Mary in a Coptic Church in Egypt

understanding of God and his relationship to God. All of these groups were expelled from the Church and labelled as heresies.

> **Exercise**
> Write a short paragraph on each of the following doctrines, noting why they were condemned as heretical: Apollinarianism, Monophysitism, Nestorianism, Patripassianism.

Jesus as Son of God

Christological controversies

In the early Church's quest to define precisely the exact nature of Jesus Christ, theologians were painfully aware of the importance of their task. They began with the established fact that Jesus was a real human being. The NT talked in this way, and located him in his social context – he was born a Jew and knew the Jewish scriptures, quoting from them often. But the NT writers were aware that Jesus was somehow different from other humans, though they did not elaborate on exactly how he was different. This was the task that the second-century theologians began to explore.

They began with significant statements in the NT, such as Paul's confession that 'Jesus is Lord' (Romans 10:9), and Jesus' statement 'I and the Father are one' in John's Gospel (John 10:30). They took these as the beginning of their Christology, believing that Jesus Christ was indivisibly one: simultaneously fully divine and fully human. The theologians' task was to demonstrate how these two ideas could be held together. Most theologians agreed with this task, but there were other groups who, although assenting to most Christian beliefs, disagreed with this early interpretation of the person of Jesus Christ.

Virgin birth: The doctrine that Jesus was born to Mary without the normal methods of procreation

Ebionities: A Jewish-Christian group who believed that Jesus was human, but also the Messiah. They rejected the virgin birth

Ebionitism

The first of these were the Ebionites. This was a group that emerged out of a primarily Jewish-influenced form of Christian belief that wanted Christians to observe all aspects of Jewish law and practice. They solved the problem of the humanity and divinity of Jesus by denying his divinity. For them, Jesus was an ordinary human, the offspring of Joseph and Mary. Jesus was seen as spiritually superior to other humans, but similar in all other respects. He was selected by God's Holy Spirit in the way that the Old Testament Prophets, such as Samuel or Elijah, had been. The Ebionites rejected the **virgin birth** but proclaimed Jesus as the Messiah, who would return to earth to rule everyone in the name of God.

The **Ebionities** did not last long as a Christian sect. This was largely because the early Christian movement, through the preaching journeys of St Paul, appealed to Gentile (non-Jewish) audiences, and the Jewish thought-forms that distinguish Ebionitism were not understood by the Gentiles. Christianity developed largely in the

Gentile world, using Gentile ideas. Another, more significant, threat came from a diametrically opposed view of Jesus that came to be known as **Docetism**.

Docetism

The name for this belief comes from the Greek verb *dokeo* (to seem or to appear), and this gives the clue to its belief that Jesus was definitely divine, but only 'appeared' to be human. The first references to this group come from the letters of Ignatius of Antioch (c.35–110), Bishop of Antioch in Syria. In two of his letters (to Christian communities at Trallia and Smyrna, respectively), he states clearly that some were ruling that Christ merely appeared to suffer at his crucifixion. Ignatius makes it clear, however, that Christ 'really and truly did suffer, just as he really and truly rose again. His passion was no imaginary illusion' (*Trallians* 9 in *Early Christian Writings: The Apostolic Fathers*, trans. Maxwell Staniforth, Penguin, 1968, p. 97). The first explicit mention of the name 'Docetists' is by Serapion of Antioch (c.200 CE).

According to English theologian **J. N. D. Kelly** (1909–97), it is very likely that the roots of Docetism lie 'in the Graeco-Oriental assumptions about divine impassibility and the inherent impurity of matter' (*Early Christian Doctrines*, 5th rev. edn, A & C Black, 1980, p. 141). Rather than being a specific **heresy** on its own, Docetism is more like an attitude or tendency in theology to think of Jesus as totally divine, to the exclusion of his humanity.

Docetism was particularly prevalent in the second century, especially in **Gnosticism**, with writers such as Marcion (85–160) (see *ibid.*, p. 57) and Valentinus (100–60). According to **Alister McGrath** (1953–present), Valentinus taught that Christ 'was a redeemer figure who awakened the divine spark within humanity, enabling it to find its way back to its true home. In order to save those who were held captive by the body, the Saviour "let himself be conceived and he let himself be born as an infant with body and soul"' (Alister E. McGrath, *Christian Theology: An Introduction*, 6th edn, Wiley-Blackwell, 2016, p. 216). McGrath warns, however, that Valentinus never calls himself a Gnostic, so we need to be cautious in calling him one.

Docetism: The belief that Jesus was divine, and only appeared (*dokeo*) to be human

Heresy: A belief that is at variance with the offical view of the Church

Gnosticism: From the Greek *gnosis*, meaning 'knowledge'. Refers to a number of linked beliefs that claimed to have special knowledge of God, but varied from official church doctrine

Arianism

The most developed and complex example of the debate about the person of Jesus Christ came in the fourth century with **Arius** (c.260–336), a priest in Alexandria in Egypt. Arius preached that Jesus, the Son of God, was not eternal, having been created by God to aid in the creation of the world. This meant that Christ was not God by nature, but was changeable. His position as Son of God was awarded by God for

> **Exercise**
> Find out about other heresies, either ancient or more recent. Make a display showing ones you find particularly interesting.

aiding in the process of salvation. Arius' teaching spread through the Church quickly and led to the Council of Nicaea in 325.

Councils of Nicaea and Chalcedon

The Council of Nicaea was an important moment in the history of Christianity in general, and Christology in particular. At the command of the Emperor Constantine, about 300 bishops from all over the Christian world attended a 'council' there (modern-day Iznik in Turkey). After many theological discussions concerning the relationship between Jesus' human and his divine nature, **Arianism** was proscribed. This council went a long way towards defining what true Christian belief was. It was not until a later council, at Chalcedon (an area in modern-day Istanbul, Turkey) in 451, that the line was finally drawn under exactly what constituted authentic Christian belief. Part of the text, called the **Chalcedonian Definition**, says:

> We, then, following the holy Fathers, all with one consent, teach men to confess one and the same Son, our Lord Jesus Christ, the same perfect in Godhead and also perfect in manhood; truly God and truly man, of a reasonable soul and body; consubstantial with us according to the manhood; in all things like unto us, without sin; begotten before all ages of the Father according to the Godhead, and in these latter days, for us and for our salvation, born of the virgin Mary, the mother of God, according to the manhood; one and the same Christ, Son, Lord, Only-begotten, to be acknowledged in two natures, inconfusedly, unchangeably, indivisibly, inseparably; the distinction of natures being by no means taken away by the union, but rather the property of each nature being preserved, and concurring in one Person and one Subsistence, not parted or divided into two persons, but one and the same Son, and only begotten, God the Word, the Lord Jesus Christ, as the prophets from the beginning have declared concerning him, and the Lord Jesus Christ himself taught us, and the Creed of the holy Fathers has handed down to us.
> (Chalcedonian Definition of Faith)

> **Arianism:** The beliefs of a heretical group founded by Arius, who preached that Jesus was not God by nature, but aided in the process of salvation

> **Chalcedonian Definition:** Definitive statement on the nature of Christ – that he was co-equal with God. Finalized at the Council of Chalcedon in 451 CE

Son of God

In the NT, Jesus was given several titles – 'Son of Man', 'Messiah', 'Saviour', 'Lord' – but the most important for our purpose here is 'Son of God'. This term is also used in the Old Testament, either generically where the Israelites are described as 'sons of God' (Ex. 4:22), or for those who have the characteristics of God. The title is also used more specifically for King David and his successors (2 Sam. 7:14). In many places in the NT, it is used specifically of Jesus, though Jesus does not use it to describe himself. St Paul uses it of Jesus, who 'had been declared Son of God because of his resurrection' (Rom. 1:4); the author of the book of Hebrews uses it several times to compare Jesus to the Jewish High Priest. For example (Heb. 4:14), 'Since, therefore, we have a Great High Priest who has passed through the heavens, Jesus the Son of God, let us hold fast to the faith we profess.' In John's Gospel, the term 'son' is used exclusively for Jesus. Other believers are called 'children' of God.

Mark begins his Gospel with the words 'The beginning of the gospel of Jesus Christ, the Son of God' (1:1). After his baptism by John the Baptist, when Jesus comes out of the water, 'a voice came from heaven: "You are my beloved Son; in you I take delight"' (1:11).

Jesus' knowledge of God

Did Jesus know that he was the Son of God? The answer to this question depends upon whether the questioner has a 'high' Christology or a 'low' Christology.

- **High Christology** means to look 'from above' at Jesus and his divine nature. According to the beginning of John's Gospel, Jesus is the *Logos* (Word) sent from God to save the world (1:1: 'In the beginning was the Word, and the Word was with God, and the Word was God'). The author of the same Gospel later has Jesus say (14:6): 'I am the way, and the truth and the life. No-one comes to the Father except through me.' The 'I am' statements by Jesus are very powerful because they are reminiscent of God's statement to Moses (Ex. 3:14) when he reveals his holy name as 'I am'.
- **Low Christology** means to look 'from below' at Jesus and his knowledge of God. This view starts with the things that Jesus did, his teaching in parables, his care for the poor and sick, and his relationship with the Jewish leaders. Having established Jesus' human characteristics, Low Christology then moves on to think about his divinity.

> **High Christology:** Looks at Jesus 'from above', declaring his divine origins
>
> **Logos:** Title for Jesus - the 'Word' in John's Gospel (1:1)
>
> **Low Christology:** Looks at Jesus 'from below', focusing on the things Jesus did and said, e.g. parables, healing, etc.

How human was Jesus?

Jesus' birth (Incarnation)

Only two of the Gospels, Matthew and Luke, relate the narrative of Jesus' birth. Mark's Gospel says nothing about it, and begins when Jesus is an adult and is baptized. John's Gospel begins with a philosophical account, in the Platonic tradition, of the '**Incarnation**', the coming of the 'Word' into the world of humans.

Pope John Paul II (1920–2005) followed this statement of High Christology, in an **Encyclical** Letter (1998) (repeated in Alister McGrath, *Christian Theology: An Introduction*, 6th edn, Wiley-Blackwell, 2017, p. 207): 'In the Incarnation of the Son of God we see forged the enduring and definitive synthesis which the human mind of itself could not even have imagined: the Eternal enters time, the Whole lies hidden in the part, God takes on a human face.'

The 'Polish Pope', as he was nicknamed, declared that Jesus, in the Incarnation, was truly God and truly human. When Mary gave birth to Jesus, she was a virgin and Jesus was fully human. Mary was later given a title of her own - ***Theotokos*** — which means 'God-bearer'. This reflects the thought

This mother will exercise her authority to teach her child wisdom, morality and many other things

> **Incarnation:** A high Christological term meaning that Jesus was God 'in the flesh'
>
> **Encyclical:** This is a letter from the Pope to cardinals, bishops, clergy and, sometimes, to all Roman Catholics. These letters usually concern social issues or church doctrine
>
> ***Theotokos:*** Title for Mary, mother of Jesus, who gave birth to God (*theos*). The term means 'God-bearer'

that Jesus was not only human, but truly and wholly God. Jesus had a dual role, to redeem humans from their sins and, as God, to reinstate the perfection from before the Fall. This is why the birth of Jesus is called the 'Incarnation', God putting himself into a human body, in order that humans could return to their original state.

> **Exercise**
>
> Read the extract below and analyse Hitchens' statement. To what extent do you agree with him? How important is the narrative of the virgin birth for Christians?
>
> **The virgin birth**
>
> In a 2007 article in the *Spectator* newspaper which asked well-known public figures whether they believed in the virgin birth, atheist Christopher Hitchens said:
>
> > I no more believe that Jesus was born of the virgin Mary than I believe that Krishna was born of the virgin Devaka, Horus was born of the virgin Isis, Mercury was born of the virgin Maia or Romulus was born of the virgin Rhea Sylvia. As the preceding examples help to demonstrate, parthenogenesis would in any case not be proof either of divine paternity or of the truth of any subsequent preachings. The authors of St Matthew, whose account cannot be squared with the one offered by Luke, in any case seem to have mistranslated the Hebrew word *almah*, meaning 'young woman', from the original legend in the book of Isaiah. Christianity insults our intelligence as well as our innate morality by insisting that we believe absurdities that are drawn from the mythology of paganism and barbarism.
> >
> > (*Spectator*, 12 December 2007)
>
> There are two significant things to be said here. The first is Hitchens' point concerning other 'virgin' births in ancient religions. It is well known that the idea of a virgin birth for a person who becomes the founder or leader of a religion is not unique to Christianity. Some, like Hitchens, would argue that this fact raises important questions for our understanding of the significance of the virgin birth of Jesus. Does the idea that Jesus' birth was not unique lessen his importance as the founder of Christianity, his position as Son of God and, ultimately, as the saviour of the world?
>
> The second important point in Hitchens' statement concerns the word *almah* in the quotation from Isaiah 7:14, which has been translated as 'virgin' in Matthew's account of Jesus' birth. This word has a double meaning. It can mean 'virgin', i.e. a woman who has not had sexual intercourse. It can also mean 'young woman', i.e. a female who may or may not have given birth. The Gospel writer had to make a conscious choice of which meaning to include in his account of the birth story of Jesus. He chose 'virgin', perhaps because that word made the importance of Jesus greater and more spectacular than simply reporting that a young woman gave birth to a baby boy. Choosing 'virgin' made the significance of Jesus' birth much more important, and this would lead to more people believing it and becoming Christians because of it.

Jesus' miracles

When asking the question 'How many miracles did Jesus perform?', it seems like there ought to be a simple answer, but there is not. This is because the same miracle is recorded in more than one Gospel, but perhaps with different details. John's Gospel records seven 'signs' performed by Jesus that are all 'miraculous'. Given these difficulties, however, it is generally accepted that Jesus performed at least thirty different miracles (including John's 'signs').

Jesus performed different sorts of miracle. Some involved the healing of sick people – even people who had died – casting out demons, nature miracles, and so on. All of these were considered impossible for any human to do. This means that God must have been working through Jesus, reinforcing the belief that Jesus was the Son of God. Many Christians today still believe that miracles happen. Some have been healed of diseases or 'incurable' medical conditions. At the French pilgrimage site of Lourdes, for example, many people have been healed of life-challenging illnesses, and many more go there in the hope of being healed.

Jesus' resurrection

The resurrection of Jesus is, for Christians, the single most important event in the history of the world. This is because they understand that Jesus gave up his own life in order to save the world from sin. His death was **salvific**. Christians believe that Jesus died in order to wash away the sins of all the world, resulting in a restoration of the relationship between God and humans. Although the Pharisees believed in life after death, there are only two references to it in the Old Testament:

Salvific:
The idea that Jesus' death saved humans from their sins

Isaiah 26:19

> But your dead will live, Lord; their bodies will rise
> let those who dwell in the dust wake up and shout for joy
> your dew is like the dew of the morning; the earth will give birth to her dead.

Daniel 12:2–3

> Multitudes who sleep in the dust of the earth will awake: some to everlasting life, others to shame and everlasting contempt. Those who are wise will shine like the brightness of the heavens, and those who lead many to righteousness, like the stars for ever and ever.

Both these references from late biblical Judaism project their belief in resurrection far into the future. Jesus' resurrection, however, took place on the third day after his death. In early Jewish thought (pre-exile), Jews did not believe in an afterlife. It was only during their exile in Babylon that the Jews learned of the Babylonians' belief in an afterlife. This discovery sparked Jewish belief in life after death. A bodily resurrection would therefore have seemed very odd to Jews of the early period. Later, the post-exilic Sadducees developed a view that, on death, a person would descend to the 'pit' of **Sheol**. They would remain there for a long time, existing as 'pallid empty shades in a land of nothingness' (Anthony Towey, *An Introduction to Christian Theology*, 2nd edn, Bloomsbury T&T Clark, 2018, p. 121). Those who arrived in Sheol were not to expect much of their surroundings or themselves. King Hezekiah prayed to God (Isa. 38:18): 'Sheol cannot thank you. Death cannot praise you; those who go down to the pit cannot hope for your faithfulness. The living, only the living can praise

Sheol:
In late Jewish theology, it was thought that, when a person died, they descended to an underground pit, where they would stay for an undefined time

The Person of Jesus Christ

you.' The quotation above comes from the late period in Jewish eschatological thought, when resurrection was an established belief.

Jesus' resurrection goes against this Jewish background. Interestingly, all the Gospels are quite consistent in recording the narrative. Everyone concerned – the women who went to the tomb, the disciples – believed that Jesus' body had been stolen, a not uncommon occurrence, or (as Matthew conjectures) that an earthquake had dislodged the stone. Whatever the historicity of the events around the discovery of the empty tomb, Jesus' followers were transformed from their dejection and defeat into renewed and purposeful people again.

Later, Paul preaches 'what we have testified about God, that he raised Christ from the dead. But he did not raise him if in fact the dead are not raised' (1 Cor. 15:15). Paul makes it clear that, if Jesus was not in fact brought back to life, Christianity would be pointless, sins would not be taken away and people would have no hope of living again after death. It is at this point that resurrection becomes a central part of Christian belief. Salvation becomes dependent on believing that Jesus was resurrected. (Romans 10:8–9).

> **Exercise**
> Explain to someone who is not religious how Jesus' resurrection could have happened.

Quest for the historical Jesus: A historical/theological search to ascertain who Jesus really was

Stretch and challenge: the quest for the historical Jesus

Since the nineteenth century, biblical scholars have used scientific methods to attempt to find out who Jesus really was, as a historical figure. The 'quest', as it became known, has returned a variety of results, and has been divided into three reasonably distinct phases.

The first quest

The scholar **Albert Schweitzer** (1875–1965) published *The Quest of the Historical Jesus: A Critical Study of its Progress from Reimarus to Wrede* in 1906 (English translation 1910, 2nd edn 1913). In this book, Schweitzer surveys all of the many previous studies on the historical Jesus, concluding that the understanding of who Jesus was had changed significantly, depending on the views of each author. His own conclusion was that Jesus should be understood in the context of late Jewish **eschatology**. Jesus preached about the end of the world, proclaiming that God would bring this about in the near future. His preaching was focused on exhorting people to repent their sins and turn back to God.

Eschatology: The doctrine of the Last Things, when God's judgement of individuals would determine their ultimate fate

The primary intention of the 'first quest' authors was to try to ascertain the 'historical Jesus', i.e. who Jesus actually was, by stripping out all the seemingly 'supernatural' or 'divine' elements. German biblical scholar **David Strauss** (1808–74) was one of the first to attempt this task. In his *Life of Jesus* (1835), he rejected all the miracles of Jesus, calling them 'myths' that had been added to the original biography, in order to enhance the status of Jesus.

Some more radical scholars, such as **Bruno Bauer** (1809–82), even concluded that there never was a 'historical' Jesus because none of the sources were historically reliable, as they had been overlaid with layers of 'myth'. The first quest for Jesus effectively came to an end with the 1896 publication of *The So-Called Historical Jesus and the Christ of Faith* by German scholar **Martin Kähler** (1835–1912). Kähler concluded that it was impossible to separate the historical Jesus from the Christ of Christian faith. Instead, Christians should aim to understand how the Christ of faith had influenced history.

The second quest

Schweitzer's *Quest of the Historical Jesus*, with its damning criticism of previous books, hammered the final nail in the coffin of the 'first' quest. There was, for a time, a feeling amongst scholars that the attempt to find the historical Jesus was a fruitless and impossible task. It is generally recognized that a lecture by German scholar **Ernst Käsemann** (1906–98), on 20 October 1953, inaugurated the 'second quest period' of Jesus research. Käsemann argued that, although the narratives about Jesus are largely theological, it is still possible to detect some historical information about him. To do this, tools of historical analysis had to be used systematically to yield effective results. He used the criterion of dissimilarity to compare statements by Jesus with the Jewish context of the time. If they were dissimilar, the statement of Jesus was probably authentic. Another criterion, that of embarrassment, was used to good effect, on the basis that the authors of the NT would not invent any story that would be embarrassing to them. So, for instance, while the basic facts of the baptism of Jesus may be historically correct, the inclusion of the 'dove' and the 'voice from heaven' may be later additions to the text. This could have been embarrassing because Jesus (who was sinless) was baptized by John (who taught the forgiveness of sin). Placing John above Jesus in this story would have been an embarrassment to the early Christians, but it was included in the NT because it was believed to be true.

The third quest

Scholars continued to be divided about suitable criteria, however, and the second quest came to an end in the early 1970s. By the 1980s, there was a renewed interest in the search for the historical Jesus. In 1992, British New Testament scholar **N. T. Wright** (1948–present) referred to the growing number of approaches from different scholars as the 'third quest'. A few of these responses were aimed at a non-academic audience. For example, Hugh Schonfield (1901–88) attempted to reconstruct the life and teaching of Jesus in *The Passover Plot* (Hutchinson, 1965) and, more recently, Dan Brown's *The Da Vinci Code* (Corgi, 2009), though it did not claim to be historical, raised the profile of the historical Jesus for a public audience.

The third quest has, perhaps, been categorized by criticism of the previous quests, particularly of the criteria that had been used to establish what was authentic historical material in the NT. The Irish-American scholar **John Dominic Crossan** (1934–present), for example, argues that Jesus was a poor Jewish peasant who attempted to break down the power structures of first-century Jewish society by associating with those on the edges of society (the poor, lepers, etc.) and by criticizing those in power (the Pharisees and other religious groups).

Another American biblical scholar, **Ed Sanders** (1937–present), sees Jesus as a prophetic figure who wanted to restore Judaism to its former glory. In his 1993 book, *The Historical Figure of Jesus* (Penguin, 1995), he returns to Schweitzer's idea that Jesus was a preacher of eschatology. Sanders believes that Jesus wanted to usher in a new age for Israel, focusing on a new Temple, with himself as God's representative.

N. T. Wright has taken a different line of argument. He criticizes Sanders' approach but agrees with some aspects of it, notably the idea that Jesus offered something new and different, particularly his relationships with ordinary Jewish people, identifying them as the people of God. The third quest has lacked coherence, with scholars from many parts of the world advocating very differing views of who Jesus was. As British theologian Alister McGrath notes: 'There is significant disagreement concerning whether Jesus is to be seen against a Jewish or Hellenistic background; about his attitude to the Jewish law and its religious institutions; about his view of the future of Israel; and about the personal significance of Jesus in relation to that future' (*Christian Theology: An Introduction*, p. 242). Despite all these disagreements, however, it seems that the search to find the historical Jesus will continue, as innovative perspectives and techniques arise.

Jesus the teacher of Wisdom

The word 'wisdom' in this section may be interpreted in two ways. First, 'wisdom' may mean that Jesus spoke 'wise' words to the people who listened to him preach. Alternatively, 'wisdom' may have a more technical meaning. In the Old Testament, and in the ancient world more generally, there was a type of literature called Wisdom literature. The canonical books of Job, Proverbs and Ecclesiastes are recognized as Wisdom literature. Several other books, including the Psalms, and some of Jesus' parables, are given the title also, but some scholars dispute this. The authentic Wisdom books emphasize the importance of true wisdom. 'Wisdom' is a feminine noun in Hebrew and is often portrayed as a woman. In Proverbs 9:1–6, Wisdom is a high-ranking woman who can employ a messenger; she may invite the 'simple' to a banquet in her large house. In Proverbs 8:6, she is a counsellor and teacher.

Jesus' use of parables

Jesus spoke in parables – this is an acknowledged form of Wisdom literature. Parables are a form of thinking that turns the accepted wisdom of the day on its head. For instance, it might say that possessing money and power are only temporary states, which will fade because they are not durable. Instead, people should put their faith in God and in loving their neighbour as themselves, because these are durable virtuous actions and beliefs. Many of Jesus' parables pick up on this theme of turning an individual's life around by confronting them with a more satisfying alternative. For example, Mark chapter 5 recounts three separate stories in which peoples' lives are completely turned around – a demon-possessed man (vv.18–20); a sick woman (vv.25–34); Jairus' daughter (vv.35–43).

Theologian **Stephen Pattison** (1953–present) (*The SCM Guide to Theological Reflection*) points to the picture in the Gospels of Jesus as an itinerant sage, touring round from village to village with a message of social radicalism that would have resulted in him getting into trouble with the authorities. This kind of behaviour was subversive of the established order and might have led to Jesus' fateful execution. He spoke about the first being last and the last first, a form of egalitarianism, as his vision of the Kingdom of God. Scholars such as Crossan (*The Historical Jesus*, Harper Collins, 1991) believe that Jesus was a Wisdom teacher with a revolutionary message for the people of Israel. This concerned a coming kingdom that was egalitarian and was being made available for them by God. This appealed to the ordinary people and agricultural workers who were being exploited by the Romans, who were commercializing the area. Crossan's view has much to commend it. There were many other teachers in this long-standing Wisdom tradition. Many of these taught in parables, as Jesus did, so it could be possible that Jesus was indeed a teacher of Wisdom. The suggestion also fits well with more modern rationalist ways of looking at the past, that are dismissive of miracles, resurrection and the idea of a virgin birth. So Jesus is seen in an entirely naturalistic framework in the context of his day. He is seen as a man

- who preached about how to overcome social norms
- who had women followers
- who taught about healing people and including them in the Kingdom of God.

In the Beatitudes (Matt. 5), Jesus picks out the meek, the hungry, those who mourn and those who strive to be peacemakers. Jesus asserts that all of these are 'blessed'. By using this kind of language, Jesus overturns the accepted framework of society. According to German New Testament scholar Gert Theissen, by using synagogues to talk to the disciples and the ordinary people, Jesus corresponds to the contemporary notion of a rabbi.

Another reason to recommend Jesus as a teacher of Wisdom is that it sits comfortably alongside other world faiths. British theologian John Hick edited a book called *The Myth of God Incarnate*, in which it is argued that traditional Christian doctrines such as the virgin birth should be re-interpreted to make them more consistent with other world faiths. So, Jesus may be seen alongside Moses or Jeremiah or Muhammad (PBUH), Guru Nanak, St Francis of Assisi or other significant Prophets around the world. In a multi-faith world, the picture of Jesus as a teacher of Wisdom who challenges self-centredness, and encourages people to be loving towards others, sits positively alongside the traditions of wisdom in other cultures and faiths and can be helpful for believers.

Arguments against Jesus as a teacher of Wisdom

There are several counter-arguments to understanding Jesus as a teacher of Wisdom. If Jesus had been only a teacher of Wisdom and had no intention of becoming a legitimate political leader, then he seems like a rather innocuous and inoffensive minor character in first-century Israel. It would be very odd for the Romans to have taken any notice of such a person, never mind wanting to execute such a harmless preacher. The well-known Christian scholar and writer C. S. Lewis attempted to persuade people that there are only two possible choices about Jesus – either he was a lunatic or he was God. Lewis' view is that it would be illogical to call Jesus a lunatic, so he must be God. Lewis continues that it does not make sense to ask, if he was merely a harmless itinerant preacher, 'Why would he have had the sign above his cross saying "the King of the Jews"?' Such a message would imply that Jesus, in his parables, was claiming to be a king (*Mere Christianity*, Collins, 1956, pp. 55–6).

> **Exercise**
>
> Do you agree with Lewis that there are only two choices about Jesus? Are there other ways of thinking about Jesus? Is there anything illogical in thinking of Jesus as merely a teacher of morals?

A second criticism concerns the connection between the idea of Christ being both God and human, and salvation. The fourth-century theologian **Gregory of Nazianzus** (c.329–90) famously said: 'That which he has not assumed, he has not healed. That which is united to his godhead is also saved' (Letter 101, 'Against Apollinarius', line 218). In traditional Christian belief, if God has not united his human nature to his divine nature, then there can be no hope of salvation. St Paul said: 'If Christ has not been raised, your faith is futile; you are still in your sins' (1 Cor. 15:17). **Dietrich Bonhoeffer** (1906–45) asserted: 'When God's son took flesh, he truly and bodily out of pure grace took on our being, our nature, ourselves, so that we are him. Wherever he is, he bears our flesh, he bears us. In the Incarnation and his resurrection, we belong to him because we are in him' (*Life Together* [1939], SCM Press, 1954, p. 33).

There is a much more fundamental claim made in Orthodox Christianity. According to this tradition, Jesus is not just a human being who teaches wise parables and sayings, he is also a fundamentally different kind of being, related to God the Father as the Eternal Son, and therefore this is the only way that salvation for humans can be brought about. This assertion claims something far more unique and exclusive for Jesus the Son of God. This view would be dissatisfied with the idea that Jesus was (only) a teacher of Wisdom.

Jesus as liberator

Jesus as a challenge to political authority

There is some evidence in the Bible that Jesus was a political figure, who criticized the ruling Roman political regime. The 'political' Jesus claimed authority and challenged the religious and political authorities through his teaching. He asserted 'render to Caesar the things that are Caesar's, but to God the things that are God's' (Matt. 22:21) in answer to whether taxes should be paid by the Jews to the Romans. Jesus' response here may be seen as somewhat lacklustre, seemingly acquiescing with this punitive tax on the Jews. He performed healings to marginalized groups, such as publicans and lepers, outside the acceptable channels. He was known as a friend of sinners, eating and drinking with them. In including the marginalized within God's Kingdom, and excluding those who were pompous in their religiosity, Jesus removed them from their usual place at the head of the table. This seems to make Jesus a subversive character. In the parable of the Good Samaritan (Lk. 10:25–37), the hero was a Samaritan, a people hated by the Jews, not a Pharisee, Sadducee or scribe. By telling this parable, Jesus was placing himself against the legitimate Jewish religious authorities, and seemingly with the **Zealots**, a Jewish revolutionary group who wanted to take arms against the Romans to force them out of Israel. One of Jesus' disciples was Simon, 'the Zealot'. Jesus talked of the coming Kingdom of God in apocalyptic terms, saying God would return, ushering in a cataclysmic Day of Judgement and settling all accounts. All of these ideas are in opposition to Rome and its power. John the Baptist had begun this movement of renewal and repentance among the Jews. Jesus, having been baptized by John, joined it in his desire to establish a kingdom opposed to that of Rome. This view has been taken up by Liberation theologians (see chapter 12), some of whom think of Jesus as a liberator, a revolutionary who wanted to achieve justice for all people. In the words of the Colombian Liberation theologian **Camilo Torres Restrepo** (1929–66), 'If Jesus were alive today, he would be a guerrillero' (Emily Wade Will, *Archbishop Oscar Romero: The Making of a Martyr*, Resource Publications, 2016, p. 68). Jesus would stand with the poor, and would take the side of Liberation theology's emphasis on the preferential option for the poor. (See p. 190.) Jesus is seen as the liberator of the poor and oppressed, as someone who was just as interested in institutional injustice and sin as he was in personal wrongdoings. Another important Liberation theologian, **Leonardo Boff** (1938–present), said: 'A Christology that proclaims Jesus Christ as the Liberator seeks to be committed to the economic, social and political liberation of those groups that are oppressed and dominated. It purports to see the theological relevance of the historic liberation of the vast majority of people in our continent' (L. Boff, *Jesus Christ Liberator*, Orbis Books, 1972, p. 266).

Many Christians believe that the liberation that Jesus brought is universal and transcends national boundaries. Jesus' liberation attacks the foundations of injustice and exploitation. Another liberation theologian, **Gustavo Gutierrez** (1928–present), taught that Jesus the liberator eliminates the political and religious confusion of being limited to a purely spiritual plane. Liberation theologians want

Zealots: Revolutionary Jewish group who wanted to take up arms against the Romans, to reclaim Israel for Judaism

> **Gustavo Gutierrez** Gutierrez is a Peruvian Roman Catholic priest and theologian, who has spent most of his life ministering to the poor of Lima. He began studying to be a medical doctor, but realized that he should be a priest instead. He studied Theology at Leuven in Belgium and in Lyon, France. He was influenced not only by Roman Catholic theologians such as Karl Rahner, but also by Protestants like Karl Barth. When Gutierrez became a priest, he worked in poverty-stricken areas of Lima. The people he met, he said, were searching for bread and for God as well. He came to understand poverty as much more than just wanting food, but as 'a way of living, of thinking, of loving, of praying, of waiting and believing, of spending free time, of fighting for life'. Along with other Liberation theologians, Gutierrez has worked tirelessly to bring about the 'preferential option for the poor' in Latin America. Of his many books, the most influential is *A Theology of Liberation: History, Politics and Salvation*.

to 'own' Jesus as a kind of Zealot figure who is anything other than politically neutral, fighting against unjust economic and social structures, and showing a bias to the poor.

Another aspect of Jesus as liberator is that he talked frequently in his parables about debtors and those who were marginalized. He wanted to lift up the poor and the weak (e.g. Matt. 5:3; 9:21; Lk. 14:13) and not be just a teacher of moral rules. An example of this is the incident where Jesus taught about the plight of those who are poor and hungry (Lk. 14:13–24). Jesus told his hearers:

> when you are having guests for lunch or supper, do not invite your friends, your brothers or other relations, or your rich neighbours; they will only ask you back again and so you will be repaid. But when you give a party, ask the poor, the crippled, the lame and the blind. That is the way to find happiness, because they have no means of repaying you. You will be repaid on the day when the righteous rise from the dead.

This advice would have been shocking and distasteful for many of the people who heard Jesus' teaching. It is an example of the radical nature of Jesus' teaching. It was aimed at the complacency and social blindness of the well-off in Israel, attempting to persuade them to think of someone other than themselves.

Jesus as a challenge to religious authority

Jesus often came into conflict with the Jewish religious authorities, especially the Pharisees. One such incident is recorded (Mark 11:27–33) when 'the chief priests, scribes and elders' challenge Jesus' authority to overturn the tables of money-changers in the Temple court. Jesus' response was to ask them a question – did the authority of John the Baptist to baptize people come from God, or from humans? This was a question that would trap the religious authorities. If they answered 'from God', Jesus would ask why they refused to accept the Baptist's message. If they declared that John's authority was merely human, the crowd would turn against them. When they declined to answer, Jesus side-stepped their criticism of him and, in turn, refused to answer them.

Jesus also challenged religious authorities in some of his parables. For instance, in the parable of the Good Samaritan (Lk. 10:25–37), Jesus praised a Samaritan for coming to the assistance of a wounded Jewish man, who had been attacked and left for dead by robbers. He spoke of how a rabbi and a Levite, both members of the most important religious groups in Jerusalem, had chosen not to help the wounded man. The Samaritans were a group who were considered by most Jews as being ritually impure, because they married non-Jews. Jesus' point in this story was twofold:

- first, to teach that, whenever anyone is in need – regardless of where they come from or which religion they are members of – they should be helped
- second, to criticize the religious authorities for not helping, putting their religious duties before the value of human life.

Difficulties with the view of Jesus as liberator

At his trial, Jesus was at pains to say 'My kingdom is not of this world. If it were, my servants would fight to prevent my arrest by the Jewish leaders. But now my kingdom is from another place' (John 18:36). In the Garden of Gethsemane, at the time of his arrest, he told Peter to put away his sword. The Roman Governor, Pontius Pilate, when Jesus is on trial, certainly did not think of him as a revolutionary leader, but rather as a dreamer (cf. Mark 15:14: Pilate asks the Jewish leaders 'What crime has he committed?'). Of course, Jesus is not initially seen as a threat to Caesar, so there is a potential problem of painting him as a revolutionary Zealot, despite the fact that Simon the Zealot was one of his disciples.

In 66 CE, the Zealots attempted a revolt against Rome and, for three years, Israel had independence and even minted its own coins. In 70 CE, however, the Roman general Titus surrounded Jerusalem and crucified many Jews, sold thousands into slavery and forced others to perform in the gladiatorial arena. These horrific punishments were a warning to every other Roman province that, if any of their citizens attempted to revolt, this was what would happen to them.

It is very difficult to see Jesus as a kind of early vanguard of a Jewish revolutionary movement such as the Zealots, and the attempt to do so is highly questionable. Jesus may have offered a fresh interpretation of Jewish beliefs and taken the title Messiah, but this is not enough to define him as a revolutionary liberator.

Michael Grant (1914–2004) relates, in his book on Jesus, that Herod Antipas had Jesus killed because he thought that Jesus was a political danger: 'Galilee was always turbulent … In this tense atmosphere, Jesus' repeated assertions of the dawning and imminent consummation of a kingdom other than that of Antipas, namely the Kingdom of God, could well be considered unsettling and seditious.'

Grant points out that the title 'Zealot' was derived from the Aramaic term *qan'an* or Hebrew *qanna*, meaning 'ruthless zeal in the service of God'. He says that, at the time of Jesus, the 'Zealots' were focused on defending the Jewish religion, and it was only thirty years after Jesus that they became politicized and raised a revolt against the Romans (Michael Grant, *Jesus*, Phoenix Giant, 1977, pp. 131–2).

In evaluating Jesus as liberator, it is important to remember that his teaching was explicitly religious, and rarely political in nature. Certainly, to understand Jesus as a revolutionary Zealot is to remove him from all the gentler, loving characteristics that describe him and his teaching throughout the Gospel accounts.

FURTHER READING

Reza Aslan, *Zealot: The Life and Times of Jesus of Nazareth*. The Westbourne Press, 2013

Helen Bond, *The Historical Jesus: A Guide for the Perplexed*. Bloomsbury, 2012

Helen Bond, *Jesus – A Very Brief History*. SPCK, 2017

Bart D. Ehrman, *How Jesus Became God*. HarperOne, 2014

Dalai Lama XIV, *The Good Heart: A Buddhist Perspective on the Teachings of Jesus*. Wisdom Publications US, 2016

Richard E. Rubenstein, *When Jesus Became God: The Epic Fight over Christ's Divinity in the Last Days of Rome*. Harcourt & Brace, 1999

Alan J. Spence, *Christology: A Guide for the Perplexed*. Bloomsbury, 2008

Thought Points

1. The Apostles' Creed is in three sections; explain why the section on Jesus is much longer than those on God and the Holy Spirit.

2. 'Jesus was just a human being.' Make a list of the arguments for and against this statement.

3. Do you think that the 'quest for the historical Jesus' had any value? Explain your reasons.

4. Why do Christians worship Jesus?

5. 'In first-century Israel, there were lots of Prophets, preachers and miracle workers, so Jesus was not unique.' Explain and evaluate this claim.

6. Some theologians make a distinction between 'the Jesus of history' and 'the Christ of faith'. Explain what this distinction means and what its implications are for understanding Christology.

7. 'Jesus' teaching on morality is much more relevant today than any other beliefs about him.' To what extent do you agree with this statement?

SECTION III
LIVING

CHAPTER 5
Christian Moral Principles

LEARNING OUTCOMES
In this chapter, you will be learning about
- the diversity of Christian moral reasoning, and practices and sources of ethics, including
  - the Bible as the only authority for Christian ethical practices
  - Bible, Church and reason as the sources of Christian ethical practices
  - love (agape) as the only Christian ethical principle which governs Christian practices

Church tradition: The official teaching of the Church on important matters of doctrine, based on what Christians have believed and practised over time

Natural Law: Aquinas defined this as 'right reason in accordance with human nature'

Magisterium: The teaching authority of the Roman Catholic church

Introduction

This chapter concerns how Christian believers make their ethical decisions about the world in which they live. For many, the Bible will be the first source of moral authority. For some, it will be the only source to glean how they should act in a difficult situation or with a problem they must solve. For others, it will be the teaching of the Church, or **church tradition**. How the Church has reacted to an ethical problem in the past will guide Christians now about what decision they should make on an ethical problem. This way of making ethical decisions is usually combined with the use of reason. It may also be guided by **Natural Law**, and perhaps by searching their conscience, or by abiding by what the **Magisterium** declares.

Some of these ways of making moral decisions are linked with particular denominations within Christianity, for example Natural Law and the Magisterium, which are prevalent in the Roman Catholic church. The Bible and reason tend to be used more

by Protestants, while believers in any denomination may use conscience to make moral decisions.

For other Christians, unconditional love (agape) may be the prime way of making ethical decisions. **Situation Ethics**, founded in the 1960s by American theologian **Joseph Fletcher** (1905–91), taught that morality must not have rigid rules, but decisions must be made on a case-by-case basis.

Even this very brief introduction indicates the diversity concerning what Christian ethics are and how they might be used. In the rest of this chapter, we will look at three strategies or principles that Christians may use in making moral decisions.

> **Situation Ethics:** Joseph Fletcher's liberal theory of ethics, based on Jesus' command to 'love' one's neighbours, based not on laws but on the situation at the time

The Bible – theonomous ethics

The Bible is not just a single source of morality, it is a collection of diverse views about what morality is, and how and by whom it should be administered. What these sources have in common is the belief that they all derive from God. The Bible is a collection of different books that span over 1,000 years, and reflect different cultures and social contexts. The one thing that unites them is the belief that the one God they all believe in wishes them to behave in ways that are consistent with his will. There are three main contexts for biblical ethics – the Torah, **the Prophets**, and the NT.

> **The Prophets:** A major part of the Old Testament is made up of prophetic writing. It took various forms, such as messages about social justice, or criticism of the Old Testament Jews when they had gone against God's laws

The Torah

Torah is the Hebrew word for 'law', and 'the Torah' is considered to be the books of law, given by God to the Israelites, through their leader, Moses. Jews and biblical Christians believe that 'the God of Abraham heard our groaning when we were slaves, rescued us from Egypt and made us a people with a covenant' (Ex. 6:5).

The Torah records ethical decisions and rules made in a period of Jewish history when the Jews were enslaved by the Egyptian empire and forced to endure hard labour and deprived of food and resources. Chief among these were the Ten Commandments or **Decalogue**. The Ten Commandments were understood as a **covenant** that God made with the Israelites/Jews. It is in the form of a **suzerainty treaty**, which acknowledged and confirmed that God would be their king and they would be his faithful people. Like other suzerainty treaties, it begins by naming the great king and proclaiming the good things he has done (Ex. 20:2), then proceeds to lay down rules about the people's loyalty to the king (Ex. 20:3–17), and ends with assurances of blessings as long as the people fulfil the covenant agreement (Ex.23:22–33). The essential thing about this kind of treaty is that both sides agree to live according to its rules. These rules are absolute: they are not dependent on circumstances. The people who make the covenant are bound absolutely. For the Jews, the Ten Commandments must be followed without exception.

When Christianity began to emerge, most of its adherents had been brought up as Jews and therefore knew the Ten Commandments and lived according to them. Some of the Commandments (1–4) are 'corporate' and relate to everyone in the community.

> **Decalogue:** Another name for the Ten Commandments

> **Covenant:** A mutually binding agreement between God and his followers

> **Suzerainty treaty:** This was an ancient Hittite treaty between two unequal partners – the more powerful suzerain and the less powerful vassal, who must submit to the suzerain. The Ten Commandments are written in this form

Others (5–10) are 'personal' and relate to individuals. The difficulty for Christians today when they assent to following these Commandments is that not all of them can be obeyed – at least, not literally. For instance, numbers 4 (about the Sabbath) and 10 (about 'coveting') both mention attitudes to 'slaves' and this cannot be taken literally today. An interpretation must be made to make this 'relevant' to a different kind of society.

The Prophets

Many of the Prophets mentioned in the Old Testament were social reformers, but most were tasked by God to remind the Israelites of their covenant responsibilities. Amos and Hosea, for instance, who lived in the eighth century BCE, both preached that Israel, the covenantal community, had rejected God's covenant. In Hosea 4, the Prophet rants at length at the people because, instead of faithfulness to the covenant, there is 'swearing, lying, murder, stealing and committing adultery'. In the same chapter, he also reveals how they sacrificed to pagan gods and engaged with temple prostitutes, thereby breaking most of the Commandments. The Prophet tells the people that, if they do not turn back to God's Commandments, severe punishment will be their fate.

Earlier, in the ninth century BCE, the Prophet Elijah, when summoned by God and asked why he was in a cave near Horeb, replied: 'The people of Israel have forsaken your covenant, torn down your altars and put your prophets to the sword. I alone am left and they seek to take my life' (1 Kings 19:10). God tells Elijah to return to Damascus, anoint Jehu as king and order him to kill all the Israelites who have sinned against God.

Another theme in prophetic ethics is that of providing help and justice to the poor and needy. Often, this concerns peoples' physical needs, rather than their spiritual ones. For example, in Isaiah 3:14–15, it says: 'The Lord opens the indictment against the elders and officers of his people: It is you that have ravaged the vineyard; your houses are the spoils taken from the poor. Is it nothing to you that you crush my people and grind the faces of the poor?'

In Isaiah 10:1–2, the Prophet warns of God's justice awaiting those who fail to live up to the standards that God expects: 'Woe betide those who enact unjust laws and draft oppressive edicts, depriving the poor of justice, robbing the weakest of my people of their rights, plundering the widow and despoiling the fatherless!'

The Prophet asks what these unjust people will do when God calls them to account. He suggests that they will have all their power and wealth taken away and they will be forced to 'cower among the prisoners or fall among the slain' (verse 3).

There is a great deal of preaching from the Old Testament Prophets calling people to account for their failure to live up to God's Commandments and ethical standards, and an equal amount of commands and warnings to these people to ensure that they fulfil their part of the covenant with God.

The New Testament

In all four Gospels, there is a consistent view of the ethical teaching of Jesus of Nazareth. He began his ministry by announcing confidently that the Kingdom of God would arrive soon and his preaching was proclaiming it. He spoke with authority, calling on people to repent their sins, and to reform their character and their deeds so that they could be counted worthy of joining this Kingdom. He was convinced that God's kingdom was close to being initiated, so he spoke with authority and urgency, making a radical demand for people to put their house in order before it was too late for them to receive God's blessing.

The focal point of Jesus' ethical teaching is seen in the **Sermon on the Mount** (Matt. 5–7). Most scholars believe that this is a compilation by the Gospel writer of Jesus' teaching on ethics. There are three distinct but connected sections in the Sermon.

> **Sermon on the Mount:**
> A compilation of Jesus' teaching on morality in Matthew 5–7

- First, there are the **Beatitudes** (Matt. 5:3–12). This is a series of statements, some of which appear contradictory, for instance:

    > Blessed (happy) are the poor in spirit; theirs shall be the kingdom of heaven
    > Blessed are the sorrowful; they shall find consolation
    > Blessed are the gentle; they shall have the earth for their possession.

    Jesus seems to be turning people's expectations upside down, and this would have caused great surprise to his audience. He says that God's kingdom will be inhabited by the poor, the rejected in society, the vulnerable and so on, not the rich and successful self-righteous members of society. Jesus calls the former group the 'salt of the earth' (5:13) and the 'light of the world' (5:14–15), whose 'good works' bring glory to God (5:16).

> **Beatitudes:**
> Part of Jesus' teaching about social justice in Matthew 5

- The second section of the Sermon on the Mount makes demands on the followers of Jesus, especially in connection with how they worship. They must not be ostentatious in their worship, calling attention to themselves and showing how 'religious' they are. Their focus must be on the central beliefs of being a Christian. This is summarized in the words of the Lord's Prayer (6:8–15), blessing God's name, hoping for God's arrival to create his (spiritual) kingdom, asking God for daily sustenance, asking forgiveness for their sins and exhorting God to keep them from 'the evil one' (verse 13).
- The final section reminds Christians that the way to salvation and heavenly reward is difficult and not everyone will succeed (7:21: 'Not everyone who says to me, "Lord, Lord", will enter the kingdom of heaven, but only those who do the will of my heavenly Father'). True believers will follow the **Golden Rule** – 'Always treat others as you would like them to treat you' (7:12). Jesus' teaching in the Sermon on the Mount declares that God has initiated a new relationship with humans. The sermon is a message of 'good news' (Gospel) that sets out its stall, showing people how to live in relationship with God. This includes not just worship of God, but performing good actions that will help others survive in a sometimes cruel and unjust world, and help them to achieve salvation into God's kingdom.

> **Golden Rule:**
> 'Do to others what you would wish them to do to you': Jesus quotes Leviticus 19:18 in the Sermon on the Mount (Matt 7:12)

Problems with the Bible-only approach

Many millions of conservative evangelical and Fundamentalist Christians use the teaching of the Bible as their only guidance for how to make ethical decisions. This is known as the doctrine of ***sola scriptura*** (from Latin, 'by scripture alone'). This approach creates an important issue for those Christians who take biblical statements literally. They believe that the Bible contains the actual words of God and that every statement in the Bible is literally true. The Ten Commandments, as we mentioned above, seem to presuppose that having slaves is socially acceptable. There is no condemnation of keeping slaves: it seems perfectly acceptable to have them, with the only caveat being that they are to be treated reasonably. The only way to avoid this apparent difficulty with reading the biblical text literally is to attempt to 'explain it away' for modern readers and Christian believers. This is usually done by acknowledging that the Commandments arose in an ancient society where the culture was very different from that of the twenty-first century. The difficulty with this kind of explanation is that, if this Commandment cannot be taken literally, then maybe the others should not be taken literally either?

There are many different styles of writing in the Bible. If they were all written by God, shouldn't we expect them to be written in a consistent style, to aid people's understanding of its teaching?

There are apparent contradictions in the Bible. To give just two examples:

Sola scriptura: Some Christians attempt to derive moral principles from the Bible alone

On the permanence of Earth

> Ecclesiastes 1:4 – 'Intelligent purpose has existed from the beginning.'
> 2 Peter 3:10 – 'the heavens will disappear with a great rushing sound, the elements will be dissolved in flames, and the earth with all that is in it will be brought to judgement'.

Seeing God

> Genesis 32:30 - Jacob called the place Peniel, 'because', he said, 'I have seen God face to face, yet my life is spared'.
> John 1:18 - 'No one has ever seen God.'

> **Exercise**
>
> Carry out an internet search for 'contradictions in the Bible'. Choose three to explain and discuss with your friends and/or classmates. What conclusions can you draw from this exercise?

Heteronomous ethics: Bible, Church and reason as the sources of Christian ethical practices

Introduction

As we have seen above, for many Protestant Christians, the Bible alone (*sola scriptura*) is believed to be sufficient for living a Christian life. In the post-biblical period, however, when Christianity was developing into a recognizably separate and different religion from Judaism, it quickly became apparent that not all believed the same things. There were groups that claimed to be Christian but had different beliefs. One example concerned the Docetists (from Greek *dokeo* – 'to appear') who believed that Jesus was divine, but only appeared to be human. This forced the early Christians to debate and think carefully about other sources of authority.

The **apostles** (the twelve disciples minus Judas Iscariot) had been endowed with authority by Jesus himself – 'Jesus summoned his twelve disciples and gave them authority over unclean spirits, to cast them out, and to heal every kind of disease and every kind of sickness' (Matt. 10:1). The word 'apostle' literally means 'messenger', and all of the apostles undertook some missionary work. The role of an apostle in the early Church, however, consisted of much more than going out to gain converts to the new faith. The apostles were seen as specially appointed leaders responsible for the founding, establishment, growth and development of the Church.

In addition to the original disciples, there were others in the early Church called apostles. James, Jesus' brother, became the leader of the Church in Jerusalem. Paul and his friend Barnabas also bore this title. In his letters, Paul refers to several others as apostles. It seems that the authority of an apostle, particularly the original group, was an authority that was conferred upon them. This authority could then be passed on to others, but it should always ultimately be derived from Jesus himself.

> **Apostles:** Jesus' twelve disciples minus Judas Iscariot

Roman Catholic ethical principles

Tradition

Tradition is an important source of authority for Roman Catholics. For many people, the past has enormous value. The fact that something has been done for hundreds or thousands of years gives it a strong sense of authority. If many people in the past have felt that a particular belief or practice is correct, then it seems arrogant for anyone to reject it without some overriding reason. Religion is an aspect of human existence that particularly values continuity, stability and the wisdom of the past. It is not that change and development are not recognized or valued in themselves, but rather that they should take place within the context of an accepted body of belief and practice that can be used to measure the value or quality of new ideas.

Christianity has been a powerful force for positive change in societies, but often by way of upholding traditional values, such as justice, in situations where they have been neglected. For example, the movement to abolish slavery in Britain was led

> **Tradition:** How the Church has reacted to an ethical problem in the past. It is an important source of authority in the Roman Catholic church

by William Wilberforce on the basis of biblical ideas about equality and justice. His inspiration was the converted slave-trader John Newton (the composer of the hymn 'Amazing Grace').

'Tradition', as a theological concept, has mostly been associated with the Roman Catholic church. Roman Catholics understand tradition as coming ultimately from Jesus Christ. For them, it is a living gift that Christ gave to the apostles and that has been handed down from generation to generation. Tradition is how the Holy Spirit makes the risen Jesus present amongst Christians today.

> **Exercise**
>
> The word 'Tradition' actually means *handing down* something to someone else. The capital 'T' is used for 'Sacred' Tradition to distinguish it from traditions that are just customs or habits.
>
> Look up the following references in the Bible and see what they have to say about the source of Tradition: 1 Cor. 13:23; 1 Cor. 15:3; 2 Thess. 2:15; 2 Tim. 1:11–14; 2 Tim. 2:1–2; Jude 1:3.

Roman Catholics believe that the apostles were commissioned to pass on the authentic Tradition. This Tradition is therefore firmly rooted and legitimized in the apostles. The apostles dedicated their lives to this mission of passing on the message of Jesus, and then appointed other faithful Christians to succeed them and carry on the work.

The Roman Catholic church has affirmed this idea. The document called *Dei verbum* was written after Vatican II (1962–5) and contains definitive teaching on the meaning of Tradition for all Roman Catholics. It includes the following statements, showing that Tradition comes from Christ and was handed down by the apostles:

> In His gracious goodness, God has seen to it that what He had revealed for the salvation of all nations would abide perpetually in its full integrity and be handed on to all generations. Therefore Christ the Lord in whom the full revelation of the supreme God is brought to completion . . . commissioned the Apostles to preach to all men that Gospel which is the source of all saving truth and moral teaching, and to impart to them heavenly gifts. This commission was faithfully fulfilled by the Apostles who, by their oral preaching, by example, and by observances handed on what they had received from the lips of Christ, from living with Him, and from what He did, or what they had learned through the prompting of the Holy Spirit. The commission was fulfilled, too, by those Apostles and apostolic men who under the inspiration of the same Holy Spirit committed the message of salvation to writing.
>
> (*Dei verbum*, 7)

The Magisterium

The institution of the Papacy in Roman Catholic Christianity is traced back to Jesus, who appointed Peter and his successors as shepherds of the Christian flock. At the end of John's Gospel (21:15–17), Jesus gives Peter the authority to lead the followers of Jesus with the words 'feed my sheep'. One of the many titles of the Pope is 'successor of St Peter, Prince of the Apostles'. This authority was confirmed in the statement from Vatican II: 'The Roman Pontiff, as the successor of Peter, is the perpetual and visible source and foundation of the unity both of the bishops and of the whole body of the faithful' (Vatican Council II, *Lumen gentium*, 23).

Pope Francis

One of the most important roles of the Pope is to unify the people of God. The Pope appoints senior figures to assist him with this task. From time to time, a Papal Encyclical will be published throughout the Church, when guidance is needed, particularly on moral issues, such as abortion or euthanasia. All Roman Catholics are expected to follow this teaching, as it encapsulates the Magisterium, or official teaching of the Church:

> It is clear, therefore, that sacred tradition, Sacred Scripture and the teaching authority of the Church (the Magisterium), in accord with God's most wise design, are so linked and joined together that one cannot stand without the others, and that all together and each in its own way under the action of the one Holy Spirit contribute effectively to the salvation of souls.
>
> (Vatican Council II, *Dei verbum*, para. 10)

Papal Encyclical:
This is a letter from the Pope to cardinals, bishops, clergy, and sometimes to all Roman Catholics. Encyclicals are important because they send an important message to the Church, usually about issues of social importance, or about Church doctrine.

Papal Infallibility: This is a dogma, not a doctrine, teaching that Papal statements made *ex cathedra* cannot contain error. Declared at the First Vatican Council, 1869–70

Associated with the power of the Papacy and the Magisterium is the dogma of **Papal Infallibility**. This was declared at the First Vatican Council in 1869–1870. This states that, because of Jesus' promise to Peter that he would be the leader of the 'church' (Matt. 16:18), the Pope (who is traced back to Peter) is believed to be incapable of error 'when, in the exercise of his office as shepherd and teacher of all Christians, in virtue of his supreme apostolic authority, he defines a doctrine concerning faith or morals to be held by the whole Church' (First Vatican Council, *First Dogmatic Constitution on the Church*, ch. 4, 9).

In Roman Catholic theology, there are several areas in which the Pope might speak 'infallibly': on revelation, scripture, tradition and the Magisterium (the teaching role of the Church). If the Pope wishes to speak 'infallibly', he speaks *ex cathedra* (i.e. 'from the chair' – that is, the symbol of his authority). What he says will have to conform to already-established beliefs understood as being derived from scripture and tradition. *Ex cathedra* statements are considered to have Apostolic and divine authority. This power was declared in 1870, and has only been used extremely rarely. The best-known example was when, in 1950, Pope Pius XII defined the doctrine of the Assumption of Mary as an article of faith.

Natural Law

In Romans 1:20, the apostle Paul argued that God's law may be seen in the world: 'Ever since the creation of the world, his invisible nature, namely his eternal power and deity, has been clearly perceived in the things that have been made.'

Christian theologians, particularly **Thomas Aquinas** (1225–74) in the thirteenth century, used this statement to develop a belief that, because God has made his moral law clear in the world, humans can have no excuse for disobeying it. God provided humans with the power of reason, so that they would be able to discern God's law in nature. Aquinas thought there were four kinds of law:

- **Eternal law** – was the mind of God. This could only be seen in terms of its effects in Natural Law and in 'moving all things to their due end'. The wisdom of God was reflected in his creation and sustaining of nature, but could not be known directly by humans.
- **Divine Law** – was revealed in the laws and moral precepts of scripture, providing a corrective to the fallenness of humans. Aquinas believed that human reason was not so impaired by the Fall as to be unable to think correctly about ethics. The revelation of scripture and the worship of the Church supplemented our understanding of the divine purpose and motivated our moral life with an inspiring vision of divine perfection and holiness. Yet it was not exhaustive in directing our moral conduct or applying to all circumstances, and, here, natural and human law both express and supplement Divine Law.
- **Natural Law** – is innate to all of nature, which is ordered by the Divine Lawmaker. Morality is human beings reasoning correctly. They can discern primary goods that are worth pursuing by their innate knowledge and natural inclination. God has ordered nature with essences and inclinations that are suited to their purpose or end goals. The **Synderesis** rule (that good is to be done and evil avoided) is innate in humans.
- **Human law** – is derived from Natural Law, and these laws are seen to be an extension of divine and Natural Law. What begins in nature is, through custom

Synderesis: Aquinas' view, as part of his Natural Law theory, that good is to be done and evil avoided

and usefulness, established in human laws through practical reasoning and experienced judgement (*phronesis*).

For Roman Catholic Christians today, Natural Law is still an important source of authority, particularly when it comes to moral issues. One of the strengths of Natural Law is that it appeals to people's sense that morality is more than just people's opinions about what is right and what is wrong. It upholds the idea that some things have intrinsic value. This means that they apply to everyone, not just some people. Another strength is that, because these moral laws come from God, they are absolute, and must always be obeyed. Moral decisions about abortion, for example, do not depend upon the circumstances at the time, but are always the same, regardless of who is involved or what their circumstances are. Natural Law has a very important voice in the discussion of Roman Catholic views on moral issues.

Protestant ethical principles

Stanley Hauerwas (1940–present)

American Methodist theologian Stanley Hauerwas has been a controversial figure in the Protestant tradition because he has argued that Christian ethics can only be done legitimately within the worshipping Christian community. He was heavily influenced by the theology of Karl Barth in this view. He argues that Christian ethics has lost its theological voice because it has attempted to make itself 'relevant' to a non-Christian world. For Hauerwas, this is a fundamental mistake. Christian ethics is based on the Bible and the life and teaching of Jesus. The ethical teaching of Christianity is for the Christian community and it evolves within that community. As such, Christian ethics would have to change to make it appropriate to the non-Christian world, but, if it did so, it would no longer be Christian ethics. Secular ethics and Christian ethics are fundamentally different. As Steven D. Cone says: (for Hauerwas) 'communities are always particular, and they are defined by their stories; Christian communities can only rightly be defined and formed by the story of Israel and Jesus' (*Theology from the Great Tradition*, T&T Clark, 2018, p. 540).

Autonomous Christian Ethics: love (agape) as the only Christian ethical principle that governs Christian practices

Beginnings

Autonomous Christian ethics, as the name suggests, is person-centred, rather than Bible- or Church-centred. Each individual may think about what he or she considers ethical action, and there is no single correct or incorrect action for each ethical problem. Ethical decisions are individual, so there are no universal rules. This means that an individual Christian does not necessarily have to consult the Bible or the teaching

> **Autonomous Christian ethics:** Person-centred ethics. Used by Fletcher in his Situation Ethics

Christian Moral Principles

of the Church in order to make his/her decision about an ethical issue. The Bible is still a special book, but it is not considered the ultimate source of wisdom for ethical advice, even for some Christians.

St Augustine famously said: 'Love, and do what you will. If you keep silence, keep silence in love; if you speak, speak in love; if you correct, correct in love; if you forbear, forbear in love. Let love's root be within you, for from that root nothing but good can spring' (*Epistola Joannis* 7.8).

'Agape' is one of four Greek words for love. Each describes a different kind of love:

- *eros* – sexual love
- *storgé* – family love
- *philia* – friendship love
- *agape* – unselfish love.

Jesus taught that agape is the kind of love that Christians should show to everyone they meet, whether they are strangers or friends or family members. Agape is the love that Jesus showed when he chose to be a sacrifice and allowed himself to be crucified for the sake of all humans. This is why his followers ought always to 'love' everyone they meet.

This is why St Paul said: 'Love is patient, love is kind; love is not envious or boastful or arrogant or rude. It does not insist on its own way; it is not irritable or resentful; it does not rejoice in wrongdoing, but rejoices in the truth. It bears all things, believes all things, hopes all things, endures all things' (1 Cor. 13: 4–7).

Agape love is the deciding criterion by which an individual Christian may choose the most loving thing to do in any given situation.

Several modern Christian theologians, both Roman Catholic and Protestant, have developed their ideas concerning an autonomous Christian ethics.

Roman Catholic views

The Swiss Roman Catholic priest and theologian **Hans Küng** (1928–present) is a liberal Roman Catholic and openly criticized the Roman Catholic church when he believed it to have failed to uphold the teaching of Jesus. He also rejected the doctrine of the infallibility of the Pope. He had a particular concern about the environment, and believed that the world was heading towards self-destruction. He taught that the Church must speak out urgently to the world so that a '**global ethic**' could be established in order to save the natural environment from being destroyed. His motivation was Jesus' command to 'love your neighbour', as Jesus had defined this as anyone that you encounter, not necessarily only Christians.

Küng's teaching was censored by the Magisterium of the Church, and his licence to teach in Roman Catholic universities was removed in 1979. He was still able to officiate as a priest, and allowed to teach at the Protestant University of Tübingen.

More generally, the Roman Catholic church widens the horizons of this debate beyond only using the Bible for guidance, by appealing to Tradition. This is the view that God has imparted his holy will to the apostles, and they pass the teaching on to the next generation and so on until the present day. This is confirmed in the Catechism:

> **Global ethic:** Hans Küng defined this as the minimal consensus concerning values, irrevocable standards and fundamental moral principles

The Magisterium of the Pastors of the Church in moral matters is ordinarily exercised in catechesis and preaching, with the help of the works of theologians and spiritual authors. Thus from generation to generation, under the aegis and vigilance of the Pastors, the 'deposit' of Christian moral teaching has been handed on, a deposit composed of a characteristic body of rules, commandments and virtues proceeding from faith in Christ and animated by charity. Alongside the Creed and the Our Father, the basis for this catechesis has traditionally been the Decalogue which sets out the principles of moral life valid for all men.

The Roman Pontiff and the bishops are 'authentic teachers, that is, teachers endowed with the authority of Christ, who preach the faith to the people entrusted to them, the faith to be believed and put into practice'. The ordinary and universal Magisterium of the Pope and the bishops in communion with him teach the faithful the truth to believe, the charity to practice, the beatitude to hope for.

(Catechism of the Catholic Church, §§2032–4)

This clear summary confirms the way in which the Roman Catholic church guarantees the veracity of its beliefs and teaching through the generations, from the time of Jesus until the present day.

Protestant views

Paul Tillich (1886–1965)

Tillich was an important German Protestant theologian from the Lutheran tradition, and is well known for his contributions to Christian theology and existentialist philosophy. He taught that, if Christian ethics is to be taken seriously, there are three principles that must be observed – justice, love and wisdom. For Tillich, love (agape) was the most important of these. He said that love needs to be guided by wisdom, and both need to be given structure by the idea of justice.

In a slight shift from how Jesus had understood agape, Tillich said that all four aspects of 'love' should be included (*eros, storgé, philia*, as well as agape). He describes love as 'the drive towards the unity of the separated'. By this he means that love is the drive or will to be connected with other people and to reconnect to people from whom we have become fragmented or isolated. He criticized what he saw as a prevalent view within some Christian churches, where ethics was more about negative rules – do not eat this or that kind of food, or perform this or that social or sexual activity – rather than speaking positively about what is correct for Christians. He called this negative approach 'moral Puritanism'. For Tillich, agape love should be about each Christian individual making a positive contribution in their community, treating each other with respect and love. Agape love must act when any individual is in need. He taught that action is crucial, otherwise there can be no positive loving outcome in a situation. Agape love must be situation-centred. All laws – moral, legal, societal and even biblical ones – are not absolute if an individual situation demands that they must be broken.

Tillich's view on how love operates in Christian ethics is quite different from that of people who wish to limit themselves to the Bible or some other set of rules. He centres loving decision-making on individuals, not on institutions. Institutions have their

Christian Moral Principles

part to play, but they have to be filtered through the needs of the people involved and the ethical problem with which they are faced.

> **Exercise**
> How far do you agree with Tillich's views on love and Christian ethics?

Joseph Fletcher (1905–1991)

Act agapism: Fletcher's version of a kind of Act Utilitarianism, making ethical decisions on the circumstances of an individual's situation, not on laws

Fletcher was heavily influenced by Tillich's ideas about agape love and used them to develop his own distinctive theory of Situation Ethics. Fletcher's 'explosive book' (*Situation Ethics: The New Morality*, SCM Press, 1966) controversially set out **act agapism** as a kind of Christian parallel to Act Utilitarianism, in which love applies directly to situational judgements and not to rules. The morality of actions is to be judged on their consequences rather than on obedience to divine commands. Situationism's 'pragmatic-empirical temper' sees conscience as a verb instead of a noun, as the reason making moral judgements prior to a contextual decision, rather than some mysterious inner faculty or external source (such as the Holy Spirit) which passes judgement after the event.

This approach opened up a third way, between the legalism of rigid laws and absolute rules that often did more harm than good, on the one hand, and an irresponsible rejection of any moral law in *antinomianism* (*nomos* = 'law' in Greek) with its *ad hoc* approach that often led to inconsistency, on the other. Situationism charted a middle course of 'principled relativism'. Fletcher spoke of the one law, *agapé* (selfless love), drawing on the wisdom (*sophia*) of the Church and culture, and applying these in the moment of decision. Love decided 'then and there', using moral principles as 'rules of thumb'. Fletcher's ethics were radically contextual and worked empirically and inductively from the facts and circumstances of a particular situation, building on just four 'principles' and six 'propositions'. (For details on these, see Brown and Coffey, *Ethics for OCR*, 2nd edn, Polity, 2016, pp. 45–53.)

Fletcher thought that the moral imperative of agape love came simply from being human. The teaching of Jesus highlighted agape love as the single most important ethical principle by which Christians ought to be guided.

There may be several benefits to Fletcher's Situation Ethics – for example, that it is justified by much of Jesus' teaching and actions, and that it is a simple ethical theory that Christians now ought to be able to practise. There are, however, several criticisms to be made. For example, Jesus' teaching in the Sermon on the Mount (Matt. 5:17) tells his hearers: 'Do not think I have come to abolish the Law or the Prophets: I have not come to abolish them, but to fulfil them.'

An early critic of Fletcher's was Scottish biblical scholar **William Barclay** (1907–78), who made a number of points in his 1971 book *Ethics in a Permissive Society* (SCM Press, 1971):

(i) Fletcher's case studies were extreme and rare, not from ordinary life. This means that extreme solutions needed to be found, and these bore little

relevance to the kind of ethical decisions most people would ever have to make.
(ii) Barclay said that, if Fletcher is correct about ignoring rules, which are put in place for the protection of people and property, then every individual would have to make their own decisions every day on a whole range of issues – paying taxes, theft, burglary, rape, schooling and so on. Most people would find this at least undesirable, and probably impossible. 'Society' could not function in these circumstances.
(iii) Some rules are essential. Human beings need a framework of rules in order to live safely and responsibly in the world. Rules such as those concerning sexual abuse, murder, genocide, theft and so on are absolute, and help to form the structure of both individuals and collective society.

Ethicist Neil Messer makes the judgement that 'Fletcher's Situationism has not worn well and many Christian ethicists now regard it as little more than a historical curiosity . . . as a theological theory of ethics, it looks distinctively thin' (N. Messer, *SCM Studyguide: Christian Ethics*, SCM Press, 2006, p. 81). Fletcher saw himself as part of a long tradition of writers and theologians who fought legalism in their day with an emphasis on love and realism (including St Paul, the author of 1 John, Augustine, Abelard, Aquinas, Luther, Leo Tolstoy, Emil Brunner, Paul Tillich, Reinhold Niebuhr and Paul Ramsey). There is a feeling, however, that Fletcher has taken a selective reading of these writers and attempted to force them into the 'box' of Situationism. In 1952, Pope Pius XII rejected Situation Ethics as opposing concrete circumstances to Natural Law and God's revealed will in the Bible. He condemned it as being altogether too individualistic and subjective.

> **Exercise**
>
> **The moral life**
> Fletcher discusses a case of sacrificial adultery in which a World War II German prisoner of war can only secure her release from a Ukrainian prison camp by becoming pregnant by a Russian guard (pp. 164ff.). She takes this course of action because she has an urgent wish to be reunited with her family and to bring up her three children (plus her newborn, Dietrich, who is loved more than the rest because he brought about her freedom). Fletcher asks his readers to consider whether Mrs Bergmeier did the right thing. He says that, after Dietrich's baptism, she asks the same question of her Lutheran pastor.
>
> It is said that extreme cases make bad law, and one criticism of Situation Ethics is that Fletcher's examples build a moral system around exceptional cases that do not properly characterize the moral life. Some ethicists argue that only rule-based systems can offer the certainty that many people require to be confident when making difficult moral decisions.
>
> In another example cited by Fletcher, he argues that an unmarried couple 'living together' who love each other are more pleasing to God than a couple whose marriage is characterized by conflict and mutual disdain.
>
> Do you agree with Fletcher? Give reasons for your answer, then discuss them with other members of your class.

FURTHER READING

Victor Lee Austin, *Christian Ethics: A Guide for the Perplexed*. Bloomsbury T&T Clark, 2012

Robin Gill (ed.), *Cambridge Companion to Christian Ethics*. Cambridge Companions to Religion. Cambridge University Press, 2011

Stanley Hauerwas (ed.), *Blackwell Companion to Christian Ethics*. Blackwell Companions to Religion. Blackwell, 2011

Kenan Malik, *The Quest for a Moral Compass: A Global History of Ethics*. Atlantic Books, 2015

Neil Messer, *SCM Studyguide: Christian Ethics*. SCM Press, 2006

Jonathan Sacks, *Essays on Ethics*. Maggid, 2016

Jonathan Sacks, *Morality: Why We Need It and How To Find It*, Hodder & Stoughton, 2020

Thought Points

1. Discuss with your class what you understand by 'moral goodness' and where it might come from, e.g. politicians, religious groups, or individuals.

2. Create a list of points for and against the view that the Bible is a comprehensive moral guide for Christians.

3. To what extent do Christians actually disagree about what Christian ethics is?

4. In what ways do Protestant and Roman Catholic moral principles differ (if any)?

5. Explain the role of the Magisterium in Roman Catholic ethics.

6. 'The Sermon on the Mount is the only necessary source of morality for Christians today.' Discuss.

7. 'Christian ethics does not provide a useful guide for how Christians should make ethical decisions in the twenty-first century.' Assess the extent to which you agree with this statement.

CHAPTER 6

Christian Moral Action

LEARNING OUTCOMES

In this chapter, you will be learning about the teaching and example of Dietrich Bonhoeffer on

- Duty to God and duty to the State
- Church as community and source of spiritual discipline
- The cost of discipleship

Introduction

Throughout history, the Church has been in conflict with the State. Both fascist and communist states sought to remove, or at least control, Christianity in the twentieth century because the Church was seen to be a challenge to the authority of the State. As Giuliana Chamedes explains:

> The state has a different origin, and a different purpose [from the Church]. Both Thomas Aquinas and the Church taught that citizens do not have the state as their end; instead, it is the state that is made for citizens. Furthermore, the state never can 'completely remove individual rights insofar as it is not the source of those rights'. As Popes since Pius IV had declared, according to Thomist teachings, human beings did have rights, although those rights were derived not from the state, and much less from the revolutionary principle of liberty, but instead from the Thomist rule to live life in accordance with reason and in devotion to God.
> (G. Chamedes, *A Twentieth-Century Crusade – The Vatican's Battle to Remake Christian Europe*, Harvard University Press, 2019, p. 171)

Here, one can see the conflict: totalitarian states wanted full rule and total control over their people. The Church, however, was arguing against this as its belief was that people should be ruled by God.

If a key requirement of the State's law is undermining a person's faith, what should they do? This is the key question Dietrich Bonhoeffer faced when living in a Nazi state

Dietrich Bonhoeffer at Finkenwalde

> **Dietrich Bonhoeffer (1906–1945)** Bonhoeffer was a Lutheran theologian who studied at Berlin and Union Theological Seminary, New York City. He was influenced by Karl Barth and Reinhold Niebuhr. He spoke out against the 'Nazification' of the German churches, and returned to Germany to join the **Confessing Church**, which opposed Hitler. He set up a community at Finkenwalde, was (wrongly) linked to a plot to assassinate Hitler, imprisoned in 1943 and executed in April 1945. He wrote a number of books that have been very influential since his death, notably *The Cost of Discipleship* (1937), *Life Together* (1939) and the posthumously published *Letters and Papers from Prison* (1951).

Confessing Church:
A breakaway group within German Protestantism that disagreed with Hitler's attempt to make churches an instrument of Nazism

led by Adolf Hitler. His response to this has had a profound and lasting effect on modern Christian thought and Christian Moral Action.

Who was Dietrich Bonhoeffer?

Dietrich Bonhoeffer was born to Paula and Karl Bonhoeffer on 4 February 1906 in Breslau, Germany (which is now part of Poland). He was raised in the Lutheran tradition, which was founded (although not intentionally at first) by Martin Luther (1483–1546), a German monk and professor who was famed for posting ninety-five theses against the practice of indulgences in 1517. It is very possible that Bonhoeffer was highly influenced by Luther, as there are some strong similarities in the thought and actions of both men.

Luther was discontented with the Church. He could see contradictions between what the Bible taught and current Church practices (including corruption and abuse). He taught that many of the rituals and works the Church expected from lay people were not only unnecessary but also a stumbling block to salvation. He taught that salvation comes from the grace of God and faith in Jesus Christ alone, rejecting traditions such as priestly celibacy, the Latin version of the Bible (Luther advocated for the scriptures to be available to the laity in their own language so that they could understand it), liturgy, and doctrines such as purgatory and transubstantiation. He was advocating for the laity to achieve a full understanding of the grace of God, not through ritual and dogma, but through a deep understanding and acceptance of the scriptures.

Luther initially hoped for Church reform, as opposed to creating a schism within the Church. When this reform proved to be impossible, he continued to spread his teachings, regardless of his excommunication and many threats to his life.

In 1912, Bonhoeffer's father became a professor of psychiatry and neurology and the family moved to Berlin. Bonhoeffer lived an idyllic lifestyle and loved the outdoors; however, this was all to end in 1914 with World War I. His older brother, Walter, was killed in action and it is believed that this traumatic event was part of the reason Bonhoeffer went on to study theology. His family was not keen on the idea of him studying this subject, as they were not a church-going family (although his mother ensured the family kept to the traditions of Lutheran Christianity). From an early age, however, Bonhoeffer had a clear concept of how he wanted the Church to reform, which persuaded his parents to support his goals.

Bonhoeffer studied Theology at Tubingen University and in 1930 completed his doctorate on Act and Being – a radical interpretation of Lutheranism in which he proposed that the Church, not the State, should be involved in decisions concerning justice. He believed that far too much power and authority was given to the State, and that the rules it imposed undermined the purpose of Christianity. After completing this doctorate, Bonhoeffer travelled to New York, to study at the famous Protestant Union Theological Seminary. It was here where, for the first time, he was able to experience different forms and styles of worship. He became committed to encouraging churches to build relationships with one another without racial or geographical boundaries.

Hitler became Chancellor of Germany on 30 January 1933 and, with almost impeccable timing, Bonhoeffer was invited to deliver a radio broadcast entitled 'The Younger Generation's Altered View of the Fuhrer', in which he was deeply critical of what he coined the 'leadership principle'. He said:

> If the leader tries to become the idol the led are looking for – something the led always hope from their leader – then the image of the leader shifts to one of a mis-leader, then the leader is acting improperly toward the led as well as toward himself. The true leader must always be able to disappoint. This, especially, is part of the leader's responsibility and objectivity. The leader must lead the led from the authority of the leader's person to the recognition of the true authority of order and office. The leader must lead the led into responsibility toward the social structures of life, toward father, teacher, judge, state.
> (Bonhoeffer, *Berlin 1932–1933*, Dietrich Bonhoeffer Works 12, Augsburg Fortress, 2009, p. 280)

However, to Bonhoeffer's great annoyance, nobody was able to hear these words as the microphone had deliberately been turned off. He was able, however, to have his lecture printed and distributed to friends and acquaintances.

From this moment, Bonhoeffer, having decided to return to Germany, had actively placed himself against the state and began to work on its demise. He became a member of the Confessing Church (a group of clergy who refused to accept that only Aryan Germans could become members of the Church, denying the laws of the State, accepting only Christ and the Bible as ultimate authorities). He joined the Resistance movement (**Widerstand**) and was under investigation by the Gestapo because of his role in training clergy in the Confessing Church.

> **Widerstand:** The resistance movement that Bonhoeffer joined

In 1939 he returned to the USA for a brief visit but he knew it was clear that, if he wanted to remain true to his beliefs, he had to return to Germany to fight against the state and overthrow the Nazi regime. Until this point, Bonhoeffer had always considered himself to be a pacifist; however, he changed this to the belief in 'secular pacifism', due to the fact that he felt pacifism was a secular concept and failed to prepare a Christian for the Kingdom of God. This idea of 'secular pacifism' can be summed up by a statement sometimes attributed to Bonhoeffer: 'Silence in the face of evil is itself evil. God will not hold us guiltless. Not to speak is to speak. Not to act is to act.' His choice to join the Resistance against the Nazi state could not be called intrinsically 'good' as Bonhoeffer believed that, in the real world of harsh choices or 'terrible alternatives', all choices made had inevitable bad consequences. In a letter to his American friend, Reinhold Niebuhr (1892–1971), he explained:

> I have come to the conclusion that I have made a mistake in coming to America. I must live through this difficult period of our national history with the Christian people of Germany. I will have no right to participate in the reconstruction of Christian life in Germany after the war if I do not share the trials of this time with my people . . .
>
> . . . Christians in Germany will face the terrible alternative of either willing the defeat of their nation in order that Christian civilization may survive, or willing the victory of their nation and therefore destroying our civilization. I know which of these alternatives I must choose; but I cannot make that choice in security.
>
> (Bonhoeffer, *The Way to Freedom*, Collins, 1966, p. 246)

Bonhoeffer saw Christian ethics as a responsibility – something that required action, as opposed to the traditional 'comfortable' view of Christian life with church services and community gatherings. He was acutely aware that, for many Christians, life was a struggle of loss, challenge and persecution and this led him to a profound sense of discipleship, accepting that his Christian life would contain an amount of suffering and sacrifice as a result of the responsibility attached to his Christian ethics, following Mark 8:34 'Whoever wants to be my disciple must deny themselves, take up their cross and follow me.' Some Christians today are both inspired and challenged by this approach to their faith and their understanding of what being a Christian actually entails.

Duty to God and to the State

Bonhoeffer moved back to Germany during the rise of the Nazi Party when the policies of Hitler were growing in power and popularity. Many German Christians incorporated the Nazi policies into their Christian belief. This led to a division in the German Protestant church between the Nazi-controlled German church and the Confessing

Church which sought to keep religion and politics entirely separate. Hitler was aiming to defeat any opposition to his party, so merged his Nazi politics and Christian tradition into one. This did not come without conflict, as Rodger Charles states:

> In the elections of March 1932, that is before Hitler was Chancellor and the constitution and civil liberties had been undermined, the Bishops advised their people to vote for the Centre party because Hitler's version of Christianity was not that of Christ. But it was too late; of the 12.5 million Catholic voters, only 5.5 million took the advice. They were in a familiar and uncomfortable dilemma, that of reconciling their Catholicism with their German nationality, but it was a particularly painful one at this time.
> (R. Charles, *Christian Social Witness and Teaching*, Vol. I: *Catholic Tradition from Genesis to Centesimus Annus*, Gracewing Publishing, 1998, p. 76)

As a result of these votes (and many more), Hitler was accepted into power and worked to incorporate Nazi ideology into Christianity. A spokesperson for the German Christians (Hermann Gruner) stated: 'The time is fulfilled for the German people in Hitler. It is because of Hitler that Christ, God the helper and redeemer, has become effective among us. Therefore National Socialism is positive Christianity in action . . . Hitler is the way of the Spirit and the will of God for the German people to enter the Church of Christ' (Geffery B. Kelly et al., 'Dietrich Bonhoeffer: The Life of a Modern Martyr', *Christianity Today*, 2012, p. 22).

As Nazi Germany began to take control, their hold over the German Christians became more apparent. Some leaders of the German Christian church began to wear brown uniforms in allegiance with **National Socialism** and began to promote the Aryan Clause, prohibiting any ministers of Jewish descent from working for the Church. Some even campaigned to remove the Old Testament from churches because of its links with Judaism. Hitler was seen as the leader of Christianity, and his words were held to have as much authority as those of Jesus. Many German Christians joined the Nazi Party, believing that Hitler was the embodiment of Christian moral values.

Bonhoeffer saw this enthusiasm for Hitler and the Nazi regime as cult-like, and his criticism of the Nazi Party brought him into conflict with it as soon as they came into power. He believed that they distorted the Christian call to worship in order to allow continued persecution of the Jews.

National Socialism: The Nazi Party

Obedience to God's will

> Only he who believes is obedient, and only he who is obedient believes.
> (Bonhoeffer, *The Cost of Discipleship*, new edn, SCM Press, 2015, p. 54)

For Bonhoeffer, discipleship and obedience came hand in hand. When Jesus called his disciples, they did not respond with a profession of the liturgy or a deep discussion of their personal philosophy, they simply obeyed what Jesus asked them to do. Bonhoeffer believed that, based on the teaching of the Gospels, all Christians are called to discipleship – all are called to be followers of Jesus and therefore must be obedient to his will.

This raised some concerns for Bonhoeffer. Traditional Christian teaching states that Christians have a duty to obey the State because, as Luther taught, there are two kingdoms ordained by God: the spiritual kingdom governed by the Church, and the political kingdom governed by the State. As St Paul preached, 'Everyone must submit himself to the governing authorities; for there is no authority except that which God has established. The authorities that exist have been established by God' (Romans 13:1). Bonhoeffer, however, was not concerned about whether he should follow the government; rather, his concern was whether the will of the Nazi Party was in line with the will of God – and it is this which led him to question the concept of being or doing 'good' and instead to focus on the will of God and being obedient to that:

> Whoever wishes to take up the problem of a Christian ethic must be confronted at once with a demand that is quite without parallel. He must from the outset discard as irrelevant the two questions which allow him to concern himself with the problem of ethics, 'How can I be good?' and 'How can I do good?' and instead of these he must ask the utterly and totally different question 'What is the will of God?'
>
> (Bonhoeffer, *Ethics*, Augsburg Fortress, 2009, p. 161)

This could be seen to beg the question 'How can one truly know the will of God?', to which Bonhoeffer responded that God's will is only clear in the moment of action. As Petra Brown states:

> For Bonhoeffer, God's will is revealed in each particular moment of that relationship in a way that makes a claim on the individual separately from ethical norms. Bonhoeffer describes the result of God's will and its relationship to morality as follows: 'There are no ethical principles enabling Christians, as it were, to make themselves moral. Instead, one has only the decisive moment at hand, that is, every moment is of potential ethical value. Never, however, can yesterday decisively influence my moral actions today. I must rather always establish anew my immediate relationship with God's will.'
>
> (Petra Brown, *Bonhoeffer: God's Conspirator in a State of Exception*, Palgrave Macmillan, 2019, p. 133, quoting Bonhoeffer, *Works: Barcelona, Berlin, New York, 1928–1931*, Fortress Press, 2008, p. 365)

Being obedient to God's will, for Bonhoeffer, is an act of faith. In order to be obedient to God's will, one must abandon responsibility to all other forms of authority and follow Christ alone, no matter how much of an inconvenience this may be. A person's faith should not be something that fits neatly around what they want their life to be, and if necessary they must leave their old lives behind in order to be obedient to God's will and follow Christ's example – even if that does mean rebelling against the State.

This was controversial for Bonhoeffer as he was stating that being a follower of Christ demands that one must have an immediate and single-minded obedience to Jesus and his teachings. This then opens up the possibility of civil disobedience – he was stating that Christians do not need to follow the laws of the land as long as they are following the teachings of Christ and doing God's will. Bonhoeffer was calling for 'single-minded obedience'. Matthew 14 provides an example of single-minded obedience to Christ when Peter risks his life to obey the commands of the Lord:

> Jesus immediately said to them: 'Take courage! It is I. Do not be afraid.'
> 'Lord, if it is you', Peter replied, 'tell me to come to you on the water.'
> 'Come', he said.
> Then Peter got down out of the boat, walked on the water and came toward Jesus.
>
> (Matt. 14:27–9)

This is an example of how so many things could have stood in the way of Peter's almost 'thoughtless' obedience. As a human, Peter could have applied logic, reason, experience to this situation, but, instead, he chose to trust in God and follow obediently without question. When he did, he was rewarded by a miracle – up until the point he started to question, at which point Jesus had to save him. For Bonhoeffer, it is only through Jesus that this single-minded obedience is possible. It is only when one is able to step away from attachment to this life, with its knowledge and experience, that Christians are able to step into a situation where absolute unquestioned faith is possible, even if that requires doing something that is uncomfortable (such as questioning authority).

> **Exercise**
> Do you think that it is compulsory for Christians to believe in miracles? Does belief in miracles mean that Christians must put their knowledge of science to one side?

Leadership

Justification of civil disobedience

The *Webster's New World Encyclopedia* (Prentice Hall, 1992) defines civil disobedience as 'The active refusal to obey certain laws, demands and commands from a government or of an occupying power without resorting to physical violence.' Elizabeth Schmermund states: 'This definition hinges on the belief that laws themselves can be unjust and that it can be a moral obligation to disobey these unjust laws. Few people would disagree that laws are created by fallible men and women and, thus, can be imperfect and, even more, reflect the prejudices of the time in which they are enacted' (E. Schmermund, *Civil Disobedience*, Greenhaven Publishing, 2017, p. 7).

It could be argued that this definition is particularly relevant when considering Bonhoeffer's justification of his civil disobedience against the Nazi regime. In believing he had a responsibility to obey the will of God, Bonhoeffer justifies his civil disobedience by the fact that he believes Christians had a responsibility to monitor the State as well as to serve God's will. The laws he witnessed coming to pass he believed to be unreasonable and against the teachings of Christ. In believing that God's grace is for all, he could not see how excluding a race of people could be Christlike. He saw this as unjust, hence having a moral obligation to disobey these unjust and unreasonable laws, stating:

> The failure of reasonable people is appalling; they cannot manage to see either the abyss of evil or the abyss of holiness. With the best intentions they believe that, with a little reason, they can pull back together a structure that has come apart at the joints. In their defective vision they want to be fair to both sides, and they are crushed between the colliding forces without having accomplished anything at all. Bitterly disappointed that the world is so unreasonable, they see themselves condemned to ineffectiveness. They withdraw in resignation or fall helplessly captive to the stronger party.
>
> (Bonhoeffer, *Ethics*, p. 78)

Bonhoeffer could see that he was surrounded by reasonable, intelligent people who could see the evil that was surrounding them but were resigned to not being able to resist those in power. They either did nothing or joined the stronger party in defeat, as people were seduced by the power of Nazism. He also said, 'There is no standing amid the ruins of one's native town in the consciousness that at least one has not oneself incurred guilt' (*ibid.*, p. 204) – i.e., a person is just as guilty for standing by and doing nothing as they would be for being one of the crowd who destroyed the town.

Many people in the German church thought that Hitler was a great leader, managing to impose order over what they saw as a disordered state. However, the marginalization of Jews and other minority groups, plus the unashamed disregard for the value of their lives, were grossly against the teachings of Christ. Bonhoeffer felt he had a Christian responsibility to defend these teachings. As a Christian, he believed he had a responsibility to the State as well, and this was the key to the justification of his civil disobedience:

> For the sake and purpose of Christ there is and ought to be worldly order in state, family and economy. For the sake of Christ the worldly order is subject to the commandment of God. It is to be noted that there is no question here of a 'Christian state' or a 'Christian economy', but only of the rightful state and the rightful economy as a secular institution for the sake of Christ. There exists, therefore, a Christian responsibility for secular institutions, and within a Christian ethic there exist propositions which relate to this responsibility.
>
> (*ibid.*, p. 269)

He was not arguing for a Christian state – rather, a moral state; and if the people in power are not building a 'rightful' secular state or economy, then a Christian must take responsibility to fight against this power. This left Bonhoeffer with the dilemma that Clements describes as: 'Praying for national victory which would mean the end of a Christian civilization, or praying for the defeat of their country so that a Christian order could survive' (Keith Clements, *What Freedom? The Persistent Challenge of Dietrich Bonhoeffer*, Wipf and Stock Publishers, 2011, p. 79). His duty to God was more important than his duty to the State, so the choice for him was clear. Hitler needed to be removed from power.

As a result of this, Bonhoeffer refused to accept the laws of the Nazi regime. He spoke out openly against the party, losing his much-loved job at the university as a result of this. Yet he was adamant that he must obey what he believed to be the will of God. Richard L. Rubenstein explains: 'He is frequently cited to show that within Germany there was both individual and institutional Christian resistance against the Third Reich. "If we claim to be Christians", Bonhoeffer wrote, "there is no room for expediency. Hitler is the Anti-Christ. Therefore we must go on with our work and eliminate him whether he is successful or not"' (Richard L. Rubenstein and John K. Roth, *Approaches to Auschwitz: The Holocaust and its Legacy*, Westminster John Knox Press, 2003, p. 262).

Even the Confessing Church began to falter under the pressure of Hitler. Initially, Hitler had no stable or consistent policy for ruling over the Christian church, although many Church offices were searched and taken over by the police. A young secretary for the Minister of Education, Dr Wilhelm Stuckart, suggested controlling Church appointments and finances by putting churches under the control and power of a government department. At this suggestion, Hitler appointed Hannz Kerrl, a former Minister of Justice, as Minister of Church Affairs, which made the freedom and existence of the Confessing Church much more restricted. Many people were leaving the Church under pressure of persecution as the Nazi State now demanded that all church pastors take a personal oath to Hitler. Some pastors within the Confessing Church left and joined state-controlled churches to avoid punishment or persecution.

This extended Bonhoeffer's civil disobedience. He justified it by giving evidence from the Bible that supported the six propositions found in the **Dahlem Declaration**, made in 1932 by the Confessing Church:

(i) We are one church
(ii) The Church requires a church administration
(iii) The church administration can be appointed only by the Church itself; it serves only the proclamation of the Gospel and the proper congregational life
(iv) The proclamation in the Church is bound to the Church's commission
(v) Obedience to a heretical church government is disobedience to Christ
(vi) The Church leaves the concern for the future to its Lord

> **Dahlem Declaration:** The Confessing Church made a declaration in 1934 challenging the legitimate authority of the Reich Church

In his work *Conclusion of the Church Struggle*, Bonhoeffer argues that the only way to end the struggle of the Church is to remove it completely from state affairs, mirroring the beliefs of the Dahlem Declaration.

Eventually, Bonhoeffer was made a member of German military intelligence by his brother. Due to him speaking out so openly against Hitler, the Gestapo had banned him from public speaking and he was at risk of arrest. This role within military intelligence gave Bonhoeffer the opportunity to work as a double agent. He used the links he had in his role to pass on information to the Allies and used the information to smuggle Jews into safety in Switzerland. It was this that ultimately led to his arrest.

Bonhoeffer's role in the Confessing Church

Bonhoeffer understood the role of the Christian church in terms of a community of believers who should all share a sense of 'spiritual discipline'. He stressed the importance of the Church being a 'visible community' – not only of spiritual discipline but also as a light for others, in the spirit of Proverbs 31:8, which asks: 'Who will speak up for those who have no voices?'

Bonhoeffer used the Sermon on the Mount (Matt 5–7) as inspiration for the concept that he and other followers of Christ should be like 'salt' and 'light'. As Paul Spanring explains:

> Salt seasons and preserves food; thus the primary function of the church is to influence and shape the whole of society with gospel truths. It is the soluble nature of salt which allows it to penetrate and season the whole. This apparent strength makes it difficult to identify the individual kernel . . . and the gathered church perceives its primary role to be 'light'. Unlike salt, light does not mingle or mix with darkness. By its very nature, it constitutes the opposite.
> (Paul Spanring, *Dietrich Bonhoeffer and Arnold Koster – Two Distinct Voices in the Midst of Germany's Third Reich Turmoil*, Pickwick Publications, 2013, p. 2)

As 'salt', Christians should be immersed and visible within the community – even a small amount can make a large difference to the 'flavour', and as 'light' they must not mingle with darkness. Their goodness should shine through and replace darkness with light inside a community, and they should not try to keep their beliefs hidden.

Bonhoeffer believed that no Christian can act morally in isolation. The strength of working as light and salt is that no-one can identify an individual within the whole group. So, when a person acts out of love or duty, s/he is acting out of solidarity with the whole of mankind, mirroring the beliefs of Kant. For this to happen, there was a requirement for Christianity to break the bounds of 'religion', remove itself from the middle-class institution it was becoming, and go out into the secular community, immersing it with the Gospel and sharing the love of Christ. The Church needed to escape the bounds of the building and immerse itself in a world devoid of true religion, thus being able to be the 'light' and 'salt'.

Bonhoeffer argued for '**religionless Christianity**', a bold new reformation, without the suffocating baggage of the past that contaminated the ideological beliefs of the present. Previously, liberalism had negated many religious beliefs and values as irrelevant, creating a community where denominations would be broken down and Christians could simply focus on Christ.

Religionless Christianity: Bonhoeffer's hope for a bold new reformation whereby barriers between denominations would be broken down and Christians could focus on Christ

Exercise
Discuss ways in which you think Christians might act as 'salt' and 'light' in society today.

Finkenwalde: The seminary community where Bonhoeffer taught

Bonhoeffer's religious community at Finkenwalde (1935–1937)

The Confessing Church began with Bonhoeffer and Martin Niemoller as a reaction to Hitler's German Christian movement, when he created the German Evangelical Church. In 1934, Hitler imposed the 'Aryan Paragraph' in order to eliminate Jewish influences on the Christian church. This paragraph meant, in the words of Shelley Baranowski, that 'Baptized Jews, Protestants with Jewish ancestry, and Protestants married to "non-Aryans" were forbidden to hold church office or serve as pastors' (quoted from Rubenstein and Roth, *Approaches to Auschwitz: The Holocaust and its Legacy*, p. 256). Hitler appointed a Reich Bishop to ensure this policy was upheld and adhered to. Hitler also merged church youth groups with groups of Hitler Youth, so that young people were being influenced by similarly aged members of the Nazi Party.

In the same year, the Confessing Church met at Barmen, and Karl Barth produced the foundations of the **Barmen Declaration**, stating that the primary loyalty of the Church and every individual Christian is to Christ. The Church, therefore, should morally reject any teaching which is not revealed in Christ – arguably a theological denial of Nazi socialism. The Synod of Barmen said:

Barmen Declaration: A document, largely composed by Karl Barth in 1934, setting out the Confessing Church's opposition to the German Christian movement that had accepted Nazism

> Try the spirits, whether they are of God! Prove also the words of the Confessional Synod of the German Evangelical Church to see whether they agree with Holy Scripture and with the Confessions of your fathers. If you find that we are speaking contrary to scripture, then do

not listen to us! But if you find that we are taking our stand upon scripture, then let no fear or temptation keep you from treading with us the path of faith and obedience to the word of God.

(Arthur C. Cochrane, *The Church's Confession under Hitler*, 2nd edn, Literary Licensing LLC, 2011 p. 185)

This echoes the belief that church and state should be separate and that no oath should be taken to any person or political party (including Hitler) because Christ alone is the one true leader, and that the only path a Christian should take is the path of obedience to Christ.

Finkenwalde

As the Nazis grew in power, universities began to apply Aryan law restrictions, and Bonhoeffer was approached to lead and direct a secret seminary (training new pastors). If an independent seminary funded by donations was set up, these laws could be ignored and so the restrictions could be avoided. This enabled new pastors to be trained free from the Nazi ideologies that were now inherent within the German churches. The new seminary grew and eventually moved to a disused school in Finkenwalde.

Aside from training outside the Nazi regime, Bonhoeffer used his time in Finkenwalde to develop training in practical ways of living as a Christian within society at that time. He used the space to live with his trainees as a community of Christ's disciples, and to exercise what he thought to be the most practical Christian virtue of all – discipline.

Life at Finkenwalde was very monastic: much of the trainees' time there was spent in reflection, prayer, Bible study – particularly of the Psalms – as well as singing 'spirituals', the religious songs of the Black community Bonhoeffer had spent much of his time with in America. This approach was very controversial, especially given the political situation in Germany at that time. There was an argument that quiet study and reflection were not required as much as action was. However, Bonhoeffer thought it essential that the next generation should be taught to listen to God, not politicians. This thinking may have stemmed from Luke 10:38–42 and the story of Jesus staying with Mary and Martha:

> As Jesus and his disciples were on their way, he came to a village where a woman named Martha opened her home to him. She had a sister called Mary, who sat at the Lord's feet listening to what he said. But Martha was distracted by all the preparations that had to be made. She came to him and asked, 'Lord, don't you care that my sister has left me to do the work by myself? Tell her to help me!'
>
> 'Martha, Martha', the Lord answered, 'you are worried and upset about many things, but few things are needed – or indeed only one. Mary has chosen what is better, and it will not be taken away from her.'

Perhaps Bonhoeffer was following the teaching of Jesus and listening to Christ, which, as he was taught from this passage, was the better thing to do. His work in the seminary focused on one thing (Christ) and this was the thing that mattered, reflecting Mary's decision to do the same.

The central practices at Finkenwalde included:

- **Discipline** – This was central to all other practices as part of the seminary. Discipline over oneself and towards Christ ultimately leads to action (in accordance with God's will). Discipline of the body was also important, and Bonhoeffer made sure the community of students would go on regular long bike rides.
- **Community with others** – Bonhoeffer insisted that church is not a place for the righteous, but for the forgiven. Nobody is perfect and all have sinned, yet *all* have been forgiven through Christ. Therefore, the church community and pastors should look outwards to the community, rather than inwards, and engage with the world.
- **Meditation** – The foundation of prayer. It takes a lot of discipline to be still and contemplative in a busy world. Spending time with God in meditation is an important aspect of deepening Christian faith.
- **The Bible** – Bible study and discussion were also central to life at the seminary. Engaging in the teachings of Christ and attending lectures to invoke debate and discussion allowed the trainees to prepare for teaching the Bible to the community outside the seminary, with knowledge rooted in deep, theological understanding.
- **Brotherhood** – Bonhoeffer insisted on frequent changing of roles, in order to ensure the seminary did not get stuck in its ways or begin to be stagnant in tradition. This is what he was trying to change for the Church as a whole, so it was important that it began during training. He also kept in regular contact with former students in order to maintain the sense of wider community.

In 1937, the Gestapo closed the seminary. Upon the closure, Bonhoeffer quickly wrote a book summarizing its theology and practice, called *Life Together*. This book showed how Bonhoeffer's understanding of social theology and Christian community shaped the daily life of the college. The model of the seminary was community-based, rather than an academy of people working separately to achieve different ends. John W. de Gruchy describes the daily life in the seminary as including:

> Worship, study of the bible, meditation, prayers, lectures, sermon practice, meals and recreation. Some of these belonged to 'the day together', others to 'the day alone'. Here we see the counterpoint of community and individual person, which Bonhoeffer formulated as follows: 'Whoever cannot be alone should beware of community. Whoever cannot stand being in community, should beware of being alone.'
> (John W. de Gruchy, *The Cambridge Companion to Dietrich Bonhoeffer*, Cambridge University Press, 1995, p. 125)

Exercise

Find out what 'ethos' means. What is the ethos of your school/college? Would you change it? Explain how and why.

The cost of discipleship

Bonhoeffer urged followers of Christ not to be passive followers. He likened them to the Pharisees who were good at hearing and following God's commands but did nothing to act on God's behalf. As Paul Spanring explains:

> The passion and commitment (of the Pharisees) was always to distinguish between what was good and evil. They sought to achieve this by way of weighing every possible life situation in order to arrive at an informed decision. Their motivation was to live holy lives, yet since they relied on the knowledge of good and evil they remained tied to the very essence of the fall. Christ lived and represented a total contrast to the Pharisees. Jesus simply taught the will of God. 'He lives and acts not out of knowledge of good and evil but out of the will of God.'
>
> (Spanring, *Dietrich Bonhoeffer and Arnold Koster*, p. 210)

Having knowledge of the law and acting on the will of Christ are two separate and distinct things for Bonhoeffer. To hear the law must be to do the law, again illustrated in the criticism of Martha who is busy 'doing' but not focusing on listening to the teaching of Christ. The ideal for Bonhoeffer is that ethics requires action, and action must be prompted by conscience, subject to the will of God. These ethical decisions may involve conflict in this action (such as civil disobedience), but this clearly distinguishes good and evil. Ultimately, love will overcome the disunity as it did for Christ, who went 'against the crowd' but ended his life in the ultimate sacrifice of love – atoning for the sins of all humanity.

'Cheap grace' and 'costly grace'

In his most famous book, *The Cost of Discipleship*, Bonhoeffer draws a distinction between '**cheap grace**' and '**costly grace**':

> Cheap grace is the deadly enemy of our church. We are fighting today for costly grace. Cheap grace means grace sold on the market like a cheapjack's wares. The sacraments, the forgiveness of sin, and the consolations of religion are thrown away at cut prices. Grace is represented as the Church's inexhaustible treasury, from which she showers blessings with generous hands without asking questions or fixing limits. Grace without price; grace without cost . . . the account has been paid in advance; and because it has been paid, everything can be had for nothing.
>
> (Bonhoeffer, *The Cost of Discipleship*, p. 35)

Cheap grace: For Bonhoeffer, this was grace that did not have to be worked for and is therefore false

Costly grace: For Bonhoeffer, this is true grace, that sacrifices have to be made for, and is based on 'only Christ, only scripture, only faith'

Using the ideas of Luther and Calvin, Bonhoeffer believed that authentic Christianity has three fundamental aspects:

(i) only Christ
(ii) only scripture
(iii) only faith

Anything else is merely human intervention. This thought concerned Bonhoeffer. He viewed the Church as being full of 'cheap grace' – because Christ died for all, then many accepted this grace for free. One can attend church and offer time and money, but not live the struggle that Christ did and not live life absorbed in the study of scripture. A person can preach forgiveness without the discomfort of confessing and seeking repentance. A person can be baptized and not have to change their ways. The Church was a happy, comfortable and welcoming place as Christ has already paid the price for every person's sin so no action is required to receive this grace. For Bonhoeffer, this was a Christianity without Jesus, because being a Christian means one must 'pick up one's cross' and struggle, just as Jesus did. Bonhoeffer was concerned that Christians did not feel they needed to make any changes to their lives, as the price for their sin had already been paid.

Bonhoeffer writes:

> What has happened to all those warnings of Luther against preaching the Gospel in such a manner as to make men rest secure in their ungodly living? Was there ever a more terrible or disastrous instance of the Christianizing of the world than this? What are those three thousand Saxons put to death by Charlemagne compared with the millions of spiritual corpses in our country today? With us it has been abundantly proved that the sins of the fathers are visited upon the children unto the third and fourth generations. Cheap grace has turned out to be utterly merciless to our evangelical church.
>
> (*ibid.*, p. 54)

This is a form of 'easy Christianity'. It is a self-congratulating lie that Christians tell themselves in order to live a comfortable life and share a comforting and heart-warming message. People do not generally like a challenge – certainly not one that may require a total transformation in the way in which they live their lives. 'Cheap grace' is not the grace of God, but the grace people offer to themselves. Easy Christianity is not Christianity, for Bonhoeffer, and the reliance on cheap grace made the Church a secular place, willing to take on the beliefs and values of modern society.

If cheap grace is merciless to the Church, the alternative is costly grace. It is costly because it 'costs a man his life and grace because it gives man the only true life' (Walker, *Costly Grace*, p. 29). This is the grace that a person would give up everything he owns in order to obtain. As Matthew 13:44 states: 'The Kingdom of Heaven is like a treasure hidden in a field, which a man found and covered up. Then in his joy he goes and sells all that he has and buys that field.' Obtaining this grace is something for which it is worth sacrificing all you have. As Larsen and Larsen explain:

> It is the pearl of great price to buy which the merchant will sell all his goods. It is the kingly rule of Christ, for whose sake a man will pluck out the eye which causes him to stumble, it is the call of Jesus Christ at which the disciple leaves his nets and follows him.
>
> Costly grace is the gospel which must be sought again and again. The gift which must be asked for, the door at which a man must knock.
>
> (D. Larsen and S. Larsen, *Dietrich Bonhoeffer: Costly Grace*, Inter-Varsity Press, 2002, p. 29)

This is grace that is not freely given, but requires a person to seek and work for it. It requires a person to make a change to their lives and the decisions they are making. Bonhoeffer was concerned that the Church was becoming too secularised and, in order to increase membership numbers (and therefore donations to the Church), it had lost the sense of costly grace in favour of cheap grace. The Church was now integrated with the government, and the rise in the monastic movement only seemed to separate even further those who were willing to make big changes for their religion and the Church. There appeared to be a chasm between 'cheap, secular grace' and 'costly, monastic grace'. Bonhoeffer referred to Luther when considering this, stating:

> Luther did not hear the word: 'Of course you have sinned, but now everything is forgiven, so you can stay as you are and enjoy the consolations of forgiveness.' No. Luther had to leave the cloister and go back to the world, not because the world in itself was good and holy, but because even the cloister was only part of the world.
> (Bonhoeffer, *The Cost of Discipleship*, p. 40)

Bonhoeffer was concerned that the words of Luther had been misinterpreted – yes, it is grace and grace alone which one requires for salvation, but that grace does not mean one can carry on one's sinful ways. Rather, in receiving the grace of God, a person must become fully obedient to the will of God and be prepared to change their life and ways in order to be a true disciple. As he states: 'Above all, it is costly because it cost the life of his Son. . . . Above all it is grace because God did not reckon his son too dear a price to pay for our life, but delivered him up for us. Costly grace is the incarnation of God' (*ibid.*, p. 37).

Sacrifice and suffering

In his discussion about Christian suffering, Bonhoeffer begins with Jesus' statement concerning the suffering that every disciple must embrace: 'If anyone would come after me, he must deny himself and take up his cross and follow me. For whoever wants to save his life must lose it, but whoever loses his life for me and for the gospel will save it' (Mark 8:34–5).

Here, Jesus links discipleship with suffering, specifically his suffering in the Passion – an ignominious, embarrassing and dishonourable death. Bonhoeffer comments on this passage in *The Cost of Discipleship* (p. 76), saying that to be a disciple of Jesus was not an easy choice. To be a disciple involved rejection by one's friends, suffering and possibly death. If would-be disciples rejected these outcomes, they were not true disciples. Being a true disciple of Jesus was to take the difficult route through life, just as Jesus did. It meant taking up Jesus' cross and suffering as he did, and dying in faithful obedience to God's will, as Jesus did.

For Bonhoeffer, there is a necessary link between suffering and costly grace. The suffering that disciples must bear has nothing to do with ordinary life, such as losing a job or dealing with a family member's illness. Disciples must suffer in a specific way - 'for Christ'. He says: 'Jesus as Christ is Christ only in virtue of his suffering and rejection, as the disciple is a disciple only in so far as he shares his Lord's suffering and rejection and crucifixion. Discipleship means adherence to the person of Jesus and therefore submission to the law of Christ which is the law of the cross' (*ibid.*, p. 71).

> **Exercise**
> Bonhoeffer wrote that 'suffering, then, is the badge of true discipleship'. Do you agree with him? Give reasons for your answer.

Solidarity

Bonhoeffer often talked of Jesus as 'the man for others'. Bonhoeffer could have stayed away from Germany during the war, but chose to return, accepting the risk that he would be arrested. For Bonhoeffer, being Christian meant following Jesus' example and being men/ women 'for others'. Their purpose in life was to interact with other people and help them in whatever situation they found themselves. He said 'our relation to God is a new life in "existence for others", through participation in the being of Jesus' (*Letters and Papers from Prison* [1959], ed. Eberhard Bethge, SCM Press, 1971, p. 381).

One of the things this meant for Bonhoeffer concerned the German Church's attitude to the Jews. He felt strongly that the German Church should be critical of the Nazis' treatment of Jews and should call on the State to make responsible decisions about injustice. The Church should help all victims of injustice, regardless of race or religion, and they should actively engage in resisting Nazi oppression. The injustices suffered by the Jews and other races led Bonhoeffer to become involved with the Resistance movement. He helped to raise a great deal of money to help the many Jews who were displaced from their homes and did not have any synagogues in which to worship (they had been destroyed by the Nazis). He believed that Christians must behave responsibly in the world, and being active in this way was doing just that.

Relevance of Bonhoeffer's theory in society today

Does the continued suffering of the poor and marginalized today mean that the teachings of Bonhoeffer still carry weight, or were his theological ethics culturally relative and only work in extreme circumstances (such as the rise of Nazi Germany)? It could be argued that because Bonhoeffer's ethics were *so* culturally relative, they would not stand the test of the globalized world today, with its threats of terrorism, germ warfare, satellite spying, conflicts in the Middle East, power struggles between the USA and China, and threats to Western democracies. However, if one uses Bonhoeffer's ethics to engage Christians with the globalized world in a Christ-like way, with an active spiritual conscience, then it may be suggested that he is still entirely relevant.

Stanley Hauerwas argues that Bonhoeffer's concern for truth in politics offers a much needed challenge to the pragmatism of Western politics. He believes the Church can, and should, play a special role in global politics. Hauerwas argues that, if a society had no idea of the truth but practised tolerance for practical reasons, it would quickly fall into indifference, and 'indifference leads to cynicism' (Hauerwas, *Performing the Faith*, p. 59).

As Bonhoeffer noted on many occasions, and from his own personal experience, liberal societies can undermine the truth, thus creating a void. If this void is filled by totalitarian powers, then the cynics of the society will blindly follow.

FURTHER READING

Eberhard Bethge, *Dietrich Bonhoeffer: Biography – Theologian, Christian Man for his Times*, rev. edn. Augsburg Fortress, 1999

Dietrich Bonhoeffer, *The Cost of Discipleship*, new edn. SCM Press, 2015

Dietrich Bonhoeffer, *Letters and Papers from Prison* [1959]. Ed. Eberhard Bethge. SCM Press, 1971

Petra Brown, *Bonhoeffer: God's Conspirator in a State of Exception*, Palgrave Macmillan, 2019

Stanley Hauerwas, *Performing the Faith: Bonhoeffer and the Practice of Non-Violence*. SPCK, 2004

Joel Lawrence, *Bonhoeffer: A Guide for the Perplexed*. T&T Clark, 2010

Jon Walker, *Costly Grace: A Contemporary View of Bonhoeffer's* The Cost of Discipleship. Leafwood Publishers and ACU Press, 2010

Thought Points

1. What led to the founding of the Confessing Church?

2. Would you describe Bonhoeffer as a man of principle or a man of action, or something else? Explain the reasons for your decision.

3. Should Christians ever disobey the government? Give some examples to help explain your view.

4. Make a list of three strengths and three weaknesses of Bonhoeffer's theology, then explain them to your fellow students.

5. Explain what Bonhoeffer meant by 'religionless Christianity'.

6. Are Bonhoeffer's ethics of any relevance in a multi-cultural/multi-faith society?

7. Can a religious person ever really know that they are following God's will?

SECTION IV
PLURALISM

CHAPTER 7
Religious Pluralism and Theology

LEARNING OUTCOMES

In this chapter, you will be learning about
- the teaching of contemporary Christian theology on
  - exclusivism
    - the view that only Christianity offers the means of salvation
  - inclusivism
    - the view that, although only Christianity is the normative means of salvation, 'anonymous' Christians may also receive salvation
  - pluralism
    - the view that there are many ways to salvation, in which Christianity is one path

Introduction

Western European society is based on the ideal of liberalism. This teaches that every individual may hold whatever beliefs they want, and these should be tolerated by everyone else in society, as long as their beliefs do not pose a threat to society. This idea leads to the further belief that society should be tolerant of any group that holds different or differing views from their own, because diversity leads to a culturally richer society.

In a religious context, the concept of diversity has led to a number of difficulties. Religious pluralism has to do with the diversity of views within one religion (for example, Orthodox and Reform Judaism, or Anglicanism and Roman Catholicism within

Christianity), and also to the similarities and differences between different religions (for example, between Islam and Hinduism).

Christianity arose in the context of a culturally diverse society. In the Ancient Near East, where it began, many people believed in several gods rather than just one – Greek, Roman, Assyrian, Babylonian and the gods of other cultures that the Jews had come into contact with. Christianity first developed as a sect of Judaism worshipping at the synagogue, keeping the Sabbath and the laws of the Torah. Jesus was a Jew who sometimes taught a radical interpretation of Jewish law that forced people to question their traditional Jewish beliefs.

Symbols representing different world religions

In the generation after Jesus' death, the early Christians had to confront several important questions: what was the relationship between them and traditional Judaism? Should Gentiles be allowed to join the Christian movement? If so, did they have to be circumcised? Should Christians still have to worship at the synagogue? Should they still follow the Jewish food laws? What should be the position of women in a Christian community? Should Christians attempt to convert others to become Christian? These, and many other foundational questions, may be seen in the earliest NT documents, particularly in the letters of St Paul.

At the heart of the early Christian movement was a question of **soteriology**. Christians believed that God had sent Jesus to save anyone who believed his message – the Gospel, or 'good news', he preached. They believed that Jesus had a unique relationship with God, symbolized by Jesus' informal Aramaic name for God, 'Abba', which meant 'dad'. They also believed that Jesus' death and resurrection meant that the sins of everyone who believed in Jesus' message had been wiped out by his salvific death. Because of this, they believed that every one of Jesus' followers would be saved from death and hell. Christians believed that Jesus would return to earth, possibly within their own lifetime. This gave urgency to their beliefs and they thought that they had to convert as many people as possible to Christianity, so that they could also benefit in the eternal salvation that Christians would have.

Soteriology: The doctrine of salvation

This focus upon salvation raises a wider and serious problem, not just for Christianity, but for religious thought more generally. Although different religions may define it in different ways, each religion claims to be the way to salvation. This creates a dilemma that may be put in the following way:

(i) **either** one is correct and the others are wrong
(ii) **or** they are all equally valid paths to salvation.

If (i), it may be asked why God has allowed ignorance of salvation and ethics to be so widespread. Perhaps God does not care if people go to hell / never reach heaven.

Religious Pluralism and Theology

If (ii), there seems to be something contradictory (e.g. God is Trinity *and* God is Allah *and* God is Brahman), or we are describing religions in a way that many of their adherents would not accept. For example, we might proclaim that Jesus is not literally God in human form, or that the Qur'an is not the only revealed word of God, because all religions are equally valid paths to salvation, so none is exclusively true.

British philosopher of religion John Hick says that the issue is about the type of statements being made about God. Some people think they are **cognitive**, while others think they are **non-cognitive**. Cognitive language asserts facts, or alleged facts. It conveys information, so cognitive statements are either true or false. Non-cognitive language is more complicated, because it is not necessarily about facts. It could be poetry, in which language is used metaphorically or symbolically, or scientific language, in which words mean very specific things in a particular context. Hick says that the problem with language when used in/about theology is how to decide whether religious language is cognitive (factual) or non-cognitive (non-factual).

Hick questions whether a statement such as 'God loves humans' could ever be shown to be true or false. Is it cognitive? If it is cognitive, how would you test its truth? Or is it non-cognitive? If it is non-cognitive – i.e. non-factual – this would be quite radical and shocking for Christians and members of other religions, going against the way that millions of religious believers have understood their doctrines. For example, if a non-cognitivist declared that 'God was working through Jesus', she would not understand this in a literal, factual, way; rather, she would mean it poetically or symbolically. Hick says non-cognitivist language has radical implications for our understanding of what theology is and how it should be understood. Religion would be isolated from other forms of speech and knowledge. He says, 'Religion becomes a hobby: either you like religion/poetry or you don't' (Hick, *God and the Universe of Faiths*, ch. 1: 'Theology's Central Problem', p. 10).

Theologians have suggested several different possible solutions to this problem.

One of the leading thinkers on this is Alan Race (*Christians and Religious Pluralism*; and *Thinking about Religious Pluralism: Shaping Theology of Religions for Our Times*, Augsburg Fortress Press, 2015). He developed a typology of responses that has become known as the **Theology of religions**. This falls into three broad categories, though not all scholars agree on the details of each category.

> **Cognitive/non-cognitive:** Refer to different kinds of statement: cognitive = facts / alleged facts; non-cognitive = non-facts, e.g. poetry, metaphors, symbolism

> **Theology of religions:** Alan Race's proposed solution to the difficulty of talking to members of non-Christian religions

> **Exclusivism:** The view that only Christianity offers the means of salvation

Exclusivism: the view that only one religion is true – the others are false. Those who convert to this religion will be saved; those who refuse will be excluded from salvation. The three main Abrahamic religions (Christianity, Islam, Judaism) have had this approach for most of their history. There are two somewhat different versions of exclusivism.

(i) Restricted access exclusivism: This view teaches that only the message of Christianity ('the Gospel') and a personal response to Christ with faith before you die will result in salvation. Key scholars associated with this view include John Calvin, Billy Graham, John Piper and Wayne Grudem. They teach that human nature is sinful, because of the Fall, and that only those individuals who repent of their sins and follow Jesus will be saved and attain eternal life with God. A key statement for restricted access

Christians is in John's Gospel, where Jesus says: 'I am the way, and the truth and the life. No-one comes to the Father except through me' (John 14:6).

(ii) Universal access exclusivism: The key idea here is that God wants to save everyone, not just the 'elect', as believed by restricted access exclusivists. Salvation may even happen after death – for example, from within purgatory. Key scholars who accept this view include **Gavin D'Costa** (1958–present), former Archbishop of Canterbury **Rowan Williams** (1950–present), possibly Karl Barth (some scholars debate whether he is a 'universalist', which means that everyone will be saved in the end). Universalism goes back to the influential early Christian scholar **Origen** (c.185–c.254).

Inclusivism: This view states that, although one religion is true, God may also save people from other religions who, usually through no fault of their own, do not belong to the 'true' religion. These people may be saved if they live good moral lives. Key inclusivist thinkers include twentieth-century German scholars Karl Rahner and Hans Küng, and the Doctrine Commission of the Church of England, and inclusivist thought is seen in some of the conclusions of Vatican II (1962–5).

Pluralism: there are many ways to achieve salvation because each religion contains truth and can lead to salvation in its own way. Key thinkers in favour of this include twentieth-century British scholars John Hick and Keith Ward, as well as the American scholar **Paul Knitter** (1939–present).

> **Inclusivism:** The view that, although Christianity is the normative means of salvation, 'anonymous' Christians may also receive salvation

> **Pluralism:** The view that there are many ways to salvation, of which Christianity is one way

Each of these approaches combines epistemological, ethical and soteriological questions, including what we can know about God, why God would condemn many people to destruction, and how we may be saved.

> **Exercise**
> Make a list or a grid of the three main theories in this chapter – exclusivism, inclusivism and pluralism – and make brief notes about their distinctive positions.

From a Christian point of view, there are several facts to acknowledge and ideas to sustain that exist in tension: the centrality of Christ, belief in God's involvement in the Church, the Holy Spirit at work everywhere, the goodness of other religious people and religions, the existence of other religions and confinement of Judaism and Christianity to specific parts of the world, the continuance of other religions even when introduced to and confronted by Christianity.

Exclusivism

Proponents of exclusivism, also called **particularism**, believe that Christianity is the only religion that will lead to salvation. This has been the dominant view for most Christians throughout the history of that religion. As we will see below, St Augustine

> **Particularism:** Another name for exclusivism

in the late fourth century and John Calvin in the sixteenth century were particularly important in formulating this belief. Since the beginning of the twentieth century, however, this view has been challenged from within Christianity and also by increasing knowledge and understanding of the other world religions.

Exclusivist Christians believe that the Incarnation, death and resurrection of Jesus Christ are events of universal and timeless significance. They believe that God sent his only son, Jesus, to earth to bring salvation to all humans in a once-and-for-all event. The only condition for receiving salvation is to believe in the Gospel preached by Jesus and respond to it in faith. Most Christians confirm their belief by being baptized. This is a symbol of their turning away from their past sins and being reborn into Christian life, cleansed of all their previous sins. This rebirth is necessary for salvation to be granted, and Christians must give up their old sinful life and follow the teaching of the Church. For most exclusivists, there is no other way to receive salvation.

The theologian Gavin D'Costa has sub-divided exclusivist beliefs into two sorts – restricted access exclusivism and universal access exclusivism (D'Costa, *Christianity and the World Religions*, pp. 25–33).

Restricted access exclusivism

Restricted access exclusivism is understood as the most traditional form of exclusivism. This focuses on the idea that all humans are sinful from birth and are much in need of salvation by Christ. Christ was unique because he was both fully human and fully God (as the Apostles' Creed states). As such, Christ was without sin and was sent by God to be the only person who could redeem humans (*Sola Christus*) from their sins. Humans must hear the Gospel (***fides ex auditu***) and be baptized into the Church in order to be granted salvation. Restrictive access exclusivists traditionally appeal for support to biblical statements such as:

> *Fides ex auditu*: Faith from having heard (the Gospel) – for some exclusivists, this is the only way to achieve salvation

John 14:6 – 'Jesus said to him, "I am the way, and the truth and the life. No one comes to the Father except through me."'

Acts 4:12 – 'There is salvation in no one else, for there is no other name under heaven given among mortals by which we must be saved.'

2 Corinthians 5:18–19 – 'All this is from God, who reconciled us to himself through Christ, and has given us the ministry of reconciliation; that is, in Christ, God was reconciling the world to himself.'

1 Timothy 2:5–6 – 'there is one God and one mediator between God and mankind, the man Christ Jesus, who gave himself as a ransom for all people. This has now been witnessed to at the proper time.'

One major difficulty with this form of exclusivism is that those millions of people who have never heard the Christian Gospel will automatically be excluded from salvation. What about those who have heard the Gospel but have rejected it? What of the millions of people who lived before Christ? St Augustine had taught that each individual was so lost in sin that no one could reach salvation on their own. Thus, humans do not have free will to choose to worship God. It is up to God, therefore, to choose which individuals to save. Augustine's answer to the question of why some are saved and others not, is that it is God's sovereign purpose, the divine will that cannot be known by humans, to decide which individuals will be saved and which condemned.

Following Augustine, John Calvin preached that, after the Fall, all humans were inherently sinful. As a result of this, it follows that God is not under any compulsion to save anyone. God is a loving God, however, and there are some people who will be saved by him because of their righteous actions and moral standards. Calvin began the development of what became known as Double Predestination, the idea that God chooses only a certain number of people whom he ordains to enter heaven and attain eternal life. In traditional Calvinism, this was set at 144,000, the number mentioned in Rev. 7:4–8, where 12,000 from each of the twelve tribes of Israel are mentioned. **Jehovah's Witnesses** still officially believe that this is the number of the 'elect'. Calvin's followers added that God also commands that those who are not chosen (the 'reprobate' or sinners) are destined for hell and eternal damnation. This view is sometimes called the '**Narrow exclusivist**' position.

Other exclusivist Christians take a '**Broad exclusivist**' view. This has been popular among some Roman Catholics, who teach that salvation will only be granted to those who are baptized members of the Roman Catholic church and who regularly receive the sacrament from a priest. This is still the official teaching of this church, encapsulated in the Latin phrase ***extra ecclesiam nulla salus*** (outside the Church there is no salvation). The way in which it is described has changed somewhat since Vatican II, when the church began to be more interested in making links with Christians from other denominations.

> **Jehovah's Witnesses:** A Fundamentalist sect who believe in Double Predestination
>
> **Narrow exclusivist:** Believers in Double Predestination, adding that those who are not chosen will go to hell and eternal damnation
>
> **Broad exclusivist:** Church members must be baptized by a priest and receive the sacrament regularly
>
> *Extra ecclesiam nulla salus*: Latin phrase: 'Outside the Church there is no salvation'

Universal access exclusivism

Many theologians have criticized restricted access exclusivism because of the seemingly harsh, unfair and unloving doctrine of Double Predestination. The Swiss Protestant theologian Karl Barth provided a nuanced view of exclusivism, arguing that, although salvation is only possible through Christ, at the end of history there will be an eschatological victory of God's grace over non-belief. Eventually, God's grace will triumph completely and every person will come to believe in Christ. Barth affirms that Christ is the only way to salvation, but God will allow sufficient time for everyone to accept him. Scholars take passages from his *Church Dogmatics* 1.2, §17 ('The Revelation of God as the Abolition of Religion'), where he discusses whether salvation may be found outside Christianity. Some scholars have interpreted Barth's teaching as the traditional view that salvation may only be attained within Christianity. No believers in other religions (Hindus, Muslims, etc.) will be saved. He focuses on the doctrine of the Trinity, as he considers it to be unique to Christianity – therefore, only Christianity has exclusive access to God: 'It is the doctrine of the Trinity which fundamentally distinguishes the Christian doctrine of God as Christian – it is, therefore, also, that which marks off the Christian concept of revelation as Christian, in face of all other possible doctrines of God and concepts of revelation' (*Church Dogmatics*, 1.1, p. 346).

This is one interpretation of Barth's position, but there is another way of understanding his view – as that of a universal access exclusivist. Some scholars believe that Barth argues that God's revelation transforms all religions, not just Christianity. This is because all religions are human constructs, attempting to understand God. No religion can legitimately claim to have full knowledge of God. They also argue that Barth's teaching on the Trinity can be understood as teaching that religious believers from religions other than Christianity may also be saved.

Universal access exclusivists must be able to answer the same difficult questions as the restricted access exclusivists: what happens to people who lived and died before Christ came to earth? What is the position of members of other religious traditions, such as Hinduism, Islam or Judaism? Will they be saved? One answer, given by the Roman Catholic church, is that the state of purgatory allows an opportunity for non-Christians to learn about and experience the message of salvation in the Gospel. If they repent and accept the redemption offered by Christ, they will be saved. Roman Catholics believe that salvation is possible for every person who has ever lived - this is **universal salvation**. But this universal salvation must be fulfilled within the Church, therefore there can be no salvation outside the Church (*extra ecclesiam nulla salus*), because this would be universalism, which Roman Catholics reject.

> **Universal salvation:** Roman Catholics believe that non-Christians, and those who have rejected Christianity, will have an opportunity of salvation while in purgatory

The Roman Catholic church's position changed only after Vatican II (1962–5), the general purpose of which was to gather together in Rome church leaders from all over the world to discuss the place of the Roman Catholic church in the modern world. One set of discussions concerned the relationship between the Church and non-Christian religions, as well as with other Christian denominations. As a result, the Roman Catholic church became more outward-looking than before and this led to several important reforms. There had been a number of historical events that led to these changes.

> **Globalization:** The movement of people around the world, resulting in exposure to different cultures and religious traditions

- The world is now more connected than ever before. **Globalization** in the twentieth century has increased the inter-connectedness of individuals, countries and religions around the world.
- The migration of people, because of improvements in transport and as a result of war, has increased the interaction between people from different faiths.
- The experience of the Holocaust and Christianity's reassessment of its own teaching have led to a more open approach to other cultures and religions.
- Confronting the issue of anti-Semitism and relations with Judaism, which is a legitimate religion in its own right, has led to greater understanding, as well as self-reflection, by Christians.
- As a result of events such as the Crusades, the Holocaust and other significant events, it was logical for those who had never encountered or had little experience of other faiths to assume the monopoly of their own religion.
- The closer people come into proximity with other religions, the more they ask questions about their own religious beliefs and those of others. This challenges the exclusivity of their own religious beliefs.

'The Temple of All Religions', Kazan, Russia. A symbol of interfaith harmony

Inclusivism

As the term might suggest, inclusivism is the view that knowledge of God may be gained implicitly, not only through *fides ex auditu*. Some theologians are unhappy with the exclusivist position that salvation is only possible through the Christian church. They believe that Christianity is true, but that this truth may be found in different ways. It was a way of thinking that emerged during the nineteenth century in India, when British and other Europeans encountered religious faiths other than Christianity, especially Hinduism. One of the most significant books to be written at this time was by English theologian **F. D. Maurice** (1805–72), with his *Religions of the World and their Relations to Christianity* (1846). This book was important because it marked the beginning of the end of the tradition amongst Christian missionaries of being entirely negative about other faiths. Other books from different authors followed, and the idea that other religions might have intrinsic value emerged. The question that followed concerned the relationship between these religions and Christianity. Over time, the entirely exclusivist position amongst Christians changed to an increased interest in inclusivism.

Gavin D'Costa, mentioned before, distinguishes two main forms of inclusivism: **Structural inclusivism**, and **Restrictive inclusivism**.

Structural inclusivism: Karl Rahner's view that believers in any religion whose structures allow openness to God's grace are capable of salvation

Restrictive inclusivism: The view that God considers non-Christians, even though they may practise ethical lives, as not capable of salvation, unless they become Christians

Structural inclusivism: Karl Rahner

Rahner had studied Philosophy under Martin Heidegger, an atheist existentialist, and learned much from him that had an important influence on his own thought. Rahner used Heidegger's analysis of human nature and his central concept of 'Being' (*Dasein*) to develop his own views on the capacities of human beings. He begins by stating that human beings are, by nature, limited in their knowledge of the world and in their understanding of themselves and others. Because of this limited knowledge, humans must accept that they are mortal. This recognition leads them to search for their 'being', and they will find that it is something that defies definition. Rahner claims that this is the point when people encounter God and his infinite grace, the source of Being.

Rahner concludes from this discovery of the divine Being that it is not unique to Christianity, but is present in other religions as well. Many of the world religions teach that their adherents must act ethically, selflessly and lovingly towards each other, and their forms of worship create the opportunity to find God. In Rahner's view, however, it is only in Christianity that individuals will experience the full revelation of God's saving grace, because of the life and work of Jesus Christ. God can save individuals even if they are not able to understand that it is Christ who is responsible for their salvation. If they treat others with respect, kindness and love, they are following Jesus' example.

Rahner was one of the most important theologians in the discussions at Vatican II, and he helped author the significant document *Lumen gentium* (A Light to the Nations). Rahner's influence may be seen in the following extract: '[members of other faiths, who] through no fault of their own, do not know the Gospel of Christ or His Church, but who nevertheless seek God with a sincere heart, and moved by grace, try in their actions to do His will as they know it through the dictates of their conscience – those too may achieve eternal salvation' (*Lumen gentium*, 1964, ch. 2.16).

Anonymous Christianity

One of Rahner's contributions to thought on the relationship between Christianity and other faiths is his idea of '*anonymous Christianity*'. He uses the relationship between ancient Judaism and the beginning of Christianity as an analogy to explain the relation between Christianity and other religions. Any institution or religion may allow individuals to learn about God's love and grace, but this is only partial truth. It is only through learning about and accepting the Incarnation of Christ that the fullness of God's greatness will be discovered. Only then will members of other religions be saved and become Christian.

Christianity, therefore, has a unique position because it is founded on what Rahner called God's 'ultimate act of revelation', when God sent his only son to earth in the Incarnation. Because of this unique act of God, Christianity is the religion by which all other religions must be judged. Rahner saw the danger in this conclusion, however, as it seems to create a barrier between Christianity and all other religions and thus exclude them from salvation. This applied especially to those believers from non-Christian religions who lived before the beginning of Christianity and did not hear the message of Jesus. Rahner's problem was that this did not seem compatible with Christianity's message of an all-loving, all-wise and omnibenevolent God.

Rahner rejected exclusivism and posited that there must be an element of truth in non-Christian religions, so that, when a Hindu, or Muslim, or member of another religion hears about the revelation of Jesus and the salvation he offers, they have an opportunity to convert to Christianity and therefore attain salvation. He says: 'For this reason a non-Christian religion can be recognized as a lawful religion (although in different degrees) without thereby denying the error or depravity contained in it' (*Theological Investigations*, Helicon Press, 1966, Vol. V, p. 121).

Rahner takes this point from several biblical passages, including St Paul's encounter with Greek philosophers at the Areopagus in Athens (Acts 17:22–3), where Paul applauds their religious beliefs in the Greek gods, but the altar to 'the unknown God' is a way for them to come to know the Gospel of Jesus.

Rahner is here disagreeing with Roman Catholic church teaching. The official view of the Roman Catholic church is that non-Christians can only receive God's love and grace by converting to Christianity and becoming members of the Church.

Rahner's final argument discusses the Church's role in salvation. He argues that the Church cannot be separate from all other religions, but it can play an important part in teaching about Christian beliefs and practices in the non-Christian and non-religious world. He calls this the 'visible' church, whose task is to tell non-Christians about how they can be saved from their sins and brought to salvation in what he calls the 'invisible church'.

> **Exercise**
>
> Look up Romans 2:14–16 and Matthew 25:33–40. Analyse each passage and discuss to what extent they support Rahner's idea of 'invisible Christians'.

Restrictive inclusivism

Restrictive inclusivism is a variation on Structural inclusivism. This view may be driven by the thought held by many individual Christians and church leaders that exclusivism appears to be very cruel and harsh towards the millions of adherents of religions other than Christianity. Why would God, being a loving God, condemn so many religious people to eternal damnation? Surely, God would wish to seek a way of allowing salvation to these people. After all, it is not the fault of Hindus, Jews, Muslims, Sikhs and so on that they were not born into Christian families. Restrictive inclusivism, therefore, puts forward the idea that, although God will make 'suitable provision' for those who have not heard the Christian Gospel but naturally live according to general Christian views, such as Natural Law and conscience, they will still not receive salvation by God. The religious life of a non-Christian can, according to this theory, only be a preparation for (Christian) salvation. This view is held, officially or unofficially, by many Christians across many denominations, including Roman Catholics, Protestants and Orthodox churches. Non-Christians will still have to convert to Christianity and accept the salvation offered by God through Christ.

Criticisms of inclusivism

John Hick thought that Rahner's phrase 'anonymous Christians' was paternalistic and patronizing, offering 'honorary status granted unilaterally to people who have not expressed any desire for it' (Hick, *God has Many Names: Britain's New Religious Pluralism*, John Knox Press, 1986, p. 68). Hick continues his criticism of inclusivism by saying:

> All these thinkers [notably Rahner and Hans Küng] who are trying so hard to find room for their non-Christian brethren in the sphere of salvation, are still working within the presuppositions of the old dogma. Only Christians can be saved; so we have to say that devout and godly non-Christians are really, in some metaphysical sense, Christians or Christians-to-be without knowing it . . . We have to realise that the universe of faith centers upon God, and not upon Christianity or any other religion.
>
> (ibid., pp. 70–1)

For Hick, the 'old dogma' is the paternalistic, imperialistic, European Christian view that non-Christian religions are somehow second class by comparison with 'the one true faith'. From this mountain-top position, all other religions must be inferior. For Hick, this view fails to study sufficiently the interior structure and core beliefs of the other religions. This is what makes it both patronizing and paternalistic, and ultimately wrong-headed.

American evangelical theologian Trevin Wax agrees that the inclusivist position is arrogant, and provides three reasons to justify his view.

- If a person's individual response to the salvation offered by Jesus is not paramount, then evangelism is only an attempt to force one's own religious preferences on others. Wax says this is a smug approach, because a Christian is merely giving his/her opinion, rather than carefully argued theological arguments. It would be like saying 'I think Jesus is better than Muhammad' or even 'I prefer coffee to tea.' There is no deep meaning in inclusivism.
- Inclusivism is patronizing to non-Christians. Christian inclusivists take the view that their beliefs about Jesus' salvation are correct. This leads to the supplementary conclusion that the views of every other religion are incorrect. There is no certain evidence, however, to justify this kind of statement. It is merely an opinion, and it allows Christians to feel 'superior' to members of any other faith group.
- Inclusivism makes Christians myopic. Christian evangelism should be directed at *all* people, not only those who are already Christian, but Sikhs and Hindus and all other religious traditions too. Inclusivism leads to a diminution of evangelism.

(Trevin Wax, 'The Arrogance of Inclusivism', The Gospel Coalition, 26 April 2011)

Pluralism

Pluralism is the view that no single religion has a monopoly on theological truth. Each religion may be different in the ways it expresses its views and formulates its doctrines, but there are commonalities among religions, including having the same ultimate goals in life – living ethically, celebrating difference, salvation or enlightenment. The apparent differences between religions are superficial, based only on cultural differences and the use of language. The result of this is that religions are not in competition with each other, and it would be counter-productive or pointless to attempt to convert individuals from one religion to another.

The main spokesperson for pluralism in the Western world is John Hick. He was brought up as an evangelical Christian. When he became Professor of Theology at the University of Birmingham, and encountered people from many other religious faiths, including Hindus, Muslims and Sikhs, he learned a great deal by their example in the communities they lived in. Their worship, care for others, ethical lives and commitment to helping people outside their own community, forced Hick to reassess his own beliefs, particularly his view that Christianity was the only path to salvation. Would a loving God condemn all non-Christians to hell, just because they were not Christian?

Hick wrote:

> As soon as one does meet and come to know people of other faiths a paradox of gigantic proportions becomes disturbingly obvious. We say as Christians that God is the God of universal love, that he is the creator and Father of all mankind, that he wills the universal good and salvation of all men. But we also say, traditionally, that the only way to salvation is the Christian way. And yet we know, when we stop to think about it, that the large majority of the human race who have lived and died up to the present moment have lived either before Christ or outside the borders of Christendom. Can we then accept the conclusion that the God of love who seeks to save all mankind has nevertheless ordained that men must be saved in such a way that only a small minority can in fact receive this salvation?
> (Hick, *God and the Universe of Faiths*, p. 122)

Hick believed that it was possible for **transcendent theism** to be shown to be true or false. He declared that a revolution was needed in theology, like that of Copernicus in the field of science, to move away from a Christ-centred view to a God-centred one. He wrote that it was necessary to move away from 'the dogma that Christianity is at the centre to the realization that it is *God* who is at the centre, and that all religions ... including our own, serve and revolve around him'.

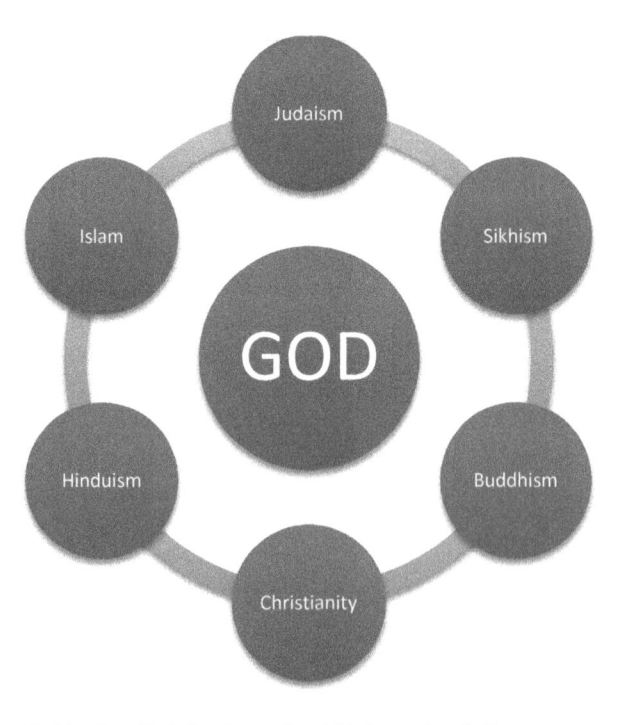

Hick's view that theology should take a pluralistic approach, seeing Christianity as merely one way among others of understanding God

Pluralism:
The co-existence in one place of many different groups: nationalities, religions, ethical viewpoints, class, sexuality and gender

Transcendent theism:
Hick's term for the view that Christianity needs to move away from a Christ-centred view to a God-centred theology. This would lead to the recognition that all religions revolve around God

Hick's philosophical underpinning

Both exclusivism and inclusivism begin with a theological justification of their position. Hick's pluralist approach begins with a philosophical underpinning that he takes from Immanuel Kant. It was immediately clear to Hick that not all religions are theistic. Buddhism, for example, is non-theistic. He learned from Kant's epistemological distinction between two kinds of knowledge – the **noumenal** and the **phenomenal**. The noumenal is the world as it really is, whereas the phenomenal is the world as humans see it. We see things from our own perspective, subjectively, as they relate or appear to us. Different people may see the same object in a different way. Humans do not see the world as it really is. For Kant, the way humans understand God belongs to the phenomenal category. This is why humans have developed different ways of thinking and speaking about God, using different concepts, rituals and ways of talking. God, for Kant, was in the noumenal realm, which is why humans are not capable of understanding God's true nature. Hick uses Kant's concept of the *Ding an-Sich*, or 'thing in itself', to explain why, although humans can have no real understanding of God noumenally, they can have some theoretical understanding of God, but this is only partial.

> **Noumenal:**
> Hick used Kant's term for the world as it really is
>
> **Phenomenal:**
> Hick used Kant's term for the world as humans see it

Hick's ultimate point is that no one religion can have a 'perfect' understanding of 'God'. Each religious tradition is culturally, sociologically and psychologically different from the others, and their understanding of the divine is necessarily different from that of the others. For Hick, these differences are not ultimately important. Every religion falls short of the truth because no human is capable of attaining noumenal understanding of God. It does not matter that each religion has differences from the others. What is important for Hick is that humans, whatever their religion, are engaged in the search for God. British theologian Alister McGrath (*Christian Theology* p. 423) quotes Hick's *Second Christianity* (2nd edn, SCM Press, 1994): 'These different human awarenesses of and responses to the Real are informed by and reciprocally inform the religious traditions of the earth. In them are reflected the different ways of thinking, feeling and experiencing which have developed within the worldwide human family.'

McGrath raises some problems with Hick's point here. McGrath says that it is clear that the various religious traditions of the world are radically different in their beliefs and practices. McGrath disagrees with Hick because some of the practices in, say, Christianity and Hinduism, are very different in both kind and significance. Hick appears not to see this as a problem. He writes:

> Yahweh exists essentially in relation to the Hebrews, the relationship being defined by the idea of covenant. He cannot be extracted from this role in Hebrew historic experience. And as such, Yahweh is a quite different divine persona from Krishna, who is God's face turned towards and perceived by hundreds of millions of people within the Vaishnavite tradition of India.
>
> (Hick, *Second Christianity*, quoted in McGrath, *Christian Theology*, p. 424)

McGrath compares Hick's point here with the eighteenth-century Deists in Britain who propounded a 'universal rational religion of nature' that became corrupted through time. McGrath also wonders whether Hick is actually talking about the

Christian God. He accuses Hick of setting to one side the central idea in Christianity – that of God's revelation in the person of Jesus Christ. For most Christians, the central tenet of Christian belief is Christocentric. Christianity could not be Christianity without Christ. McGrath says 'Hick's desertion of Christ as a reference point means abandoning any claim to speak from a *Christian* perspective' (*Christian Theology*, p. 424).

Hick had disagreed with this criticism in his famous and contentious book, *The Myth of God Incarnate*. Here, he, and other authors, had written that the Incarnation of Christ was a 'myth' and should be abandoned by Christianity. Hick understood the term 'Incarnation' to be symbolic, or a metaphor to explain Jesus' feeling of closeness to God. Over time, this myth became objectified and treated as a fact – that Jesus actually was the Son of God. Hick also referenced the same process with the Buddha, who became transformed from the inspirational and enlightened teacher Gautama into the embodiment of the Dharma, the eternal Buddha.

Hick wanted Christianity and other religions to leave behind these unhelpful myths, moving forward to a different way of expressing their faith that would be relevant and meaningful for the current generation, and not remain tied to an ancient and inappropriate mode of speech and thought. Hick also believed that Christianity needed to leave behind the doctrines that had been formulated at Nicaea (AD 325) and Chalcedon (AD 451). Among others, these councils had established the divinity of Christ and the doctrine of the Trinity. He believed that these no longer had any value for twentieth-century Christians, as they appeared obscure and difficult to understand, and should be thought of as myths. If these were disposed of, Christianity would become more vital and relevant to modern Christians. It would also allow members of other religions to take truth and meaning from Jesus' teaching, which would 'enlarge the relationship with God to which they have already come within their own religion' (*The Myth of God Incarnate*, p. 181).

McGrath notes (*Christian Theology*, pp. 421–2) that an alternative way of understanding the relationship between Christianity and other world religions is emerging, known as 'parallelism', a variant of inclusivism. One scholar who has written about this is Joseph A. DiNoia (1943–present). In his *The Diversity of Religions* (Catholic University of America Press, 1992), DiNoia calls for religious diversity to be taken seriously. He argues that Christians can value their own faith and express their convictions about it, but also respect the faith of those who are members of other religions. DiNoia is a Roman Catholic priest, and argues that Christians must acknowledge the profound differences between Christianity and the other religions. While Hick and others have focused on structural similarities between the different religions, DiNoia points out the significant differences, and argues that the most appropriate way to show respect for each religion is to appreciate these differences properly, and to acknowledge the distinctive goals these religions have.

Another American theologian, Mark Heim (1950–present), criticizes Hick and two other pluralist theologians, Wilfred Cantwell Smith and Paul Knitter, because they all start from a Western liberal position. Heim says that their conclusions will be obvious – they will force other religions into the straitjacket of their own presuppositions, and therefore not allow them to celebrate their own thought forms, doctrines and ways of expressing their beliefs according to their varied cultures.

> **Exercise**
>
> In Fyodor Dostoyevsky's novel *The Brothers Karamazov*, the main characters, Ayosha and Ivan, discuss a utopia in which no-one suffers again. This 'utopia', however, is founded on torturing one child to death. Ivan says he would reject it. He thinks this world's suffering cannot be justified by the existence of heaven. So perhaps one could reject God and salvation even if one understood it. But it is not clear that Ivan does understand because part of the message of Christianity is that the intense joy and peace of heaven are not fully comprehensible from within this life.
>
> Discuss this passage with your classmates. How does this relate to Hick's ideas on pluralism? Does the passage make sense? Do you agree with Ivan's argument? Can you provide a counter-argument?

FURTHER READING

Gavin D'Costa, *Christianity and World Religions*. Wiley-Blackwell, 2009

David F. Ford, *Interreligious Reading After Vatican II: Scriptural Reasoning, Comparative Theology and Receptive Ecumenism*. Directions in Modern Theology. Wiley-Blackwell, 2013

John Hick, *God and the Universe of Faiths*. Oneworld Publications, 1993

Hans Küng, *Christianity and World Religions: Paths to Dialogue*. Orbis Books, 1993

Alan Race, *Christians and Religious Pluralism: Patterns in the Christian Theology of Religions*. 2nd edn. SCM Press, 1993

Alan Race and Paul Hedges, *Christian Approaches to Other Faiths*. SCM Core Text. SCM Press, 2008

Karl Rahner, *The SPCK Introduction to Karl Rahner: A Brief Introduction*. SPCK Publishing, 2007

Thought Points

1. Consider the claim that 'there is no real difference between all religions'.

2. 'Only one religion can be true.' Critically assess this view.

3. 'Rahner's idea of "anonymous Christians" is patronizing and hurtful to non-Christians.' To what extent do you agree with this view?

4. Karl Barth taught that true knowledge of God can only be found in the life, death and resurrection of Jesus Christ. Critically assess this view.

5. 'A pluralist view of religion is the only view that makes any sense of the world.' Consider this statement.

6. To what extent do you agree that inclusivism is just another version of universal access exclusivism?

7. Do you think that a God who is worthy of worship could be a God who does not save people?

CHAPTER 8
Religious Pluralism and Society

LEARNING OUTCOMES
In this chapter, you will be learning about:
- the development of contemporary multi-faith societies
  - reasons for this development
- Christian responses to inter-faith dialogue
  - how Christian communities have responded to the challenge of encounters with other faiths
- the **Scriptural Reasoning Movement**
  - methods and aims
  - how mutual study of sacred scriptures can aid understanding of different and conflicting religious truth claims

Introduction

In 2019, the population of Greater Manchester was 2,710,074. It is a multi-cultural city, made up of people from many countries around the world. It is also a multi-faith city, made up of 48.7% Christian, 24.7% who stated they had no religion, 15.8% Muslim, 1.1% Hindu, 0.8% Buddhist, 0.5% Jewish, 0.5% Sikh, 0.1% Atheist.

In this survey, 34,774 people did not make any statement about religious affiliation, so they may have been Humanists or agnostics; 1,946 people identified as a Jedi Knight, and 150 people said they believe in Heavy Metal. Greater Manchester is a pluralist city, both ethnically and religiously.

126 | PLURALISM

> **Pluralism:**
>
> In the context of society, 'pluralism' means the co-existence in one place of many different groups: nationalities, religions, ethical viewpoints, classes, sexualities and genders.

Pluralism in Britain has increased since the 1950s. Commonwealth citizens were brought to Britain to make up labour shortages in industry after the end of World War II. The shift towards the de-regulation of companies and free market economies increased the movement of people across national boundaries (as part of the reduction of economic barriers in general). Globalization involves the movement of people (modes of travel – by air, sea, road and rail – became quicker and cheaper), and made it easier to have contact with people in other parts of the world and therefore to be exposed to other views and different religious traditions. This began more than 200 years ago, when Britain was a leading nation in the slave trade, taking thousands of people from different countries and religious traditions from their native lands and forcing them to work as slaves in British colonies. This may have meant being in domestic service, or being taken to work in British overseas plantations. No precise figures are available. World War II produced millions of displaced people, and more recent events, such as wars in the Middle East,

Religion in Manchester	
Christian	48.7
No Religion	24.7
Muslim	15.8
Hindu	1.1
Buddhist	0.8
Jewish	0.5
Sikh	0.5
Athiest	0.1
Other	7.8

Multiculturalism in 21st-century Britain

Religious Pluralism and Society | 127

Windrush Generation: An example of the movement of (mostly Caribbean) people from one part of the world to another (Britain)

have done the same (as of early 2019, there are approximately 65 million displaced people – within a particular country – and refugees – moved to a different country – around the world). One famous example of this was 'the **Windrush Generation**', named after the ship that transported thousands of people from the British Commonwealth to live in Britain. The first consignment of 500 people arrived at Tilbury docks on 22 June 1948, and there are now about 500,000 members living in Britain. Many of these are from Caribbean countries such as Jamaica, whose people practise an evangelical form of 'Black' Christianity, and this has caused them difficulty in integrating with other Christians because their form of worship is quite different from traditional Protestant and Roman Catholic worship. In 2018, about 25 per cent of Christians in London identify as Black Christians, and many of these are members of the Baptist denomination.

Inter-faith dialogue

Problems and challenges

Most people in Britain, even if they do not live in a major city or have never met anyone from a different country, tradition or race, will have some knowledge and understanding of the wide diversity of customs and beliefs around the world, even if it is only from studying world religions in RS lessons! Most people will have neighbours, friends, relatives and others they come across in their daily lives who come from a different religious, racial or cultural tradition. This is just part of living in the twenty-first century. Supermarkets stock foods from different parts of the world, airports have multi-faith prayer rooms, TV programmes will feature actors or presenters from different countries or religious traditions. There is also the fact of large numbers of people who reject any form of religious belief, defining themselves as agnostic or atheist. So, we can say that there are three important strands concerning **inter-faith dialogue** to be considered:

Inter-faith dialogue: The process of learning to understand and communicate with people of different faiths

Christianity → Other religions → Non-religious

For some Christians, religious diversity can be a positive experience, as they can learn new things about people of different faiths, or their own faith. They may also reflect on the similarities and differences between faiths. Christianity, of course, developed out of a different faith, that of Judaism, so Christians may wish to find out more about the origins of Christianity to enhance their own understanding and, perhaps, make links with any Jewish neighbours they may have in their own community. Engaging with people of different faiths or of none can encourage Christians to think more deeply about their own faith. This can be challenging for them, because they may not have looked objectively at their own beliefs, as if from the point of view of someone who either believed in a different religion or had no religious beliefs at all. Some Christians will find this rewarding, in the sense that, when they read the Bible or attend a church service, they will think actively about each reading they hear, or the words in the sermon or hymns they sing, or the meaning of the symbolic actions in the eucharist, and so on. This can be very educational and uplifting for them. For other Christians, however, it may be somewhat upsetting or even threatening, because they might believe that the way they worship and what they believe is the only 'true' faith and all others are wrong. If this were to be the case, these Christians would be unlikely to want to engage with any other religion, or even other Christian denominations. An example may be the long history of religious segregation in Northern Ireland.

General Christian responses

Inter-faith dialogue stands within a more general structure of Christian theology. If it did not, it would be very difficult to give it any real meaning. The word 'dialogue' is central to understanding what inter-faith relations are about. Meaningful dialogue between members of different faith communities needs to be positive, creative and open-ended. It must be capable of communicating with individuals of other religions and those of none, to break down stereotypes and existing prejudices, and to build up mutual respect and co-operation amongst the participants. The dialogue must also recognize areas where they differ and attempt to reach an understanding of these differences. Inter-faith dialogue is not about trying to convert anyone from one faith to another, or about attempting to demonstrate the superiority of one faith over another. All participants wish to learn about and benefit from the beliefs of others.

Official church responses

There have been several responses from Roman Catholic, Jewish, Muslim and Anglican religious groups on the subject of inter-faith dialogue. Each group presents their own views and ideas in a spirit of openness and friendship, seeking to engage with the other faiths and those of no faith.

(i) **Roman Catholic:** *Redemptoris missio* (Mission of the Redeemer), subtitled 'On the permanent validity of the Church's missionary mandate'. Pope John Paul II issued this as a Papal Encyclical in 1990. It aims to explain why Roman Catholics must try to continue to convert people and how they can do so sensitively, while always respecting and learning from what is good in other religions.

The Pope also explains that Jesus Christ is the one saviour of the world and that it is only through Christ that God may be known. Christians may learn truths from members of other faiths, but, at the same time, they must attempt to convert them to Christianity.

One section of *Redemptoris missio* (55–7), subtitled 'Dialogue with our brothers and sisters of other religions', explains how a Roman Catholic might engage in dialogue with someone with a different faith. The Pope states:

Redemptoris missio: A Roman Catholic Encyclical in response to questions about how Roman Catholics should interact with people of different faiths

In the light of the economy of salvation, the Church sees no conflict between proclaiming Christ and engaging in interreligious dialogue. Instead, she feels the need to link the two in the context of her mission *ad gentes* (to the Nations). These two elements must maintain both their intimate connection and their distinctiveness; therefore they should not be confused, manipulated or regarded as identical, as though they were interchangeable.

(Section 55)

Salvation is available to all people, without exception, regardless of which religion they belong to. The only stipulation, according to the Pope, is that they must accept Jesus Christ as the only means to effect salvation. Although he is insistent on this point, the Pope makes it very clear that members of other religions must be treated with respect and kindness in inter-faith discussions.

The Pope also acknowledges that there will be different levels of dialogue in the process. Some possible converts may be academics, others may be at a lower level of engagement in the dialogue. Christians may practise their understanding of the faith at whichever level they are able to do so. The Pope also acknowledges that the process may be difficult, and misunderstanding may occur, but perseverance is important. He says:

> I am well aware that many missionaries and Christian communities find in the difficult and often misunderstood path of dialogue their only way of bearing sincere witness to Christ and offering generous service to others. I wish to encourage them to persevere with faith and love, even in places where their efforts are not well received. Dialogue is a path toward the kingdom and will certainly bear fruit, even if the times and seasons are known only to the Father (cf. Acts 1:7).

(Section 57)

Exercise

Read the following statement and decide whether you agree with it. Give your reasons and discuss them with your fellow students.

'In the end, God decides who is saved. God wants to save everyone and does it through Christ. How that happens "we can only be agnostic about". But "the fullness of relationship with God is possible only in Jesus Christ, who is the definitive revelation of God".'
(The Doctrine Commission of the Church of England, *The Mystery of Salvation*, ch. 7: 'Christ and world faiths')

Alan Race developed the categories of exclusivist, inclusivist and pluralist (see p. 111):

- exclusivists believe that salvation comes through explicit faith in Christ, or through the church
- inclusivists see salvation coming ultimately through Christ, but inclusive of everyone, or of particular people in other religions
- pluralists understand that there are many paths to salvation, including any of the major religions and possibly spiritual groups or individuals.

(ii) **Justin Martyr** and other Apologists in the early centuries of emerging Christianity (i.e. Christians explaining Christianity to their peers in the Greek world) saw Platonism as a philosophical preparation for Christianity, and Christianity as the *true* philosophy. Other early Christian theologians rejected this, especially **Tertullian** (c.155–c.220), who famously stated: 'What indeed has Athens to do with Jerusalem? What concord is there between the Academy and the Church? What between heretics and Christians? With our faith, we desire no further belief. For this is our primary faith, that there is nothing which we ought to believe besides' (Tertullian, *Prescriptions against Heretics*, 7).

In the more recent history of Christianity, there are several examples of genuine dialogue between religions:

- **St John of Damascus** represented Christians in the court of the Ummayad caliphate in the seventh century.

> **St John of Damascus (c.675–749)** St John of Damascus was a Syrian monk and priest, one of the founders of the Eastern Orthodox church and a strong defender of icons. He is a Doctor of the Roman Catholic Church. He wrote several books explaining Christian beliefs, including *Against Heresy; On Right Thinking; An Exact Expression of the Orthodox Faith; On Dragons and Ghosts*. He also wrote poetry and hymns.

- Nineteenth-century Christian missionaries in India started to understand the depth of other religions, and the fact that other religions continued to exist despite attempts to convert people to Christianity. They started to ask whether God had a 'saving purpose' for these religions.
- John Nicol Farquhar (1861–1929) argued that Hinduism was an excellent faith, but in the end he still believed that Jesus died for peoples' sins and was 'the fulfilment and goal of all the religions of the world'.
- Karl Barth believed that, with the exception of Christianity, all religions were human constructions and therefore not really valid. Barth is difficult to categorize precisely, however. He said that Hinduism was not true belief. When asked how he knew this, since he had never met a Hindu, he replied, 'I know that *a priori*.' Yet he thought that *all* people are redeemed in Christ, which is an inclusivist position to take.

> **John Nicol Farquhar (1861–1929)** Farquhar was a Scottish 'educational' missionary in Calcutta. He developed relationships with Hindus, and is known for his pioneering work in 'Fulfilment theology', arguing that Christ is the fulfilment – or crown – of Hinduism. He left India in 1923 because of ill health, and spent the last six years of his life as Professor of Comparative Religions at Manchester University.

(iii) *Dabru Emet* **(Speak the Truth)** was published as a statement in September 2000. Over 150 rabbis and Jewish scholars from around the world signed it. It begins:

> In recent years, there has been a dramatic and unprecedented shift in Jewish and Christian relations. Throughout the nearly two millennia of Jewish exile, Christians have tended to

Dabru Emet (Speak the Truth): A document from Jewish leaders encouraging discussions with Christian leaders to establish common ground and dialogue

characterize Judaism as a failed religion or, at best, a religion that prepared the way for, and is completed in, Christianity. In the decades since the Holocaust, however, Christianity has changed dramatically. An increasing number of official Church bodies, both Roman Catholic and Protestant, have made public statements of their remorse about Christian mistreatment of Jews and Judaism. These statements have declared, furthermore, that Christian teaching and preaching can and must be reformed so that they acknowledge God's enduring covenant with the Jewish people and celebrate the contribution of Judaism to world civilization and to Christian faith itself.

We believe these changes merit a thoughtful Jewish response. Speaking only for ourselves – an inter-denominational group of Jewish scholars – we believe it is time for Jews to learn about the efforts of Christians to honor Judaism. We believe it is time for Jews to reflect on what Judaism may now say about Christianity. As a first step, we offer eight brief statements about how Jews and Christians may relate to one another.

The eight statements are:

- Jews and Christians worship the same God.
- Jews and Christians seek authority from the same book – the Bible (what Jews call 'Tanakh' and Christians call the 'Old Testament').
- Christians can respect the claim of the Jewish people upon the land of Israel.
- Jews and Christians accept the moral principles of Torah.
- Nazism was not a Christian phenomenon.
- The humanly irreconcilable difference between Jews and Christians will not be settled until God redeems the entire world as promised in scripture.
- A new relationship between Jews and Christians will not weaken Jewish practice.
- Jews and Christians must work together for justice and peace.

This Jewish response was enabled by the rejection by Christians, after the Holocaust, of their belief that Judaism was only important because it was 'merely' a preparation for Christianity, and that God's covenant with the Jews was thereby defunct.

Dabru Emet was written as a challenge for individual Christians as well as the religion of Christianity to rethink its doctrines, and how it reads the Jewish scriptures, as well as how it uses language in worship, politics and education.

Professor David Ford (1948–present) thinks four main tasks emerge from *Dabru Emet*: (i) 'Rereading scripture, both within the church and with Jews'; (ii) following that rereading 'into every area of doctrine, ethics, politics, worship'; (iii) 'Embedding the results of such reassessment in current Christian catechesis, curricula, liturgies, church policies, and cultural expressions'; (iv) making 'collegial engagement with Jews . . . part of normal Christian life' where they live side by side, and developing national and international conversation and collegiality. (These apply to Christian–Muslim relations too).

David F. Ford (1948–present) Ford was, until 2014, Regius Professor of Divinity at the University of Cambridge. He has written many books on theology and is one of the founders of the Scriptural Reasoning Movement.

(iv) ***A Common Word Between Us and You*** was published on 13 October 2007. In it, 138 Muslim scholars and clerics met for the first time to declare the common ground between Christianity and Islam. Every denomination and school of thought in Islam, and every major Islamic country in the world, was represented in the message, addressed to all Christians everywhere.

This is one of the most significant documents ever to have been produced relating to Muslim–Christian relations. The document opens with the words:

> In the Name of God, the Compassionate, the Merciful: A Common Word Between Us and You.
>
> Muslims and Christians together make up well over half of the world's population. Without peace and justice between these two religious communities, there can be no meaningful peace in the world. The future of the world depends on peace between Muslims and Christians. The basis for this peace and understanding already exists.
>
> It is part of the very foundational principles of both faiths: love of the One God, and love of the neighbour. These principles are found over and over again in the sacred texts of Islam and Christianity. The Unity of God, the necessity of love for him, and the necessity of love of the neighbour is thus the common ground between Islam and Christianity.

It is 'unprecedented' that religious leaders from several different faiths have met together with a common purpose. It was a common, though not final, word, implying mutual dialogue rather than conversion and **supercessionism** (Islam has always seen itself as correcting Christianity). It challenges both religions to live up to their own best teachings in ethics and politics. There is no attempt to hide the differences between the two religions, but it challenges both to look more closely at the demands made of their believers, especially on the responsibilities to live up to the teachings of their religion expected of each of them. It hopes for an on-going dialogue between the two religions, seeking to find commonalities for debate and discussion.

(v) **Rowan Williams**, then Archbishop of Canterbury, published in 2008 ***A Common Word for the Common Good*** (in conjunction with Christian leaders and scholars) in response to *A Common Word Between Us and You*. This was an attempt to explore areas of theology that the two religions had in common – for instance, shared belief in ideas concerning the love of God and love for one's neighbour. Williams wanted Christians and Muslims to decide on practical steps that would enable members of both religions to make a commitment to peaceful relations. He said: 'We can together suggest a way in which religious plurality can be seen as serving the cause of social unity and acting as a force for the common good.'

(vi) ***Sharing the Gospel of Salvation***, a document published by the Church of England in 2010, made a further contribution to inter-faith dialogue. The discussion was stimulated in 2006, when Paul Eddy, a member of the Synod of the Church of England, asked for a debate and clear guidance on whether the Church should be attempting to convert people of other faiths to Christianity. The document states that this mission is an important part of British history – for instance, the 1910 Edinburgh World Missionary Conference, where 1,200 delegates from Protestant missionary societies met together. British society has now changed and, in a multi-faith society, mission

---

A Common Word Between Us and You: A 2008 document from Muslim scholars declaring the common ground between them and Christians

Supercessionism: Where one group or religion supersedes or succeeds over another

A Common Word for the Common Good: A document representing Christian views about the value of dialogue with Islam

Sharing the Gospel of Salvation: A 2010 Church of England contribution to the discussion of inter-faith dialogue

needs to be carried out with sensitivity. The Church must show 'hospitality . . . develop good inter-faith relations . . . in the hope that [non-Christians] will come to faith and be baptized' (para. 30).

Christians should live 'authentically' according to their beliefs – that is, they must put their beliefs into practice every day. They must live with a sense of common purpose, which is to achieve the 'common good' for the whole of society, as opposed to acting out of self-interest. The Church of England has many opportunities for mission, including ministry, universities, chaplaincy, councils and networks, among others. The document provides examples of how mission might be undertaken, and advice about how Christians might work within a multi-faith society.

The document identifies four strands of different situations in which Christians may engage people of other faiths:

(i) *the dialogue of daily life* – where a Christian may start up an informal conversation about their different religious beliefs, perhaps in the supermarket, or on the street
(ii) *the dialogue of the common good* – engaging informally while doing community-based tasks
(iii) *the dialogue of mutual understanding* – this might be a more formalized debate or conversation, such as the Scriptural Reasoning Movement (see below)
(iv) *the dialogue of spiritual life* – where people of different faiths meet formally for prayer and worship.

One of the main benefits of this approach for Church of England members, and other Christian denominations, is that they are encouraged not to 'hide their light under a bushel' (Matt. 5:15), but to talk more openly about their Christian faith to other people.

> **Exercise**
>
> To what extent do you think the suggestions in the *Sharing the Gospel of Salvation* document are practically achievable?

The Scriptural Reasoning Movement

Scriptural Reasoning Movement: A forum for Christian, Jewish and Muslim people to meet and discuss theological and other issues to foster mutual understanding

'Scriptural Reasoning' is a movement that began in the 1990s when the Jewish American scholar **Peter Ochs** (1950–present) invited Jewish scholars to create a forum with the purpose of discussing Judaism's sacred texts. This group was originally called 'Textual Reasoning' and included Jewish philosophers, historians, linguists and religious leaders. After some time, they invited some Christian theologians to join the group, and later included several Muslim scholars. The enlarged group developed a strong sense that their readings, discussions and reflections were producing very interesting ideas. The next stage was to change the name of the group to 'Scriptural Reasoning' and the movement became international, with groups particularly in the US, Canada and the UK. The movement's main aim is not to convert anyone, but to deepen members' understanding of different religious traditions by studying their scriptures, and to foster long-term friendships and mutual understanding across participants and their religions.

One of the first British participants in the Scriptural Reasoning Movement was David Ford. He has been heavily involved with the movement since the late 1990s, and was influential in setting up Scriptural Reasoning as part of the **Cambridge Inter-Faith Programme**. According to their website:

> In Scriptural Reasoning (SR), participants meet to read passages from their respective sacred texts. Together they discuss the content of those texts, and the variety of ways in which their traditions have worked with them and continue to work with them, and the ways in which those texts shape their understanding of and engagement with a range of contemporary issues. The goal is not agreement but rather growth in understanding one another's traditions and deeper exploration of the texts and their possible interpretations.

Cambridge Inter-Faith Programme: One of the English focal points of the Scriptural Reasoning Movement, offering meetings, discussion, courses, etc.

A few of the themes that have been discussed include:

- detailed reading and discussion of Christian, Jewish and Muslim sacred texts
- education
- clothing and modesty
- human nature
- the role and importance of fasting
- the importance of spirituality
- the effectiveness of prayer
- the purpose of worship
- music in religion
- women and equality.

There is also an academic journal, the *Journal of Scriptural Reasoning*, to support participants on the course and other interested scholars, and to further the discussion at an academic level.

Scriptural Reasoning is different from other types of inter-faith dialogue, because it does not want simply to inform people through academic conferences. Instead, it promotes discussion in small groups of Christians, Jews and Muslims. David Ford puts forward three aims for these groups:

- **Collegiality**: reading sacred texts is a shared experience for each group. Texts are prepared in advance, then read and discussed at the meeting by the group members, who come from different faith traditions
- **Hospitality**: there has to be a spirit of openness to learning something new from the texts, and for individual views to be expressed and listened to by all members of the group. Value judgements are not made. Different faith groups may take turns to host the meetings.
- **Wisdom**: there is a feeling of commitment to a common quest – participants are looking for knowledge, understanding and an increase in their wisdom through the discussions.

The task of a Christian inter-faith theology is therefore first of all to be a genuinely Christian theology that has attended to other faiths, and so is partly formed in the drama of mutual hospitality with them, learning from their forms of engagement with God, community of faith and world, their thinking, and their communication and artistic expression. The effects of this attentiveness are often hard to identify, but it is also often evident when this dimension is lacking.

(David F. Ford, *The Future of Christian Theology*, Wiley-Blackwell, 2011, p. 146)

From his experiences in participating in Scriptural Reasoning, Ford suggests nine guidelines for interfaith practice.

1. Love God and each other, and have compassion for all God's creation.
2. Go deeper into our own faith, into each other's, and into commitment to the common good.
3. Seek wisdom through our own scripture, history, and theology, through each other's, and through engagement with arts, sciences, philosophy, and other sources of wisdom.
4. Beware of assimilating to modernity and beware of rejecting it; seek to heal and transform it.
5. Form personal relationships, groups, networks, and organizations dedicated to inter-faith conversation, collaboration, and education at all levels, from international to local.
6. Encourage the best communicators, artists, writers, and teachers to spread the message of love of God and neighbour, drawing on the richest sources.
7. Cultivate a long-term vision of a habitable world, created and sustained by God for the good of all.
8. Create signs of hope within and between the faiths, inspired by the letter *A Common Word Between Us and You* and the responses to it.
9. Do all this for the sake of God and God's good purposes.

(ibid., p. 12)

Scriptural Reasoning in practice

Participants from the three religions meet in groups to read and reflect upon a scripture passage from one or more of the faiths. This will have been decided before the meeting. The aim is not to reach agreement, but to be open to discussion of differences of opinion about the passage, and to be willing to learn from it. The result is often a deeper understanding of others' and one's own scriptures, as well as the development of strong bonds across faith communities.

Possible outcomes

(i) **Learning and understanding** – Participants learn more about other faith communities through what is often at their heart – scripture. It can deepen people's understanding of their *own* scripture and wider tradition. This is because their group will contain people from different traditions to their own, and this will help to give each one a new or different perspective on the text being studied. When this happens, it can enhance one's own understanding of scripture.

(ii) **Exploring differences** – The process of Scriptural Reasoning allows participants to appreciate the things they have in common, as well as their

differences. There may be common ground on which the whole group can agree, but there can be disagreement, too, and, if consensus is not reached, members can 'improve the quality of their disagreements'.
(iii) **Friendships** – With time, as relationships between members of the group grow, traditional stereotypes of the 'other' are broken down, barriers are dismantled and, at best, participants develop lasting friendships underpinned by an appreciation of difference as well as an understanding of common values.

> **Exercise**
>
> Read the following statement, discuss it with your class, then write down your reaction to it. Do you think that scriptural reading among people of different religious traditions is genuinely possible, or can it only be an academic exercise?
>
> 'Scriptural Reasoning is a genuine opportunity for committed religious people to engage in inter-faith practice without undermining particularity: here is a way to deepen one's own faith commitment and deepen one's engagement with members of other faiths simultaneously.'

Criticism of Scriptural Reasoning

The vast majority of people who participate in the Scriptural Reasoning Movement find it enjoyable, educational and spiritually uplifting. There are some, however, who are less convinced by its efficacy.

- Some participants have found, perhaps because of the members in their group, that there is a danger that the views of one of the religions may not be the 'official' or orthodox teaching of that religion. This could lead to a misunderstanding, and possibly seriously skew others' views of that religion.
- As there is no 'right answer' in discussions, who will decide which interpretation is acceptable or reasonable?
- Following from the previous point, although it is intended that each religious tradition is treated with respect and integrity, some people have argued that the process of Scriptural Reasoning leads to a relativizing of scripture. All beliefs are treated as equally valid, because participants are not allowed to be judgemental.
- As Scriptural Reasoning has expanded, members from non-Abrahamic religions have been invited to participate. The difficulty with this is that Buddhism, Hinduism and Sikhism have very different origins, textual traditions and ideas about deity.

Inter-faith dialogue and social cohesion

Social cohesion concerns the feeling of shared belonging at home, in communities and societies; of respecting and valuing other members of the group; of enjoying a sense of shared goods. Socially cohesive groups are more likely to achieve common aims and have a network of friendships. It is the opposite of alienation, distrust, friction between communities and individuals. A *modus vivendi* arrangement in society is one where people simply live together without much social cohesion, but it tends to be fragile. For example, as soon as one group gets more power, it can oppress the other group because it feels no solidarity with them.

It is obviously difficult – if not nearly impossible – to measure, but one can get a feel for relations between groups within a community/society if one lives in a local area long enough and has contact with a sufficient number of people. Do people interact across group boundaries? Do they smile in the street and say 'hello' (this is one of the first things to disappear when citizens mistrust each other), do they help you carry your groceries or when you slip and fall?

Inter-faith dialogue has resulted in many local religious groups (from churches, mosques, synagogues) meeting, eating together, discussing, and so on, which contributes to social cohesion by promoting friendships, and reducing ignorance (which is a prime source of discrimination and fear). Effects on local areas are stronger than nationally, but it has resulted in national and international cooperation and discussion amongst religious scholars and leaders. All of this has contributed to a new mood of acceptance amongst religions, reducing tensions, reducing attempts at proselytization and increasing collegiality and working together with a common purpose and in friendship.

Some conservative religious groups see inter-faith dialogue as a mistake, so it doesn't create social cohesion with or for them. Some see wealth, educational and opportunity inequalities as far more damaging to social cohesion than religious difference, so inter-faith dialogue, in their view, is not particularly effective. Given the large amount of coverage of religion in the media in recent years, it is arguably more important to develop inter-faith relations in order to help reduce prejudice and discrimination.

Should Christians seek to convert people from other faiths?

Some Christian individuals and groups will say 'yes' to this question. They are likely to argue that we live in a society based on persuasion not coercion, on free speech not censorship. Christians feel their religion has been very beneficial to them, they have experienced God's love and forgiveness, entered a community of friendship and support, and want to share those things with others. Exclusivists will see conversion as the most important thing in life, because without it people cannot be saved by God's grace.

Other Christians will say 'no'. They will argue that it is often damaging to family relationships when people convert out of a religion. The history of anti-Semitism, anti-Islamic feeling and colonialism make it inappropriate to continue to try to convert people; it cuts against social cohesion; inclusivists and universalists can encourage people to be better members of their own religion rather than try to convert them, believing that God will still save them through Christ. Also, many Christians believe that God is the only God, so will save members of religions other than Christianity.

Does Scriptural Reasoning relativize religious beliefs?

Some people will say 'no'. They argue that Scriptural Reasoning is simply the sharing of readings of scriptures – there is no need to agree with the readings of other scriptures or take them as scripture, if participants do not wish to. Rather, their participation helps each person to appreciate more of and about their own religion. It is allowable to stick to the orthodoxy and accepted readings of one's own religion.

Others will say 'yes'. The process of reading different scriptures with others will inevitably make one see one's own scriptures and religion in a different light – as less distinct, as lacking insights or wisdom or emphases found in other traditions. Without seeking to persuade anyone of the truth of any particular view, a participant is effectively treating the scriptures as relative in terms of their truth, even if a person stands by their own view privately.

We need, however, to ask what it is to relativize religious beliefs? Now that inclusivism is the mainstream view within Christianity, its beliefs have been somewhat diminished from the previous feeling that they were exclusively true and other religions were full of error. Inclusivists still believe that Christianity is true, so its truth claims are not relativized, as those of pluralism have been. They are, however, 'situated' or 'placed' differently, meaning that they need to be reformed by contact with other views (Doctrine Commission of the Church of England, *Mystery of Salvation*).

Should Christians have a mission to those of no faith?

In some ways, this is a more straightforward question to answer. The answer, for many Christians, would be 'yes'. For these believers, someone who has no religious faith will have no hurdles stopping them converting to Christianity. They have no commitment to another religion, or to any other Christian denomination, that might cause a problem of conscience or a sense that they would be betraying their former allegiance to a religious group.

It is not difficult to imagine, however, that a non-religious person who lived with others who were practising Christians/Jews/Muslims, might find it somewhat difficult to convert to a religion. For one thing, that person might have strong reasons for not being religious. For a religious person to attempt this person's conversion could have counter-productive effects and would likely turn that person even further away from religious faith than before.

Another view concerns inclusivist Christians. They might think it perfectly legitimate to attempt the conversion of a person who is not already a member of a different religion. This is because inclusivists believe that religious believers, in a world religion other than Christianity, are 'anonymous Christians', and so attempting to convert them might not be a priority.

FURTHER READING

The Doctrine Commission of the Church of England, *The Mystery of Salvation*. Church House Publishing, 1995, ch. 7

David F. Ford, *The Future of Christian Theology*. Wiley-Blackwell, 2011

David F. Ford, *Interreligious Reading After Vatican II: Scriptural Reasoning, Comparative Theology and Receptive Ecumenism*. Directions in Modern Theology. Wiley-Blackwell, 2013

John Hick and Brian Hebblethwaite, *Christianity and Other Religions: Selected Readings*. Augsburg Fortress, 1990

Peter Ochs and Nancy Levene, *Textual Reasonings: Jewish Philosophy and Text Study at the End of the Twentieth Century*. SCM Press, 2010

Van Lal Thuam Lian, *Scriptural Reasoning as a Practice of the Common Good*. GRIN Publishing, 2016

Savasan Yurtsever, *Scriptural Unity: An Interfaith Dialogue through Scriptural Reasoning*, Vol. I, CreateSpace Independent Publishing, 2012

Thought Points

1. Explain the key similarities and differences between inclusivists, exclusivists and pluralists.

2. 'Inter-faith dialogue cannot be compatible with Christian exclusivism.' Discuss.

3. Do you think that globalization has had positive effects on religion in Britain? Explain your answer.

4. 'There is no possibility of real dialogue between theological exclusivists and the Scriptural Reasoning Movement.' To what extent do you agree with this statement?

5. 'Scriptural Reasoning cannot achieve any deep understanding between members of different religions.' How far do you agree with this statement?

6. Is it legitimate, in a 21st-century liberal society, for Christians to attempt to convert atheists or members of other religions?

7. 'Scriptural Reasoning may have some benefits for members of monotheistic religions, but it can have no relevance for any other religions.' Discuss.

SECTION V
SOCIETY

CHAPTER 9

Gender and Society

LEARNING OUTCOMES

In this chapter, you will be learning about the effects of changing views of gender and gender roles in Christian thought and practice, including:
- Christian teaching on the roles of men and women in the family and society
- Christian responses to contemporary secular views about the roles of men and women in the family and society

Introduction

Biological sex is historically determined by physical attributes. Most people when they are born are clearly one biological sex or another: male or female. Some, however, have an ambiguous biological sex and have characteristics of both. The concept of gender is fluid, and involves a combination of **gender biology** (physical attributes of a person's body), **gender identity** (the gender which a person views themselves most comfortably as belonging to, which may or may not be the same as their biological sex) and, lastly, **gender expression** (for example, clothing, tone of voice – how a person expresses their gender to the outside world).

Although most people are born with a biological sex, this is heavily influenced by factors within society – at a young age, 'societal norms' ascribe biological females to liking dolls, dresses and the colour pink, whereas biological boys are ascribed to liking cars, trucks, dinosaurs and the colour blue. One only has to walk down the toy aisle in a supermarket to note the different gender roles that are placed on people from an early age. Many people in our society tend to think in very binary terms – that there are two very distinct sexes and everybody in society belongs to one or the other. However, most recent studies state there are up to seventy-one different gender identities, showing that gender may not be as straightforward as traditionally thought (*Daily Telegraph*, 27 June 2014). It could be suggested that it is misleading, artificial and damaging to assign 'roles' to people

Gender biology: Physical attributes of a person's body

Gender identity: The gender a person views themselves as most comfortably belonging to

Gender expression: The way a person dresses, speaks and generally expresses themselves to the outside world based on binary gender when they may not ascribe to the gender they were biologically born into.

Historically, Christianity has a very chequered history when it comes to the treatment and role of women in the Church. Some Christians believe that the biblical approach to gender roles within society and Christianity (discussed later in the chapter) should be strictly adhered to. This may be due to the fact that they view the Bible as the ultimate source of authority for Christians, or indeed they may take the Genesis Creation story literally as opposed to metaphorically – therefore, God made 'man and woman' and, as a result of the Fall, man has to 'toil in the fields' and woman has to endure childbirth.

However, there are many Christians who argue that Christianity and the Christian church needs to adapt to society and the changing roles of men and women – not just because of gender identity and expression, but also for many social reasons. There are very few families who can afford for the female to stay at home while the man works to earn a living – the rising cost of houses, food and utilities means two incomes per household are needed in order to maintain a half-decent lifestyle. Another factor is access to education – the UK is very lucky in that all sexes can access appropriate education, and are encouraged to do so regardless of biological sex. If a woman has worked her whole life to achieve a good standard of education, is it right that she should be expected to stay at home 'raising a family' and not put her education to good use in employment?

This change in society has been very fast-paced. During World War I, there were not enough men to do the 'male' jobs as most men had been drafted to serve for their country. This meant that women were needed to fill in. It quickly became apparent that women were just as capable in these roles as men, bolstering women's liberation movements with the Suffragette movement. Women began to fight for equal rights to men, such as the vote, and the role of gender within society changed completely.

Callum G. Brown argues that, up to the middle of the twentieth century, women were responsible for the piety of the home, for maintaining the religious participation of the family and teaching the faith to children:

> The end of the war had been marked by the state's promotion of 'pro-natalism', of women's place being in the home where the nation needed an invigorated birth rate to overcome labour shortage. During the war, women had been drafted into a wide variety of industries and agriculture to fill the gaps left by men in active service, but this did little to alter but rather reinforced the unequal position of women in society. Though female participation in the labour market increased, domesticity was revived. In manual occupations, the idea evolved that women could combine paid and domestic work, while for middle class women there was a significant return to the domestic ideal. For both groups, labour saving devices could improve domestic efficiency.
>
> However, working women became the target of a barrage of official and popular discourses which returned them to the home and hearth and imposed on them guilt and anxiety about neglecting children and doing them psychological damage.
>
> (*The Death of Christian Britain*, pp. 170f.)

There are some who may argue that this is a social change and has nothing to do with Christianity. If so, there is no requirement for the Church to reassess its views on the roles of men and women, within the Church or society. They believe that God has established an order where men are the stronger gender, as they were first to be created, and women the weaker, because they were created from Adam. By this argument, Christians are not required to bow to the pressures of modern society.

There is a different argument, however, in which many more Christians believe that the Church should adapt to modern society, especially the changing perception of gender and society. The Church should be accepting and welcoming to all people, regardless of role within the household or gender identity. If Jesus preached the rule of agape love, surely the Church ought to show love and acceptance to all, regardless of gender identity?

Feminists have shown how men have oppressed women for centuries, denying them rights, equality, education and agency, and how Christianity historically did the same, justifying it as God's will. Given the changed nature of British society, and a more enlightened attitude to the relationship between men and women, the question arises of how to understand biblical statements and attitudes to women. Should the Bible's views on women be ignored, or might there be a way to reinterpret and realign them with more modern thought? Ethicist Neil Messer states:

> Feminist critics argue that the Church has been complicit in [the] oppression of women in many ways. For example, its power structures have tended to exclude women, particularly by restricting ordained ministry to men; and its theological traditions have reflected male interests, by using mostly male language and imagery for God and articulating Christian doctrines such as sin and redemption in ways that reflect male rather than female experience. The Church, like society at large, has tended to scapegoat women: in particular the story of 'The Fall' (Genesis 3) in a way that suggests Eve, and women in general, bear particular responsibility for the entry of sin into the world.
>
> (Messer, *SCM Studyguide: Christian Ethics*, p. 67)

Exercise
To what extent do you think that the story of the Fall (Genesis 3) has led to women being blamed for the existence of sin in the world'?

Gender and Gender Roles – The Changing View

There are now many different attitudes to gender and the roles that are ascribed to it. Firstly, there is the view that men and women are not equal and men are superior to women. This is a very long-held, traditional belief, stretching back at least as far as Plato and Aristotle. Plato did not believe that there were male and female souls, but superior and inferior. As Morag Buchan explains: 'Souls do not polarize into male and female, but into superior and inferior. The superior are deposited into male bodies associated with fathering and therefore with the "Cosmic Father", the inferior are deposited in female bodies associated with the notion of passive "Prime Matter", (M. Buchan, *Women in Plato's Political Theory*, Palgrave MacMillan, 1998, p. 46).

Ultimately, Plato believed that souls were reborn as women if they had failed as men, because men are the superior sex and women are the lesser, passive sex.

Aristotle agreed with this theory. He believed that women were more inclined towards weak behaviour and were naturally inferior to men. Aristotle viewed women as being 'defective' males who had lesser strength and intelligence.

In his *History of Animals* (608b, 1–14), Aristotle says: 'The fact is, the nature of man is the most rounded off and complete . . . woman is more compassionate than man, more easily moved to tears, at the same time is more jealous, more querulous, more apt to scold and to strike.'

> **Exercise**
> Make a list of the characteristics of woman, as described here by Aristotle. To what extent are any of them valid, given our more recent knowledge of physiology and psychology?

The second view of gender roles is that men and women are of equal value. This is the idea that, although men and women are different, they are equal in the eyes of God and therefore should be viewed in the same way. For some, this difference leads to the belief that men and women *should* have different roles, both in the home and within the Church, but that these roles should be equally valued. However, this may then lead to issues regarding how to define what are mainly 'male' and 'female' roles (such as the idea that women should not become priests as Jesus only chose men to be his disciples, or that women cannot offer the eucharist as they should not represent Christ at the Last Supper). Again, this is a challenge to society and the rise in feminism and changing views of gender roles.

Feminist theologian **Mary Daly** (1928–2010), offers a third option, arguing that women are ethically superior to men because they are inherently cooperative and caring, rather than aggressive and competitive, like men. She was inspired by philosopher Friedrich Nietzsche (1844–1900), who wrote: 'Whenever man has thought it necessary to create a memory of himself, his effort has been attended with torture, blood, sacrifice' (F. Nietzsche, *The Genealogy of Morals*, Penguin, 2013, p. 192).

Daly argues that, throughout history, men have sought to oppress women, using their brute power. Female oppression is as a result of rape, genocide and war – and Christianity is used as a tool to enforce this oppression (see Daly, *Beyond God the Father*, ch. 10).

> **Mary Daly (1928–2010)** Mary Daly was a radical post-Christian theologian, who grew up in New York State in an Irish Roman Catholic family. She wanted to study Theology but was initially told that it was unsuitable for a woman. She travelled to Switzerland and gained two Ph.D.s, in Theology and Philosophy, at the University of Fribourg. She taught at Boston College for many years, drawing attention to the inherent patriarchy and irredeemably sexist nature of Christian theology in her book *Beyond God the Father* (1973). She sees it that maleness has been closely associated with the idea of God, to such an extent that this excludes women.

The last view to consider is that gender is not as straightforward as once believed. Just because a person is born as male or female does not mean that they have to ascribe to the role that is assigned to them by that gender. Thirty years ago, if a child had been asked to describe the role of a woman, they would have said 'cook, cleaner, nurse', etc. Now, however, children might say 'mum, worker, writer, fixer'. Children are now growing up in an era where men cook and clean, and women go to work and do DIY. Society is changing at a fast pace that the Church cannot keep up with. This may be as a result of church leaders wanting to do the right thing 'theologically'. The Church must attempt to accommodate several generations of worshippers, at least some of whom would struggle to accept the changed view of genders in society. Church leaders would not wish to alienate any of their members and this may help to explain why the Church seems slow to move with the changing attitudes in society. Three examples of 'problem' areas might be allowing women to become priests, allowing same-sex marriages in church, or even hiring out the church buildings to non-Christian groups.

Christian teaching on the roles of men and women in the family and society

Globalization and ease of access to travel around the world have meant that we have a generation of children who have been raised in a multi-cultural and diverse society. They are exposed to a wide range of ideas about gender roles, and opinions. Even having easy access to the internet means they are exposed to ideas and practices outside their own traditions. There is also a wide range of views on the roles of men and women in the family and society within Christianity. According to the Bible, men and women are created and loved by God equally as they are both made in God's image:

> Then God said, 'Let us make humankind in our image, according to our likeness; and let them have dominion over the fish of the sea, and over the birds of the air, and over the cattle and over all the wild animals of the earth, and over every creeping thing that creeps upon the earth.' So God created humankind in his image, in the image of God he created them; male and female he created them.
>
> (Genesis 1:26–7)

Clearly, at the moment of creation, men and woman were created as equals and had equal dominion over the world. This may lead some Christians to conclude that men and women should have equal roles both in society and within a family setting. However, there are other biblical passages which offer further guidance on gender roles – one, importantly, being Ephesians 5:22–33, which states:

> Wives, submit yourselves to your own husbands as you do to the Lord. For the husband is the head of the wife as Christ is the head of the church, his body, of which he is the Saviour. Now, as the church submits to Christ, so also wives should submit to their husbands in everything.
> Husbands, love your wives, just as Christ loved the church and gave himself up for her to make her holy, cleansing her by the washing with water through the word, and to present her to himself as a radiant church without stain or wrinkle or any other blemish, but holy

and blameless. In the same way, husbands ought to love their wives as their own bodies. He who loves his wife loves himself. After all, no one ever hated their own body but they feed and care for their body just as Christ does the church – for we are members of his body. 'For this reason, a man will leave his father and mother and be united to his wife, and the two will become one flesh.' This is a profound mystery – but I am talking about Christ and the church. However, each one of you must also love his wife as he loves himself, and the wife must respect her husband.

This set of instructions given to the original readers reflected the view from Greek and Roman households and provides a clear set of instructions for both men and women, from both a societal and religious perspective. The main point is the fact that women should submit to their husbands as the husbands are the head of the house, but also that the husband should love his wife in the way Christ loved – even paying the ultimate sacrifice of death. In speaking of Christ and the Church, Paul is also reminding men and women that their marriage is part of a bigger picture – they are a part of the body of Christ and should work harmoniously together as part of that body.

On the surface, this passage appears to encourage a patriarchal society (one in which men have more power than women, and dominate all areas of life). However, patriarchal societies tend to be more favourable to men than women, and it *may* be argued that this passage favours women, given that men are told to love and care for their wives. Although the passage ends with the quote 'the wife must respect her husband', it expects a mutual respect from both partners in their marriage.

We may contrast this Ephesians text with one from Paul's letter to the Galatians: "There is neither Jew nor Greek, slave nor free, male nor female, for you are all one in Christ Jesus' (Galatians 3:28).

Acts 16:13–15 recounts an event during one of Paul's missionary journeys:

On the Sabbath day we went outside the gate by the river, where we supposed there was a place of prayer; and we sat down and spoke to the women who had gathered there. A certain woman named Lydia, a worshipper of God, was listening to us; she was from the city of Thyatira and a dealer in purple cloth. The Lord opened her heart to listen eagerly to what was said by Paul. When she and her household were baptized, she urged us, saying, 'If you have judged me to be faithful to the Lord, come and stay at my home.' And she prevailed upon us.

Whilst the story may appear prosaic, the fact that a woman could be converted is a contrast to the model of Greek and Roman citizenship in which the male is the head of the household and has absolute authority. The fact that God would intervene in the life of a woman separately from her husband is a huge departure from the historical context of the time. Paul and his companions then spent time teaching her about the new religion, showing that a woman was also able to be educated. This shows that at least some of the early Christians were open to treating women as equals. Lydia had her own job, dealing in 'purple cloth' (i.e. very expensive goods) and having her own home, in which she persuaded Paul to stay overnight.

Another example of the important role played by women in the NT appears in Luke 24:1–4, 9–12. This is Luke's narrative of how a group of women disciples discovered the Empty Tomb of Jesus:

On the first day of the week, very early in the morning, the women took the spices they had prepared and went to the tomb. They found the stone rolled away from the tomb, but when they entered, they did not find the body of the Lord Jesus. While they were wondering about this, suddenly two men in clothes that gleamed like lightning stood beside them . . . Returning from the tomb, they told all this to the eleven and the rest. Now it was Mary Magdalene, Joanna, Mary the mother of James, and the other women with them who told this to the apostles. But these words seemed to them an idle tale, and they did not believe them. But Peter got up and ran to the tomb; stooping and looking in, he saw the linen clothes by themselves; then he went home, amazed at what had happened.

The most interesting feature of this text is that women were the first to view the tomb that Jesus' dead body had been placed in after his crucifixion, and to hear the news of his resurrection. This was unprecedented in the biblical world. Women's testimony in the Judaism of the time was generally not valid in rabbinical court. Having women as the first witnesses of the resurrection might appear, therefore, to undermine the plausibility of Christianity.

Roman Catholic responses to feminism: *Mulieris dignitatem*

> *Mulieris dignitatem:* This papal document, 'On the Dignity and Vocation of Women', was a response in 1988 to the first two waves of feminism.

Mulieris dignitatem (On the dignity and vocation of women) is an apostolic letter written by Pope John Paul II in 1988 on the subject of the dignity and rights of women, in response to the rise of feminism. His purpose in writing this letter was to clarify the Roman Catholic position on the issues raised by feminism. In order to understand his response fully, it is firstly important to understand what feminism is. The *Oxford English Dictionary* describes 'feminism' as the 'advocacy of women's rights on the grounds of the equality of the sexes', and a 'feminist' is 'a person who supports the belief that women should have the same rights and opportunities as men'. Although this may appear as a single ideology, in fact there are many differing strands of feminism, and not all agree with one another. The many different types include liberal, Marxist, radical and Black feminism. Each of these types has its own particular focus or agenda, so, for example, Black feminism was attuned to the intersections between race and gender oppression. Feminism is sometimes seen as having three 'waves':

(i) First Wave Feminism – This began in the late nineteenth century and was primarily committed to gaining the right for women to vote. This was successful and, in 1918, the Representation of the People Act was passed, which allowed women over 30 the right to vote in 1918, and in 1928 the age limit was lowered to be equal with men.

(ii) Second Wave Feminism – This continued after women won the right to vote and focused on wider issues, such as equality in the workplace and women's reproductive rights (e.g. access to contraception).

(iii) Third Wave Feminism – This is the most recent wave, which began in the 1990s and advocates for the fluidity of gender roles and identification, and also calls for inclusivity of women of all sexualities and ethnic diversity.

Mulieris dignitatem was a response to the first and second waves of feminism. The emphasis was on respect for women – which focused on Mary, the mother of Jesus. The Pope focuses on two particular dimensions of the fulfilment of the female personality – motherhood and virginity – both of which are united in an exceptional way, though Mary has both co-existing within her. In the mutual gift of marriage, the woman plays a special role, as her readiness for motherhood implies a special openness to a new creation. The Pope states that motherhood is specifically linked to the personal structure of a woman and it constitutes a special role in this concept of shared parenting – especially during the pre-natal period. The male has no choice but to be 'outside' of this process and has to learn about fatherhood from the woman. So, whilst parenthood is a shared, common responsibility, 'the mother's contribution is decisive in laying the foundation for a new human personality' (para. 18).

In Mary, the Pope says motherhood takes on an even deeper meaning. Through her giving birth to Jesus, 'God begins a New Covenant with humanity' (para. 19). Mary's motherhood involved her listening and responding to the will of God – in which the Pope invites contemplation of the deeper spiritual meaning of motherhood (potentially referencing contraception – if one is preventing conception, then it may be suggested that one is withholding what would otherwise be the will of God). Her humility and obedience to God make her a model for humanity, not just women. The letter improves on previous Christian teaching by pointing out that Jesus promoted 'women's true dignity' far beyond the norm in his society, to the extent of causing scandal, with the implication that it becomes a Christian duty to continue to support equality for women.

Yet the Pope's version of gender equality is different from the feminist account. He prohibits abortion, whereas **Simone de Beauvoir** (1908–86) and **Shulamith Firestone** (1945–2012) think women can never be free unless they can escape 'enforced maternity'. Feminists also accuse the Pope of 'essentializing' women – taking a particular historical-cultural view of women and turning it into the essence and definition of women and femininity, so that all women have to behave and be that way (specifically, mothers or virgins). Their biological ability to have children is seen as a conscious decision on God's part to entrust them with that task:

> Consequently, even the rightful opposition of women to what is expressed in the biblical words 'He shall rule over you' (Gen 3:16) must not under any condition lead to the 'masculinization' of women. In the name of liberation from male 'domination', women must not appropriate to themselves male characteristics contrary to their own feminine 'originality'. This is a well founded fear that if they take this path, women will not reach 'fulfillment', but instead will deform and lose what constitutes their essential richness . . . The personal resources of femininity are certainly no less than the resources of masculinity: they are merely different.
>
> (para.10)

Hence, women are blocked from the priesthood because there 'must be a physical resemblance between the priest and Christ'. This point obviously makes it impossible for a woman to become a priest in the Roman Catholic church, and the papal letter was heavily criticized by many feminists because of this.

Given that Second Wave Feminists were fighting for access to contraception, this whole section of the letter appears to miss the point. Whilst it is very easy to agree on many of the points the Pope raises in the letter, he fails to recognize the issue that perhaps not all women *want* to have children. In which case, should a woman be entitled to the same amount of respect as a mother? In addition, what if a woman is *unable* to have children – some Christians may see this as the will of God. The woman may not wish for the information to be public, in which case she may be seen as a failure as a wife.

Although *Mulieris dignitatem* tries to present the role of women as mothers as a special privilege, it may also be seen as degrading to women. The Pope could be seen to suggest women are to be either mothers or virgins, there is no other alternative (with the exception of Mary). This may be seen as limiting and patronizing to women. It may suggest that sex for a woman is for the purpose of procreation alone and not for enjoyment as well.

The open letter from the Pope seems to suggest that women should be commended for their role as mothers, but dismisses everything else a woman could be, other than a mother. When looking at the different types of family (below), it is the mother who traditionally takes the primary responsibility for looking after the family, while the father works. This dynamic may be seen as grounding the idea that the woman has a special place – at home, and therefore not at work. Some people may find this demeaning and patronizing.

Does the role of a mother restrict women? Some may feel as though they must give up their own lives in favour of their children and husband, or be concerned for their career when taking maternity leave. Indeed, some may feel social pressure to become a parent, with constant reminders that 'the clock is ticking' (referencing the point that a female's ability to reproduce reduces dramatically with age). However, as Angela Davies points out: 'Not all women found marriage and motherhood restrictive. Some interviewees said they had found it liberating, especially if they had not enjoyed their jobs or were keen to cease employment. While women sometimes felt frustrated with the tedium that looking after small children could bring, they also found that motherhood imbued them with a sense of fulfillment' (Davies, *Modern Motherhood*, p. 150).

Here, it is important to point out that, although there may be a tendency to adopt a 'one size fits all' approach, both in the Church and in society, not everybody is the same. Some women may not want children at all, some may want children but not get married, some will want to remain at work, and others may be happy to stay at home and look after their children full time. This is where Third Wave Feminism has a powerful voice – allowing people to identify as individuals, as opposed to having their identity placed upon them.

Fundamentalist Protestants may take Ephesians 5 literally and may agree with the Roman Catholic view that the primary roles of a woman are those of a wife and mother. However, a more liberal approach may debunk the idea that motherhood is inextricably linked to a woman and allow the role of gender to be much more fluid. It is possible for a woman to have mothers as role models and yet not want to be a mother herself. What fits one may not fit all – and some women may choose not to be mothers, just as some men may choose not to be fathers.

Christian responses to contemporary secular views about the roles of men and women in the family and society

Should official Christian teaching resist current secular views on gender?

There is an argument to say that, given Christianity has existed for more than 2,000 years, it should have the right to resist current secular views on the fluidity of gender. The question regarding gender fluidity only began to emerge in the 1970s and one could state that it goes against all former human experience. Just because science is making it possible to alter hormones in a way that would limit or change a person's biological sex entirely does not necessarily mean it ought to happen. Technology is advancing at such a fast pace that we cannot fully understand the ethical implications of this advancement. To argue, therefore, that the Church should accept and adopt the changing view of gender is questionable.

Christians believe that God created both male and female – two binary roles – with the ultimate purpose of procreation, to have a partner for life, and to achieve mutual support within the context of raising families. It may be argued that the family bond is one of the most fundamental building blocks of society, and the concept of 'family' has existed since the beginning of history. Undermining this family dynamic goes against all historical experience. If we begin to change our view of the 'typical' family, then support networks in society will begin to weaken. Given the current situation where young people are having to move farther and farther away from close family ties in order to find work, this could lead to an increase in loneliness and depression. The *British Medical Journal* stated: 'The NHS prescribed record numbers of antidepressants last year. The number of prescriptions for antidepressants in England has almost doubled in the past decade, new figures have shown. Data from NHS Digital show that 70.9 million prescriptions for antidepressants were given out in 2018, compared with 36 million in 2008' (www.bmj.com/content/364/bmj.l1508).

This could support the claims above, given that it has been in the past decade that secular gender roles have changed beyond recognition, potentially having an adverse effect on society. Some could argue that the Christian church has a moral duty to resist this.

It could also be argued that a person who changes their gender is being wilfully ignorant of the evidence of their biology. Gender differences do exist; men and women should certainly be treated equally – however, that is not to say they are the same. Given the biological evidence, there could be no reason to pretend that the sexes are not different.

If Christianity is based on God's revelation of the Truth, it should not discard this in order to fit in with society's changing ideas. It could be suggested that the Truth is the only firm and grounded thing that society has to cling on to, so Christians should tell society the Truth in order to help it.

Women workers breaking down gender stereotypes

However, it can also be argued that, like all religions, Christianity is a historically evolving religion – as is our concept of gender. Throughout history, women have been dominated and oppressed, tied down to their role as mothers and treated as property by men in order to bear children through which to pass on their name, inheritance and property. This is the reason the concept of a woman's virginity is so important – it would rule out any other children who might bear a right to a man's inheritance, and also rules out any competition between heirs.

Recently, scientists have discovered a number of facts about gender. One of these is that some people are born homosexual and it is not a 'lifestyle choice'. Scientific studies have shown that both genes and sex hormones can play a part in a person's sexual orientation. This indicates that gender issues may not be due simply to the changing morals of society. In a 2015 article in the *Guardian*, Qazi Rahman stated:

> Sex hormones in pre-natal life play a role. For example, girls born with congenital adrenal hyperplasia (CAH) which results in naturally increased levels of male sex hormones, show relatively high rates of same sex attractions as adults. Further evidence comes from genetic males who, through accidents, or being born without penises, were subjected to sex changes and raised as girls. As adults, these men are typically attracted to women. The fact that you cannot make a genetic male sexually attracted to another male by raising him as a girl makes any social theory of sexuality very weak.
>
> (*Guardian*, 24 July 2015)

This points to the idea that God creates some people as homosexual and therefore this is 'good', as the Genesis story affirms about the Creation.

Another argument is that biological sex is not simply male or female but exists as a whole spectrum of different identities. How could it be possible that every person who has ever, and will ever, exist has to fit into two very binary camps of 'male and female'? Also, gender can be expressed in many different ways and it does not necessarily have to fit with our biological assigned sex. Our biological sex should not determine our dress, virtues, roles, and so on. Rather, it should allow individuals the freedom to express this how they want to. Just because a woman can be a mother does not necessarily mean she should be one. In the same way, it does not mean that just because I could have been an accountant, I should have been one. This is a logical error – just because you *can* do X does not mean that you *should* do X. Societies change constantly, and these changes will not threaten society. Rather, the changes make society more open and welcoming. There is no suggestion that people should dismiss the family unit altogether – far from it. The use of contraception is quite simply a way to restrict the size of a person's family in order to reduce the burden of a large family that they may not be able to afford.

Christianity is based on revelation, but this understanding of revelation has always been evolving. Secular understanding of gender is an opportunity to improve Christianity's understanding of reality. The idea is simply that not all people fit into a safe and secure, structured and accepted family. This could be a chance for Christianity to realize its role in the oppression of women. Christianity can, and ought to, help to liberate women – and, in doing so, liberate LGBTQ people and show them the love and acceptance of Christ. Then this changing society may no longer be seen as contradicting the revelation of God. Instead, it will be a part of that revelation.

FURTHER READING

Simone de Beauvoir, *The Second Sex*. Vintage Classics, 1997

Angela Davies, *Modern Motherhood*. Gender in History. Manchester University Press, 2014

Mary Daly, *Beyond God the Father: Towards a Philosophy of Women's Liberation*. The Women's Press, 1973

Daphne Hampson, *Theology and Feminism* [1990]. Signposts in Theology. SCM Press, 1996

Neil Messer, *SCM Studyguide: Christian Ethics*. SCM Press, 2006

Rosemarie Tong, *Feminist Thought*. Routledge, 2013

Phyllis Trible, *Texts of Terror: Literary-Feminist Readings in Biblical Narratives*. SCM Press, 2011

Thought Points

1. Do you think the Bible's teaching on women should be ignored, as it came from a very different kind of society a long time ago?

2. 'Most people get married for the wrong reasons, so marriage should be abolished.' Discuss.

3. 'Wives, submit to your husbands as to the Lord . . .' (Ephesians 5:22). How should feminist Christians respond to this biblical statement today?

4. Have Christian values been undermined by secular views of gender equality?

5. Explain the apparent mismatch between official Christian teaching and current secular views on gender.

6. To what extent do you think that *Mulieris dignitatem* has had a positive effect on Roman Catholic teaching on feminism?

7. Explain to a friend the extent to which the Church has been complicit in the oppression of women in the last 2,000 years.

CHAPTER 10
Gender and Theology

LEARNING OUTCOMES

In this chapter, you will be learning about the reinterpretation of God by feminist theologians, including:

- the teaching of Rosemary Radford Ruether and Mary Daly on gender, and its implications for the Christian idea of God
- Ruether's discussion of the maleness of Christ and its implication for salvation
- Daly's claim that 'if God is male then the male is God' and its implications for Christian theology

Introduction

Feminism is a movement that challenges the view that men are superior to women and that women are inferior. There are some feminists who seek to reverse this inequality and express female dominance over men – however, the vast majority simply argue for *true* and *fair* equality between the sexes.

The Vienna Declaration and Programme of Action (part 1, para. 18), adopted by the World Conference on Human Rights, Vienna, 25 June 1993, stated:

> Recent efforts to document the real situation of women worldwide have produced some alarming statistics on the economic and social gaps between men and women. Women are the majority of the world's poor and the number of women living in rural poverty has increased by 50 per cent since 1975. Women are the majority of the world's illiterate; the number rose from 543 million to 597 million between 1970 and 1985. Women in Asia and Africa work 13 hours a week more than men and are mostly unpaid. Worldwide, women can earn 30–40 per cent less than men for doing equal work. Women hold between 10 and 20 per cent of managerial and administrative jobs worldwide and less than 20 per cent of jobs in manufacturing. Women make up less than 5 per cent of the world's heads of state. Women's unpaid housework and family labour, if counted as productive output in national accounts, would increase measures of global output by 25–30 per cent.

Gender and Theology

> **Exercise**
>
> Look at the statistics below, choose what you think are the three most important and explain why.
>
> The charity Woman Kind states the following facts about violence against women:
>
> - Violence against women and girls is a global issue, with 1 in 3 women across the world experiencing violence (London School of Hygiene and Tropical Medicine, 2013)
> - Statistics show that a woman's abuser is usually somebody she knows. As many as 38% of all murdered women were killed by their partner (London School of Hygiene and Tropical Medicine, 2013)
> - Of all women killed globally in 2012, it is estimated that almost half were killed by a partner or relative, compared to fewer than 6% of men (United Nations Office on Drugs and Crime, 2014)
> - The vast majority of women across the globe have experienced violence on the streets of their cities, with 89% of women in Brazil, 86% in Thailand and 79% in India reporting harassment and abuse (Action Aid, 2016). Moreover, only 18 out of 173 countries have specific legislation addressing sexual harassment in public places (World Bank, 2016)
> - Over 700 million women alive today were married when they were under 18, and of those some 250 million were married before they were 15 (UNICEF, 2014)
> - Around 1 in 10 (120 million) girls worldwide have experienced sexual violence at some point in their lives (UNICEF, 2014)
> - At least 200 million girls and women alive today, living in 30 countries, have undergone female genital mutilation (UNICEF, 2016)
> - A European Union survey showed that 34% of women with a health problem or disability had experienced violence by a partner in their lifetime, compared to 19% per cent of women without a health problem or disability (European Union Agency for Fundamental Rights, 2014)

Statistics regarding participation and leadership in world affairs are equally bleak when it concerns the role of women and women's voices being heard in the world. British post-Christian theologian **Daphne Hampson** (1944–present) suggests that a whole new way of thinking is required – it should not be the case that women have to join and 'fit into' a male-dominated world, they should expect equal footing. It is a complete revolution in the way of thinking about the place of women within the world. She writes: 'Feminism represents a revolution. It is not in essence a demand that women should be allowed to join the male world on equal terms. It is a different view of the world. This must be of fundamental import for theology . . . as women come into their own, theology will take a different shape' (D. Hampson, *Theology and Feminism*, Blackwell, 1990, p. 1).

British Post-Christian philosopher, Daphne Hampson

> **Daphne Hampson (1944–present)** Hampson is a post-Christian theologian and former Professor of Theology at St Andrews University. She has degrees from Oxford, Warwick and Harvard universities. She argues that Christianity and feminism are incompatible. She says that a woman cannot be both a Christian and a feminist. She argues that Bible myths, such as the birth of Jesus, are framed in a male-orientated way because they were written by men and are intrinsically sexist. Myths like this cannot be reinterpreted in a feminist way and should be discarded. A better way forward is to interpret God's love in a non-sexist way. Religious belief should not be backward-looking (to traditional sexist traditions) but forward-looking to new ways in which all people can find meaning in the Christian religion.

Brief history of the role and status of women throughout history

In order to understand fully the requirement for change, one must understand ways in which women have been discriminated against openly throughout history. For example, it was not until 1975 that the 'Sex Discrimination Act' was passed by Parliament, making it illegal for employers to discriminate against job applicants on grounds of their sex. Once employers have appointed people, then they must provide equal opportunities for men and women with regards to training and promotion. However, as you may have noted in chapter 9, the societal pressures on a woman to have children may often hinder her chances at promotion opportunities as, generally speaking, it is the woman who is expected to be at home raising a family. Although this is not correct in all cases, it has historically applied to the vast majority. Changing attitudes towards gender roles are going some way to making this more equal; however, there is still some way to go and some feminists argue that this change is taking too long, reflecting historical facts regarding women in the UK, such as:

(i)   A woman could not divorce her husband until 1857.
(ii) The first woman doctor did not qualify until 1865 – indeed, this is after Dr James Barry (1789–1865) who, from the age of 20, presented himself as male both publicly and privately in order to be allowed entry into medical school and practise as a surgeon. He had been born Margaret Ann Bulkley and his birth sex only became known to the public and his colleagues after his death.
(iii) Women were not allowed to vote until 1918.
(iv) Margaret Thatcher became the first female Prime Minister in 1979.

Feminists are fighting against thousands upon thousands of years of oppression of women. Even in today's society, gender stereotypes are reinforced by terminology such as 'mankind' or 'chairman'.

Christianity had its roots in Old Testament Judaism and also developed through the classical traditions of the Roman Empire. Both of these are well known to be patriarchal societies, and so some feminists argue that many sexist attitudes have their roots in the Bible. For example, the Old Testament provides laws on how a man can divorce his wife, yet there were no such instructions for women because women were forbidden to divorce their husbands.

In Deuteronomy 22:28–9, there is an implication that an unmarried woman is her father's property. If a man rapes an unmarried woman, then he must pay compensation to her father: 'If a man happens to meet a virgin who is not pledged to be married and rapes her and they are discovered, he shall pay her father fifty shekels of silver. He must marry the young woman for he has violated her. He can never divorce her as long as he lives.' So, not only does the father receive compensation, but the woman has to spend the rest of her life married to a man who has violently attacked her.

There are a number of other ways in which sexist attitudes are ingrained throughout the Bible. For instance, Jesus calls God 'father' and he did not choose any women to be among his closest disciples. As discussed in chapter 9, the Roman Catholic devotion to Mary could be viewed as a way of encouraging Christians to see women solely in the terms of motherhood.

These historical views of woman were shared by many well-thought-of figures at the time. As Frances Beer explains:

> There are many more shades and subtleties to these complementary misogynist traditions, but to understand the legacy to which the Middle Ages were heir, one further ingredient needs to be considered: woman's perceived link with the powers of evil. 'There is a good principle which created order, light and man', observes Pythagoras, 'and an evil principle which created chaos, darkness and women'. 'Woman is the source of all evil', warns Socrates succinctly; 'her love is to be dreaded more than the hatred of men'. This notion was seized with relish by the early church fathers who saw women, beginning with Eve, as the 'devil's gateway'. Tertullian was unequivocal in placing responsibility for the Fall on women: 'You are the one who opened the door to the devil, you are the one who first deserted the divine law. . . . All too easily you destroyed the image of God. Because of (you) . . . even the Son of God had to die'. Consequently, observes St Clement, 'Every woman should be overwhelmed at the thought that she is a woman.'
>
> (F. Beer, *Women and Mystical Experiences in the Middle Ages*, Boydell Press, 2006, p. 3)

To continue this theme, Martin Luther wrote: 'Women should remain at home, sit still, keep house and bear and bring us children. If a woman grows weary and at last dies from childbearing, it matters not. Let her die from bearing. She is there to do it' (Martin Luther, *On the Estate of Marriage* [1522], Luther's Works 45, Fortress Press, 1962, p. 54).

As a result of these ingrained historical beliefs, for nearly 2,000 years ordained ministers were almost all men. Many people view this as one of the most shocking examples of how Christianity has helped to maintain the idea that leadership must always be male. However, due to the rise of the feminist movement and as a reaction to Bible passages such as Galatians 3:27–8, which states 'There is neither Jew nor Greek, slave nor free, male nor female, for you are all one in Christ Jesus', nearly all Protestant churches ordain women as ministers or priests. It was not until 1992, however, that the Church of England finally voted to do this. This positive vote came about after seventeen years of discussion and debate, outlined below:

1975: General Synod passed the motion 'That this Synod considers that there are no fundamental objections to the ordination of women to the priesthood', yet does not ask for legal barriers to be removed in order for women's ordination to be brought forward.

1978: The motion 'That this synod asks the Standing Committee to prepare and bring forward the legislation to remove the barriers to the ordination of women to the priesthood and their consecration to the episcopate' was passed by both the House of Bishops and House of Laity, but was lost in the House of Clergy by 94 votes to 149.

1981: The General Synod resolved that the order of deacon should be open to women, and passed the requisite legislation in 1985. The first women deacons were ordained in 1987.

1984: The General Synod voted for legislation 'to permit the ordination of women to the priesthood' to be prepared.

1988: The General Synod gave approval for the draft legislation.

1992: After further discussion with the dioceses (where 38 out of 44 Diocesan Synods voted in favour), the measure to permit women into ordination as priests was debated by the General Synod on 11 November and received the necessary two-thirds majority in all three Houses.

The Roman Catholic and Orthodox churches hold a different view, however. They have serious reservations about the ordination of women. In 1976, the Roman Catholic church set out its teachings about women's ordination in its *Declaration on the Admission of Women to the Ministerial Priesthood*. It defends its position with the following arguments:

(i) All the apostles were men
(ii) Christ was a man
(iii) Heretical Christian groups have tried women's ordination in the past but the experiments have never worked satisfactorily – i.e., they have not been in accordance with the rules and traditions of the Roman Catholic church.

Therefore, the Roman Catholic church at present does not feel it has the authority to admit women to the priesthood, arguing instead that women and men have different vocations but are equal in the sight of God.

Because of the fact that, historically, men have dominated the world of academic writing, most theologians and philosophers referenced in academia are men. As discussed in chapter 9, there is a shift in culture and gender roles and these societal roles are being challenged. There has been an increase in the discourse between twentieth-century female theologians, and their responses to the above issues faced by women in the past. Not all female theologians have the same goals in their thinking, however. Some suggest that there needs to be a rethink of the patriarchal structure of the Church in order to make it less sexist, whereas others suggest that Christianity is intrinsically sexist and should therefore be rejected on moral grounds by the standards of today's society.

There are, however, a number of common issues these female theologians discuss, predominantly:

- the exclusivity of male language when referencing God
- the justification for historical male dominance and female subordination in theology
- the view that only men can represent God within church leadership and society
- the view that men are more God-like than women
- the view that women are subordinate to men and that is their role within creation – should they reject this idea, then they are sinful by nature.

This chapter will focus on the two key feminist theological thinkers Mary Daly and **Rosemary Radford Ruether** (1936–), and their responses to the issues raised:

post-Christian theology – the total abandonment of traditional Christian thought
Reform feminist theology – seeks to change and rethink traditional Christian thought, but not to abandon it altogether.

> **Rosemary Radford Ruether (1936–)** Ruether is a Reformed feminist theologian, brought up in the Roman Catholic church. She studied Classics and History of Religions at Scripps College, California. She later became involved in the Civil Rights Movement and was made aware of many people who had been oppressed, particularly in the African American communities. Although she is a radical feminist theologian, she has remained in the Roman Catholic church. Her first book *The Church Against Itself* (1967) criticizes the doctrines of the Church. Her most influential books are *Sexism and God-Talk: Toward a Feminist Theology* (1983) and *Women and Redemption: A Theological History* (2012).

Mary Daly

Daly (1928–2010) was an American, post-Christian theologian who, in 1973 (during the time of Second Wave Feminism), published *Beyond God the Father: Towards a Philosophy of Women's Liberation*. Daly begins by setting out the problem as she sees it: 'If God in "his" heaven is a father ruling "his" people, then it is the "nature" of things and according to divine plan and the order of the universe that society is male dominated' (p. 13). She argues that beliefs become reflected in the way in which people live, and 'when God is male the male is God' (*ibid.*) Although Daly acknowledges that sophisticated thinkers do not take this image literally, she suggests that even people who know and intellectually accept that God is not actually male still subconsciously view 'him' as such.

Daly spoke of God being 'castrated' and how this should be done through the use of language. She believed that the term 'God the father' was inadequate, and that biblical language is androcentric (male-centred). She goes on to further her post-Christian thinking by suggesting that people (notably women) should have the courage to reject the concept of God as 'a being' and instead view God as simply 'being', therefore rejecting God the noun and embracing God the verb. In this way, God is seen as something people 'do' rather than believe 'in'.

Daly discusses the concept of Original Sin and the Fall in depth, likening it to an attempt for humanity to cope with the tragedy and unfairness of the human condition. In a patriarchal society, it would appear that the story of the Fall has entered the consciousness of humanity, and women have learned to accept feelings of guilt and blame as a result of being ultimately responsible for the Fall of 'man'. It is in this way that women have possibly contributed to their own oppression by accepting these feelings and not rejecting them. She argues that:

> The beginning of liberation comes when women refuse to be 'good' and/or 'healthy' by prevailing standards. To be female is to be deviant by definition in the prevailing culture. To be female and defiant is to be intolerably deviant. This means going beyond the imposed definitions of 'bad woman' and 'good woman', beyond the categories of prostitute and wife. This is equivalent to assuming the role of witch and madwoman. Though this might be suicidal if attempted in isolation (not less self-destructive, however, than attempting to live within the accepted categories), when done in sisterhood it amounts to a collective repudiation of the scapegoat syndrome. It is then tantamount to a declaration of identity beyond the good and evil of patriarchy's world and beyond sanity and insanity.
>
> (*ibid.*, p. 34)

Daly refers back to the Fall, suggesting that indeed women *should* fall, but only fall away from the pressures and guilt society has placed upon them. Women have been scapegoats and carried the guilt for too long. She suggests that it would be self-destructive for women to carry this burden for any longer and that women should work together to change the attitude that has historically been held.

Daly also refers to the Incarnation of Christ. Like many feminist theologians, she finds the idea of a male saviour uncomfortable and problematic. 'The idea of a uniquely male saviour may be seen as one more legitimisation of male superiority' (*ibid.*, p. 76). In other words, woman messed up the world through the Fall, so a man is sent to save it and fix all of the problems women 'caused'. Although some have suggested that Jesus himself went against traditional views at the time and could be viewed as a feminist, Daly considers this to be ultimately irrelevant. Even if Jesus was indeed a feminist, women today should not have to look to a man who existed 2,000 years ago to legitimize their views and be heard within the context of theology.

Daly is a firm believer that we live in a society in which morality has been constructed by men. Daly anticipated a 'female ethic' that was not yet developed, as Christian women were yet to stand together and be allowed to think freely about the experience of women. She suggests that our society celebrates 'phallocentric power' and this has produced an 'unholy trinity' of rape, genocide and war. This idea is inspired by Nietzsche, who stated: 'Whenever man has thought it necessary to create a memory of himself, his effort has been attended with torture, blood, sacrifice' (Nietzsche, *The Genealogy of Morals*, p. 193).

Daly believed that 'rape culture' (the first of this '**unholy trinity**') exists within the celebration of phallocentric power in society as a sense of **male entitlement**. Man will do whatever he can to get whatever he wants. Daly points to a number of examples of

Unholy trinity: Mary Daly's shocking charge against the Church, whose treatment of women has produced 'rape, genocide and war'

Male entitlement: Daly claims that men feel entitled to do whatever they want to retain power and subdue women

male domination and entitlement, including rape, but also female genital mutilation, foot binding, widow burning and other forms of violence against women. She also references the links between rape and war – both are symbols of violent oppression, and one in which rape can become a product of war, offering the example of the rape of hundreds of thousands of women in Bengal in 1971.

Daly also notes the references to rape in the Bible, using the following passage from Judges as an example: 'Look, here is my virgin daughter, and his concubine. I will bring them out to you now, and you can use them to do with them whatever you wish. But as for this man, do not do such an outrageous thing' (Judges 19:24). This relates to a group of corrupt men arriving at a house demanding to abuse one of the (male) guests, but the host offers his daughter as a substitute in order that they leave the guest alone. The men refuse the daughter, but proceed to rape the concubine throughout the night. This is not only showing that men will willingly submit to the 'needs' of other men, but also that women are viewed as property, simply put on the earth for the pleasure of men, and to be subservient to their wants and needs, regardless of the welfare of the woman concerned.

Daly did not believe that only men who physically commit the act of rape were to blame, but also men whom she describes as 'armchair rapists'. These are men who take pleasure out of watching stories of rape or abuse of women through pornography, as they are then able to use it to enhance their belief in their sense of power over women.

The second in Daly's 'unholy trinity' is genocide. If rape objectifies a woman, then it has to be argued that rape culture is one in which women are regarded as a group of objects – setting men as a whole against women as a whole. In Daly's view, there is a gender 'caste system' which gives men an unequally large proportion of power, and this is reinforced through social and cultural constructs so that, from birth, men and women accept this as the societal 'norm'. She sees a strong link between rape and genocide as both objectify the victims – the victim is not seen as a person but more as an object that can be violated for the wants and needs of the 'other'. Rape is an act of violation for the victim, but is also the victimization of one group by another.

The third and last element of Daly's unholy trinity is war, which she viewed as inevitable within male-dominated society and politics. She suggests that we live in a world of 'phallic mentality' that appears to lead to violence, and this is something women need to stand together and move away from. Men attempt to disguise the horrors inflicted on others during war by using euphemisms such as 'collateral damage' to describe the deaths of innocent civilians. Men in power defend war as 'necessary' – however, when it comes to euthanasia and abortion, these are rejected as 'murder' and 'against the will of God'. They defend war as having a 'good' result – however, the same could equally be applied to both euthanasia *and* abortion, depending on the circumstances, so the mindset of this is entirely hypocritical.

Daly rejects the idea that women would be able to restore Christianity through feminist liturgies. This is mainly because she believed that the patriarchs are so ingrained within both society and the Church that this would be futile, perhaps impossible, due to the fact that all attempts to do so would still be carried out within the context of a patriarchal tradition. She states:

> A feminist liturgy could change nothing for the 'form was theirs'. It was the 'form' that counted, no matter what the content. The form was a dead shell, and the growth of the consciousness of women is an attempt to live without such shells ... feminist liturgy is a contradiction in terms ... it is an attempt to put new wine, women's awareness, into old skins of forms that kill women's self-affirmations.
>
> (*ibid.*, p. 145)

For Daly, Christianity needs to be left behind as it is too tightly connected with oppression of women by men. Men have taken over religion and any changes that would need to be made would have to be made through them, which for Daly defeats the object. She viewed church buildings as being built and managed by men, and not only have men in the Church taken over all roles of power, but, Daly goes on to argue, they have also taken over the traditional role of women:

> Graciously they lifted from women the onerous power of childbirth, christening it 'baptism'. Thus they brought the lowly material function of birth, incompetently and even grudgingly performed by females, to a higher and more spiritual level. Recognising the ineptitude of females in performing even the humble 'feminine' tasks assigned to them by the divine plan, the Looking Glass priests raised these functions to the supernatural level in which they alone had competence. Feeding was elevated to become Holy Communion. Washing achieved dignity in Baptism and Penance. Strengthening became known as confirmation, and the function of consolation, which the unstable nature of females caused them to perform so inadequately, was raised to a spiritual level and called Extreme Unction. In order to stress the obvious fact that all females are innately disqualified from joining the Sacred Men's Club.
>
> (*ibid.*, p. 117)

Daly concludes her case by ridiculing the way the 'Sacred Men's Club' (priests) dressed by imitating female clothing, outlining the fact that these men wear skirts, and on special occasions wear 'delicate white lace tops ... silk hose, pointed hats and crimson dresses'. She continues her sarcastic conclusion, saying:

> These anointed Male Mothers, who naturally are called Fathers, felt maternal concern for the women entrusted to their pastoral care. Although females obviously are by nature incomplete and prone to mental and emotional confusion, they are required by the Divine Plan as vessels to contain the seed of men so that men can be born and then supernaturally (correctly) reborn as citizens of the Heavenly Kingdom.
>
> ('The Looking-Glass Society' in Ann Loades (ed.), *Feminist Theology: A Reader*, SPCK, 1996, p. 190)

Daly argued that this way of thinking has become second nature in society, and women continue to accept their role as being the 'other'. Once women begin to change this outlook, then men will have no choice but to think for themselves and society will then be more aware of other areas of social injustice and inequality, such as racism, classism and homophobia. Inequality will no longer be able to be justified by a God-given entitlement.

Rosemary Radford Ruether

> By becoming a servant of God, one is freed from bondage to all human masters. Only then, as a liberated person, can one truly become 'servant of all', giving one's life to liberate others rather than to exercise power and rule over them.
> (Ruether, *Sexism and God-Talk: Toward a Feminist Theology*, SCM Press, 1983, p. 121)

Ruether (born 1936) is a Roman Catholic feminist theologian who believes that Christianity is ingrained in the patriarchy and has become distorted by these patriarchal traditions. As a result, a complete reform is needed. She believes that, for Christians, the focus should be on God alone, not on following male leaders. She believes that these patriarchal influences have dominated Christianity (and therefore women in the Church) for far too long, and describes herself as an 'eco-feminist'. She believes that the Roman Catholic view on women's ordination and abortion has been influenced by these patriarchal influences, and so advocates for the Roman Catholic church to change its view on these topics. Ruether has served as a board member for the pro-choice group 'Catholics for Choice' (CFC) since 1985. She argues that, although Christianity has always absorbed cultural change to match people's real lives, it seems to be continually out of step with social progress (for example, in women not being allowed to be ordained). She argues that, if religious doctrines do not match the experiences of the people, then these doctrines need to change.

Ruether differs from Daly's view, in that she believes the Church should be reformed rather than totally abandoned. Ruether believes that God is real and that he continues to communicate with people. It is therefore not necessary to persevere with the patriarchal concept of God formulated thousands of years ago. Although Ruether disagrees with many patriarchal rules and regulations within the church structure, she remains a part of the church in order to warrant change and reform from within.

Ruether and Jesus' challenge to the male warrior-messiah expectation

The Old Testament views the messiah as God's chosen one: a future king who will deliver his people through battle and restore Israel. He would be a military king, like David, hence the name of this awaited messiah is 'the Davidic Messiah'. Ruether states that because this messiah is chosen by God, represents God and is the son of 'man', there is an explicit maleness intrinsically attached to the concept. She says: 'The messiah can only be imagined as male' (Ruether, *Sexism and God-Talk*, p. 110).

However, for Ruether, Jesus does not fit into this 'military king' expectation, so, although there was an Old Testament view of a Davidic Messiah who was inextricably linked to the concept of 'maleness', Jesus did not fit into this warrior expectation, and therefore should not be 'discarded'. Jesus was not a military leader – indeed, he rejected the use of force and only once did he show 'just' anger when turning over the tables in the Temple (Matt. 21:12–13), harming nobody in the process. It could be suggested that Jesus took on the role of the servant. Instead of dominating and exaggerating his male 'power', he sought out the weak, vulnerable, poor and oppressed, and fought against people who misused their positions of power or authority for themselves. He also refers to God as 'Abba', which signifies the close, personal relationship between a father and a child, rather than referring to God as a dominant, authoritarian being:

> Jesus revises God-language by using the familiar Abba for God. He speaks of the messiah as a servant rather than a king to visualize new relations between the divine and human. Relation to God no longer becomes a model for dominant–subordinate relations between social groups, leaders and the led . . . Relation to God liberates us from hierarchical relations and makes us brothers–sisters of each other. Those who would be leaders must become servants of all.
>
> (*ibid.*, p. 136)

Ruether refers to Jesus' opposition to the positions of religious power inherent at the time in the following examples:

- Jesus argues against positions of religious power in Matthew 21:12
- He refers to local religious lawyers and experts as hypocrites in Matthew 6:5
- He dismisses the power of Pontius Pilate in John 19:11
- He warns his disciples against using power over others in Matthew 20:25
- He washes the feet of his followers in John 13:1–17
- He points out that good leaders should be servants of their people in Luke 22:24–30

Jesus pays the ultimate price that no warrior would willingly do, and sacrifices himself for others. For Ruether, the military, male view of God is not needed. The fact that Jesus was biologically male does not matter – his importance comes through his life and teachings, which represented servanthood and self-sacrifice. These traditionally feminine qualities of wisdom are what should be focused on, not his biological gender. She argues that Christianity has got it wrong in marrying the traditional male notion of the Davidic Messiah with that of Christ, and it is this mistake that displaces women from the concept of God.

Ruether draws attention to the principle of wisdom, 'Sophia', as personified in Greek culture. The ancient Greek for 'Sophia' translates as 'clever, skilful, intelligent and wise', so these characteristics were personified in female form. It could be suggested, therefore, that, although Jesus was biologically male, his 'divine wisdom' would share in the feminine aspects of God. Ruether points out that, alongside the male images of God the Father and Son, there are more ambiguous ones of God as a spirit. In the Hebrew Bible, this spirit is aligned with the concept of 'Sophia'. This figure of wisdom is aligned with the person of Christ, as seen in 1 Corinthians 1:20, where Paul argues that this wisdom from God makes the world look foolish. Moreover, it is striking that Paul juxtaposes the true (female) wisdom with the false wisdom of (male) scholars, philosophers and wise men – arguably a proto-feminist move.

Ruether seeks a full understanding of God by challenging the use of exclusively masculine terms to refer to him. She refers to the Ancient Greek term 'Gaia' which refers to the Ancient Greek goddess of the Earth. Ruether argues that these feminine terms for God have been covered up by the patriarchy over centuries, so she is simply recovering the ancient notion of the female God rather than inventing new ways to picture God. She believes that this provides a truer notion of *Imago Dei* in that it reflects the view that *all* beings were made in the image of God – not just men – so giving a better reflection of the relationship God has with his creation.

> **Exercise**
> Make a chart and compare and contrast the views of Daly and Ruether. Discuss your findings with your class.

Is Christianity essentially sexist?

> The head of the woman is man . . . for man did not come from woman, but woman from man; neither was man created for woman, but woman for man.
> (1 Cor. 11:3–9)

There is an argument that Christianity is inherently sexist. One only has to refer to the quote above, written by Paul to the Christians in Corinth, to see that Christianity bears its roots in a very male-centric world. The man is head and woman is simply created for the purpose and use of man. This has led thinkers such as Daphne Hampson to adopt the view that, if one wants to be a feminist, then one must reject Christianity, as to be both is impossible. Hampson speaks from authority, as a graduate of Oxford and Harvard, and as a former Professor of Theology at St Andrews. She founded the **Group for the Ministry of Women**, coming from a background in the Church of England, and wrote vigorously supporting women's ordination. Indeed, it was Hampson who wrote the theological statement in favour of women's ordination circulated to all Synod members before the vote on women's ordination in 1978, in which she refuted the theological and scriptural arguments of its opponents. However, as Sharma and Young point out:

Group for the Ministry of Women: A group set up by Daphne Hampson, offering support to women and campaigning for the ordination of women in the Church of England

> The frustration of this struggle (for ordination of women) convinced Hampson that her effort was wrong-headed. The determined resistance of traditionalists to women's ordination reflected fixed, unchangeable limits to the Christian religion. Hampson decided that Christianity is incompatible with feminism and indeed with modern scientific truth. Christianity cannot be reformed to become compatible with feminism because it's root must always go back to scriptures that validate a patriarchal view of God, humanity and the world. Christianity is not only false, it is unethical, in Hampson's view. Thus, to be intellectually and ethically consistent, a feminist must leave Christianity.
> (Sharma and Young, *Feminism and World Religions*, State University of New York, 1998, p. 225)

For Hampson, whichever argument one may put forward, the counter will always be rooted in the Bible, which was written at a time of a patriarchal society. This is a fundamental rejection of the beliefs of feminism, so Christianity must be rejected on moral grounds. As long as Christianity grounds its belief in this tradition, it cannot be ethical.

Hampson states 'Christians are those who believe there has been a particular revelation in history' (Hampson, *After Christianity*, p. 51). She rejects this in favour of the idea that God reaches out to all people at all times. Therefore, traditional religion is no longer required – especially one so rooted in a single revelation during a time where men ruled over women. Individuals can interpret their own love for God without having to submit to an essentially sexist traditional history.

Other feminist theologians, such as Elisabeth Schussler Fiorenza, disagree with this view and argue that Christianity is not essentially sexist, referring to the fact that Paul also wrote that 'you are all one in Christ Jesus' (Galatians 3:28). If we read the Bible as literal, timeless truth, then some passages may appear sexist. However, if we view the Bible in its historical contexts, yet interpret it alongside our modern understanding of the world and the equal place of women today, then it can be understood without undermining women. If all this is possible, then we may see the moral messages that challenge sexism, such as when Jesus breaks societal customs like those of not speaking to women (John 4:1–42) and not touching women (Mark 5:25–34). Jesus' teachings are consistent in their message of freeing the oppressed and giving voices to those who have been silenced. Such examples may support Ruether in her belief that there is hope for a change towards a more feminist theology within Christianity without having to abandon it altogether.

The *Christa* controversy

During Holy Week of 1984, *Christa* by **Edwina Sandys** (1938–present) was displayed at the Cathedral Church of St John the Divine in Manhattan, New York City, as part of a small collection on the female divine. *Christa* is a statue of a woman representing the crucified Jesus.

Generally, the reception of this statue was positive, yet a particularly vocal group condemned the piece and attacked it as blasphemy that they considered to be changing the symbol of Christ on the cross. They highlighted how the sculpture's sexualized (i.e. female) figure brought attention to Christ's human body, which they deemed blasphemous, shocking and inappropriate.

Overruling the Dean of the cathedral, the Bishop of the Episcopal Diocese of New York ordered the removal of the statue, deeming it 'theologically and historically indefensible' (*New York Times*, 25 April 1984). In his Maundy Thursday service, he added that, although he supported the 'women's cause' both inside and outside the Church, totally changing the symbolism of Christ on the cross was 'symbolically reprehensible'.

Although supporters of the statue agree that the historical Jesus was a man, they believe that the statue conveys the concept that women as well as men are called by the Gospels to 'carry their cross'. They argue that a woman on the cross emphasizes the teaching that God acted through Jesus to save *all* humanity, regardless of race, sex or ethnic background. This statue simply helps to underline that point.

However, as Nicola Slee points out, 'Feminists themselves are divided in their response to the *Christa* figure, with a number of feminists objecting to what they see as an image which assumes the male gaze, encouraging a voyeuristic, potentially sadistic attitude towards the female body' (Slee, *Seeking the Risen Christa*, p. 45).

Christa **controversy**: A statue displayed in 1984 in St John the Divine Cathedral in New York City that caused controversy because it represents the crucified Christ as a woman

Gender and Theology

And Janet Walton adds: 'It sent shivers down my spine. It is not enough that women are battered, bruised, raped and otherwise denied a reality, it must now be glorified as suffering for the greater good' (M. Procter-Smith and Janet Walton, *Women at Worship: Interpretations of North American Diversity*, Westminster John Knox Press, 2004, p. 78).

Due to the changing attitudes with regards to the reinterpretation of the symbolism on the cross, in 2016 Edwina Sandys was invited to install *Christa* in the Chapel of St Saviour (New York) as a centrepiece of an exhibition known as 'The Christa Project: Manifesting Divine Bodies'.

Controversial statue of Jesus as feminine by Edwina Sandys

Exercise

What do you think about the statue of *Christa*?

FURTHER READING

Mary Daly, *Beyond God the Father: Towards a Philosophy of Women's Liberation*. The Women's Press 1973

Elisabeth Schussler Fiorenza, *In Memory of Her: A Feminist Theological Reconstruction of Christian Theology*. SCM Press, 1983

Daphne Hampson, *After Christianity*. New edn. SCM Press, 2012

Daphne Hampson, *Theology and Feminism*. Blackwell, 1990

Rosemary Radford Ruether, *Sexism and God-Talk: Toward a Feminist Theology*. SCM Press, 1983

Nicola Slee, *Seeking the Risen Christa*. SPCK, 2011

Arvind Sharma and Katherine K. Young, *Feminism and World Religions*. State University of New York, 1998

Thought Points

1. Look at the list below of significant women in the Bible and fill in their role or achievements. Some have been done for you.
   (a) Eve –
   (b) Hagar – the slave of Sarah (Abraham's wife). Because Sarah could not conceive, she gave to Abraham Hagar, who gave birth to his first child. Once the child was born, she then became estranged from the family
   (c) Deborah – The only female judge mentioned in the Bible. Known as a powerful Prophetess
   (d) Delilah –
   (e) Ruth – Loyal and virtuous
   (f) Martha –
   (g) Women at Tomb –
   (h) Phoebe – Helped out in the early church. Her role was described as that of a deacon

2. 'Men and women could never be equal – physically, emotionally, psychologically or in any other way.' Discuss.

3. Is feminism irretrievably sexist?

4. 'To be female is to be deviant by definition in the prevailing culture.' To what extent do you agree with Mary Daly's statement?

5. Look up Numbers 31:17–18 and Judges 19:24 in the Old Testament. Should the Bible be edited to take out passages that are obviously repugnant to modern readers?

6. 'Jesus was a man and so were his disciples, so priests should be male.' Discuss.

7. Is it justifiable in the twenty-first century that the Roman Catholic church still refuses to ordain women as priests?

SECTION VI
CHALLENGES

CHAPTER 11
The Challenge of Secularism

LEARNING OUTCOMES
In this chapter, you will be learning about the rise of secularism and secularisation, including the views that:
- God is an illusion and the result of 'wish fulfilment' (Freud and Dawkins)
- Christianity should play no part in public life (secular humanism)

Introduction

Many have argued that Christianity, and religion in general, have been the cause of many social ills throughout history (from Israel vs Canaan in 2000 BC, through to the Muslim Conquests, the Crusades, the Buddhist Uprising and the Lebanese Civil War – and, in recent times, the threats of Islamic militant groups such as al-Qaida and Isis). This is leading many modern atheists such as Richard Dawkins to argue that religion should be kept out of education, government and social life altogether, stating that 'Religion is the root of all evil' (from the title of Richard Dawkins' two-part TV series *The Root of all Evil?*, Channel 4, Jan. 2006).

European intellectuals have developed powerful arguments for active secularisation of society since the eighteenth century. Auguste Comte (1798–1857) held the view that religion would eventually give way to **secular positivism**, and that the power of scientific reasoning would rid society of all its false views of the world.

The concept that religion and state should be separated has been reinforced by the role of militant Islamic groups and attacks such as 9/11, and the London, Paris and Manchester Arena bombings. With attacks such as these taking place, it is hard to ignore the fact that, regardless of how society attempts to remove religion from

Secular positivism: The idea of a society based on scientific reasoning and without the need for religion

state, religion continues to play a major role within the Western consciousness. The ripple effect of these attacks has caused many societies to reconsider whether more effort should be made to exclude all religions from all public life, as noted by the timeline below.

The Magen David (Star of David) is a universally recognised symbol of Judaism

> **Timeline of European legislation regarding religious symbols in public**
> 2003: German court rules in favour of an Afghan-born teacher who wants to wear an Islamic scarf to school, but says states can change that law locally if they wish – a law which half of German regions go on to ban
> 2004: France's national assembly begins bill debating a ban on all religious symbols (including Muslim headscarves, Kippas and Christian crosses) in schools
> 2010: Belgium votes to implement the ban on wearing the burqa and niqab in public
> 2011: France becomes the first European country to ban women from wearing the burqa or niqab in any public place outside of a person's home, other than when worshipping in a religious building or travelling in a car.
> 2014: European Court of Human Rights upholds France's law banning the burqa
> 2016: UK Prime Minister David Cameron states he would back sensible rules regarding Muslims wearing full-face veils, but would rule out a full public ban
> 2017: Austria's government agrees to prohibit full-face veils in courts and schools
> 2017: The European Court of Justice rules that employers can ban staff from wearing visible religious symbols, as long as the company has a policy on such procedures and this policy is strictly adhered to
> 2018: Danish parliament votes to ban garments that cover the face, including Islamic veils.
> (Matthew Weaver, 'Burqa bans, headscarves and veils: a timeline of legislation in the West', *The Guardian*, 31 May 2018)

One can see from this timeline that, in the Western world, religious symbolism is becoming less and less accepted in society, yet there is a powerful argument to say that, if it is properly understood, religion is a fundamentally important aspect of society and has brought enormous benefits to civilization. Regardless of this, it is clear that, throughout Europe, religion is becoming a largely private matter, often described

The Challenge of Secularism | 175

Secularisation:
The view that public and private life should be entirely separate. Religious belief should not be in the public domain

as '**secularisation**', which is the view that public and private life ought to be entirely separate. This provides a public space for discussion and debate concerning what is common to all and the law, leaving religious belief to reside in the private space of the home.

Jose Casanova explains three ways in which people refer to secularisation:

1. The decline of religious belief and practice in modern society. Some suggest this is a normal universal, human development process.
2. The privatization of religion, something which again is seen as normal and something required for living in a modern liberal democracy, where religion should be private and should not be seen in public (for instance in the wearing of symbolic clothing in places of work).
3. The secular separation of spheres of state, economy, science, which are set free from religious institutions as a new norm (for instance the religious sponsorship of state funded schools).

(Jose Casanova, *Rethinking Secularization: A Global Comparative Perspective*, Brill, 2007, p. 7)

The Crucifix is a symbol of Christianity, especially for Roman Catholics

This secularisation is being reflected in modern Britain. In 2019, the Office for National Statistics showed that fewer than one quarter (24 per cent) of all marriages in England and Wales were religious ceremonies, falling by nearly a half (48 per cent less than two decades ago). The 2011 Census also showed that there was an increase in the number of people purporting to have no religion, with this figure reaching a quarter of the population.

Procedural secularism:
The role of the State is to take into account the interests of all citizens and institutions

Programmatic secularism:
The role of the State is to be purely secular; all religious practices should be excluded from public institutions, including governments, schools and hospitals

The concept of secularisation supports views of liberalism – we live happier, more just, lives without the 'superstition' of religion, and religion can be perceived as dangerous or harmful to civilized society. **Procedural secularism** describes the idea that the role of the State is to take into account the interests of all citizens and their institutions. There should be no priority or preference for a specific religion, but religions should be treated equally, along with all other institutions. **Programmatic secularism**, on the other hand, argues that the role of the State in a pluralist society is to be purely secular; that all religious views or practices should be excluded from public institutions such as the government, public events (holidays), schools and universities.

On the other hand, this view of religion being 'dangerous and harmful' is a misunderstanding of religion. Christians may argue that any person engaging in violent conduct has fundamentally misunderstood the teachings of Christianity. Jesus spoke against immoral behaviour such as violence, so, in this sense, the Christian religion is not to blame for the 'dangerous and harmful' ways of religion; it is the immoral conduct of humans that is to blame.

Sigmund Freud

The origins of secularism come from **Ludwig Feuerbach** (1804–72), a German philosopher who, arguably, paved the way for a psychological rejection of religion. In his 1841 work *The Essence of Christianity*, he argued that belief in God is merely a projection of the human mind, stating: 'what you wish to be, you make your God'. So, in striving for ultimate power, humanity wishes to be omnipotent, omniscient, omnibenevolent – these properties are projected onto God and, instead of God creating humanity, this is turned around to the view that humanity has created God. Feuerbach argues that the desire for God arises because humans can feel vulnerable and lonely in a hostile world and, by creating a higher being, they can always have somebody there who is bigger and better than anybody else – and always on their side.

Feuerbach wanted human beings to reclaim their own positive qualities, which had been projected onto God and removed from them through religion by the 'God illusion'. In doing this, he believed people had alienated themselves from their own identity by looking up to a perfect being humans have created. The requirement was for humans to take back these qualities and 'own' them. For Feuerbach, God was the projection of the unconscious mind.

While Feuerbach developed this notion, **Sigmund Freud** (1856–1939) adds a psychological foundation to religion. He was of the view that religion was the main contributor to the development of neurosis (a psychological condition with symptoms such as stress, anxiety and obsessional behaviour). This was

Sigmund Freud by Max Halberstadt

caused by natural human instincts being systematically repressed by tradition and conformity – especially within the constraints of religion. Therefore, he concludes that religion – notably Judaism and Christianity – were primary causes of mental illness, stating: 'The religions of mankind must be classed as among the mass delusions' (Freud, *Civilization and its Discontents*, W. W. Norton, 2010, p. 81).

His central claim was that religion is founded in the 'infantile' stages of human development – when a person is in need of external support and comfort before they develop powers of reason for themselves. He reaches a similar conclusion to eighteenth-century Scottish philosopher David Hume (1711–76), who believed that religion was intrinsically childish and followed by uneducated people throughout the world. People who have mentally grown up have no need for religion anymore and therefore reject its childish ways. Hume states: 'It seems certain that, according to the natural progress of human thought, the ignorant multitude must first entertain some grovelling and familiar notion of superior powers' (Hume, *The Natural History of Religion*, Oxford University Press, 2008, p. 7).

Freud adds that religion is a reversion to a childish pattern of thought in response to feelings of guilt and helplessness. As a society, people feel a need for security and forgiveness, so in this need we invent the source of security and forgiveness: God. Quite literally, God is seen as a father figure: 'The whole thing [religion] is so patently infantile, so foreign to reality, that to anyone with a friendly attitude to humanity it is painful to think that the majority of mortals will never be able to rise above this view of life' (Freud, *Civilization and its Discontents*, p. 74).

This idea of the father figure is closely connected to Freud's concept of the Oedipus Complex – in that the last stage of a boy's psychological development is learning that he cannot possess his mother. A boy then grows resentful of his father. This resentment is repressed into the unconscious mind and projected onto the idea of God (which is in some religions or cultures expressed through phallic symbols such as the totem pole). Religious belief is then a form of 'wish fulfilment' in order to restore a child's father figure, in the respect of security and forgiveness, and so religion is seen to be an infantile illusion and atheism as grown-up realism.

The concept of wish fulfilment is also explained by Freud in the following way: people see life as having a higher purpose, but what that purpose is can be difficult to discern. Freud says that people think it has to do with the soul, which is difficult to understand, but whose aim is to make life enjoyable. They believe that everything that happens in life – even bad things – expresses the intentions of a benevolent higher power. This higher power only appears to be cruel and punishing. Death is not obliteration, but the beginning of a new kind of existence that leads to something higher and better.

According to Freud, humans believe that the moral laws that civilizations have set up govern the whole universe. They are governed by a supreme court of justice that is more powerful and consistent than any human court. People believe that, in the end, all good actions are rewarded and all evil ones are punished in their post-mortem existence, a place where the suffering and hardships of life will disappear (Freud, *The Future of an Illusion*, Penguin, 2008, p. 25).

Religion is the ultimate wish fulfilment as it provides answers to questions, which humanity cannot find on earth. It offers supreme judgement and the understanding that, although things on earth may be unfair, painful and unjust, all of these wrongs will be righted upon death. Religious beliefs provide the answers that humans crave about things that cannot be discovered through experience – therefore, given that death is the only thing that humanity has not experienced, it is 'obvious' that the answers lie there.

Freud saw Christianity's obsession with sacrifice, sin and guilt as ultimately damaging. Unconscious desires of the *id* (the primitive and instinctual part of the mind which contains sexual and aggressive drives and hidden memories) are repressed by the *ego* (the realistic part of the mind which mediates between the desires of the id and the *superego*) and superego (the part of the mind which incorporates the values and morals of society, which are learnt from others – this is used to keep control of the id). Religious morality feeds the superego, which then further represses desires of the id, which causes further unhappiness and even neurosis.

Freud suggests that religious beliefs cannot be questioned, as they were passed down from our ancestors. This again would feed a person's superego, as, historically, it was deemed unacceptable to question these beliefs of the older generations, even if they were full of contradictions: 'The proofs they have left us are set down in writings which themselves bear every mark of untrustworthiness. They are full of contradictions, revisions and falsifications, and where they speak of factual confirmations they are themselves unconfirmed' (*ibid.*, p. 27).

Richard Dawkins

Richard Dawkins is an academic biologist and a committed atheist. He developed Darwin's theory of evolution in his book *The Selfish Gene* (1976), and has since published many books which attack religious beliefs, including *The Blind Watchmaker* (2006) and *The God Delusion* (2006). One of his fundamental arguments is that religion takes far too high a precedence in society, and, even if religious beliefs can be argued as being intolerant or oppressive, they are protected because society still respects them.

Dawkins reflects the beliefs of Freud, arguing that monotheistic religions are a cause of mental and physical harm, and his book *The God Delusion* urges people not only to accept atheism with pride in a world without religion, but also to accept that the 'God Hypothesis' is weak, and to realize that religion is a form of child abuse. He states his aim as being to 'raise consciousness to the fact that to be an atheist is a realistic aspiration, and a brave and splendid one' (*The God Delusion*, p. 1).

In a letter to his daughter, 'Good and Bad Reasons for Believing', Dawkins outlines three poor reasons for belief, on which Christianity is founded: tradition, authority and revelation. The problem with these is that people simply believe things because people 'have believed the same thing over centuries', but that fact alone does not make them true. He attacks monotheistic religion by questioning why anybody would believe in something for which there is no evidence, and argues that things should be subject to rational enquiry in order to be believed. For example, the evolutionary theory does not need a supernatural power to make sense of it. We are not developing towards a specific telos set out in the sky – we are simply part of an evolutionary process in which we are developing our body, mind and morality without the requirement of a higher being. For Dawkins, the scientific, reasoned, evidence pointing to evolution bears no comparison to the evidence available to support the existence of God. When reason is applied to God's existence, it demonstrates, at very best, that the evidence for his existence is inconclusive.

Dawkins refers to Stephen Jay Gould's notion of non-overlapping magisteria (NOMA): the notion that science and religion are so fundamentally different in their approach that they cannot even address the same topics. It is the attempt to distinguish the factual world of experience from the supernatural world of religion. Because religion is fundamentally different from the material world, it cannot be subject to any rational, scientific enquiry and should therefore be rejected. As Alister McGrath points out:

> Dawkins is a splendid representative of the no-nonsense 'one rationality fits all' approach of the enlightenment. Perhaps this is most obvious in his discussion of 'mystery' – a category which he cheerfully, if a little prematurely, reduces to 'plain insanity or surrealist nonsense'. We can make sense of things – or, if we can't make sense of things now, the relentless advance of science will make it possible sooner or later. Given enough time, anything can happen. Religious people who talk about 'mystery' are just irrational mystics who are too lazy or frightened to use their minds properly.
> (McGrath, *Dawkins' GOD: Genes, Memes and the Meaning of Life*, 2nd edn, Wiley, 2016, p. 143)

Dawkins argues that religious belief discourages scientific enquiry by allowing a lazy mind-set that points to 'divine mystery' before seeking scientific explanations. Unlike God, the theory of evolution is supported by a significant and widely accepted body of evidence. For Dawkins, therefore, it makes more sense to believe in this process without the need for another type of supernatural force which controls it in some way, so 'belief in a divine creator is unnecessary and delusional' as we can make sense of this as a natural process without referencing a supernatural being. As Dawkins says: 'There is something infantile in the presumption that somebody else (parents in the case of children, God in the case of adults) has a responsibility to give your life meaning and point' (Dawkins, *The God Delusion*, p. 348).

Although it could be argued that, given that science and religion are incompatible in the eyes of Dawkins, one should just accept that some people believe, others don't and that their paths should not cross as they are entirely different subjects seeking entirely different answers, and it is entirely harmless. However, Dawkins disagreed with this view of 'harmless' religion and argued that not only was it a source of conflict, but, when these religious 'truths' are taught to children, it is tantamount to abuse. He states: 'Our society, including the non-religious sector, has accepted the preposterous idea that it is normal and right to indoctrinate tiny children in the religion of their parents, and to slap religious labels onto them ... "Catholic child", "Protestant child" ... ' (*ibid.*, p. 339).

Children are initiated into a set of beliefs before they can understand what is happening to them. He also gives examples of the abuse of children by 'Christian' monks and nuns. Dawkins argues that children have the right to be raised without having their minds confused by other people's nonsensical beliefs, stating: 'Even without physical abduction, isn't it always a form of child abuse to label children as possessors of beliefs that they are too young to have thought about?' (*ibid.*, p. 315).

The notion of '**memetics**' may explain why Christianity has been a part of humanity for so long. The notion of a 'meme' first appeared in Dawkins' first book *The Selfish Gene*. He used it as an anology to genes, to explain, from an evolutionary perspective, why some kinds of behaviour, such as slogans, catch-phrases, icons, inventions, fashions and so on, were very common in human societies. Memes could survive for longer if they multiplied, becoming a 'memeplex', in which memes joined together in a mutually supportive way, similar to how genes work together in a genome. Dawkins argues that political and religious ideas and practices may be understood as memeplexes, helping memes to survive for a long time.

> **Memetics**: Richard Dawkins uses this term to explain how ideas like religion survive for a long time, just as genes mutate and multiply

> **Exercise**
> For Dawkins, 'religion' is a memeplex. How far do you agree with his view that religion has survived for so long because it is a meme?

Should Christianity play a part in public life?

Both Freud and Dawkins are examples of secular humanists (who believe that people can live good and moral lives without the need for religious adherence). Within the context of **secular humanism**, there are many differing views, from programmatic secularism, which argues that society should be active in its removal of all religion from public organizations, to procedural secularism, which states that religion may have a place in society but not be allowed any special privileges – such as having twenty-six Church of England bishops in the House of Lords, for example.

The **Amsterdam Declaration** is a set of seven statements that were agreed on at the fiftieth anniversary of the World Humanist Congress in 2002, and were adopted by the International Humanist and Ethical Union (IHEU) General Assembly. The seven statements set out the main aims of modern humanism, which are summarized below:

> **Secular humanism**: This ideology believes that people can live moral lives without the need for religious adherence

> **Amsterdam Declaration**: Seven statements agreed at the World Humanist Congress in 2002, setting out the minimum aims of modern humanism

1. Humanism is ethical: all people are worthy of dignity and autonomy. They should be allowed the greatest possible freedom which must be compatible with and not infringe the rights of others. Humanists have a duty of care to all of humanity.
2. Humanism is rational: science should be used creatively in order to help solve world problems, and not destructively. The solution to the world's problems lie in the hands of humankind and not a divine being and this should be done wisely.
3. Humanism supports democracy and human rights: democracy and development are human rights – and this is in all areas of life and relationships, it is not confined to governmental matters.

4. Humanism insists that personal liberty must be combined with social responsibility: humanism recognizes humanity's responsibility to (and, indeed, dependence upon) the natural environment. It is undogmatic, which means all can be free to receive an education free from indoctrination.
5. Humanism is the response to widespread demand for an alternative to dogmatic religion: as opposed to the major world religions whose rules are based on revelation fixed at a social point in the past, humanism recognizes that understanding of the world relies upon continuing observation and evaluation.
6. Humanism values artistic creativity and imagination: humanism affirms the need of the arts, music and literature for a person's personal development.
7. Humanism is a life-stance aiming at the maximum possible fulfilment for all: through offering ethical and rational means by which to understand and address the challenges of our times, humanism can be an accessible way of life for any person in any place.

Given that these seven statements appear fair, moral and accessible to all, there is an argument to say that humanism should form the basis of morality in public life, rather than explicitly Christian doctrines. Part of this argument is due to the fact that the place of Christianity in many areas of society is quite simply as a result of ritual and/or tradition. Take, for example, the Christian element of the House of Lords. Bishops having automatic seats in the House of Lords highlights a bias towards religion, when government should be democratic; such traditional practice fails to reflect the reality of 21st-century Britain, and it could be argued that it is dogmatic and stuck in the past. The UK is one of only two sovereign states to have religious leaders afforded automatic places – the other is Iran, an Islamic theocracy. Also, each sitting starts with Christian prayers, one example of which being:

> Almighty God, by whom alone Kings reign, and Princes decree justice; and from whom alone cometh all counsel, wisdom, and understanding; we thine unworthy servants, here gathered together in thy Name, do most humbly beseech thee to send down thy Heavenly Wisdom from above, to direct and guide us in all our consultations; and grant that, we having thy fear always before our eyes, and laying aside all private interests, prejudices, and partial affections, the result of all our counsels may be to the glory of thy blessed Name, the maintenance of true Religion and Justice, the safety, honour, and happiness of the Queen, the public wealth, peace and tranquillity of the Realm, and the uniting and knitting together of the hearts of all persons and estates within the same, in true Christian Love and Charity one towards another, through Jesus Christ our Lord and Saviour. Amen.
>
> (https://publications.parliament.uk/pa/ld/ldcomp/ldctso58.htm)

Again, there is bias towards Christianity, 'in true Christian Love and Charity . . . through Jesus Christ our Lord and Saviour'. This, again, does not reflect the beliefs of 21st-century Britain.

In September 2018, the Minister of Faith (Lord Bourne of Aberystwyth) called for more religious leaders to be appointed to the House of Lords, arguing that the twenty-six bishops currently in sitting add great value, but broader representation would be beneficial. Responding to this suggestion, Humanists UK Director of Public Affairs and Policy, Ricky Thompson, stated:

CHALLENGES

Lord Bourne's suggestions are ill-thought-out. To attempt to appoint a proportionate number of religious leaders to make up for the bishops in Parliament would mean appointing another 85 people of other faiths, and even then, that is to say nothing of representation of the majority of the population that belong to no religion. It is to say nothing of the fact that religious leaders do not represent those who are in fact religious, whether this be in their beliefs, their practice, or their social attitudes. It is to say nothing of the fact that religious people are already over-represented anyway amongst the Lords who are not bishops. And then there is the fact that such an approach would be hugely unpopular.

The only fair and equitable solution is to end the privileged place of the Church of England by removing the bishops from the House of Lords and instead allow those of all religions and beliefs equal representation in the chamber through no such special representation at all.'

(humanism.org.uk: House of Lords)

The Humanist Society believes that the only truly fair way to represent all religions in government is to have *no* religious representation whatsoever, thereby removing the Church from the State altogether.

> **Exercise**
>
> Organize a debate on the motion 'This house believes that all bishops in the House of Lords should be removed.'

The existence of faith schools may be understood as inappropriate to modern life in Britain. The British Humanist Association strongly campaign against any schools with a religious aim, stating:

> We aim for a secular state guaranteeing human rights, with no privilege or discrimination on the grounds of religion or belief, and so we campaign against 'faith' schools and for an inclusive, secular schools system, where children and young people of all different backgrounds and beliefs can learn with and from each other. We challenge 'faith' schools; admissions, employment and curriculum policies, as well as the privileged processes by which new 'faith' schools continue to open.

(Humanism.org.uk: faith schools)

The Association argues that the State should not fund schools which have a religious aim, and, indeed, that it is damaging to divide children into different religious groups, as this could end in people growing up leading separate, parallel lives, and thereby increasing ignorance of other people's cultures, and therefore intolerance. They do, however, agree that Religious Education should be taught as an academic subject within schools, but believe that there should be a reform of this in order for there to be an inclusive curriculum, teaching non-religious worldviews, such as humanism, alongside religious worldviews.

This concern regarding faith schools is widely shared. The book *Faith Schools: Consensus or Conflict?* states:

> One of the most significant criticisms voiced against faith schools in current debate is the claim that they are 'divisive'. Examples of this claim can readily be pointed to. Richard Dawkins, for instance, has argued that faith schools are 'lethally divisive' and Polly

Toynbee claims that such schools 'foil attempts at future integration', 'cause apartheid' and (in the case of Catholic schools) leave some ten percent of their places empty rather than admit 'unwashed heathen'.

(Gardner et al., *Faith Schools: Consensus or Conflict?* Routledge, 2005, p. 61)

Richard Dawkins is concerned that religious schools are teaching children 'from their earliest years, that unquestioning faith is a virtue' (Dawkins, *The God Delusion*, p. 323), and that this will have a direct negative impact on the place of science in school. Teaching the literal, fundamental and geological 'truths' of the biblical account of Creation could lead children to miss the evidence-based approach to understanding the world and the truths of the scientific, evolutionary teaching about creation.

However, there may be many reasons to suggest that faith schools have a positive influence within our society. One argument points to the fact that, historically, churches were the institutions that built schools for the poor, and many churches still own the land such schools stand on. The original faith schools, therefore, were simply built by the Church in poor areas in order to provide all children with an adequate education.

To affirm this view, the head teacher of a Scottish Roman Catholic school said:

'RE may be for some people about the knowledge and understanding of certain facts, figures, the Gospels, whatever it may be. But for me, RE is about that experience of seeing that Our Lord came upon the earth to ask of us. And putting that into the day to day life of the school. It's not just a subject because it's a human enrichment process as well. It nourishes children when you give them opportunities to reflect upon their concept of themselves and their place in the world. . . .'

The eloquence of a school leader who has publicly and professionally showcased the faith credentials of his school once more takes us to the plane where religion and education interact to constitute an 'experience'.

(Karen Conroy, James C. Lundle, David Davis, Robert A. Baumfield, Vivienne Barnes and L. Philip, *Does Religious Education Work? A Multi-Dimensional Investigation*, Bloomsbury Academic, 2013, p. 106)

For this head teacher, religious education is far from simply an academic subject and should indeed be reflected throughout the school as a whole in order to constitute an 'experience' for the children. It could also encourage young people to be more comfortable about being open and relaxed about their faith, as opposed to feeling the need to hide behind a secular society and practise their religion in the confines of their home or place of worship. In his essay 'The Challenge of Secularism', Christopher Dawson argues that secular education has a consciously atheist agenda – religion might not be discussed, but 'no religion' is acceptable. It could be argued that this is taking the secular society too far and it is becoming overtly 'anti-religious'.

Among other arguments for the continuation of faith schools is that, far from them creating a divisive culture, in fact a diverse society should have a diverse choice of schools to attend, as this will simply reflect society as a whole. If people wish to attend faith schools, then that would be their choice, but there are also non-faith schools. Given all schools have mission statements reflecting each school's values, it could be argued that faith schools are simply another type of value.

Another argument against Christianity being removed from society is that of evangelism. Spreading the word of God by public preaching or personal witness in an act of evangelism is an integral part of the Christian faith. Earley and Wheeler discuss evangelism in terms of a religious 'command' rather than an individual choice. They say:

> Consider what Jesus says in Acts 1:8: 'But you shall receive power when the Holy Spirit has come upon you; and you shall be witnesses to me in Jerusalem, and in all Judea and Samaria, and to the end of the earth.' The phrase 'you shall be witnesses' is written as a direct command of Christ. The aim is to mobilise his disciples into the world to fulfil His earlier promise as recorded in Mark 1:17: 'Follow me, and I will make you become fishers of men.'
>
> (Dave Earley and David Wheeler, *Evangelism Is . . . : How to Share Jesus with Passion and Confidence*, Broadman & Holman Publishers, 2010, p. vii)

If Christianity no longer played a part in public life, it could be argued that this command would obviously be impossible to achieve. If salvation is only available through Christ, should Christ not be accessible to all? Also, many citizens, regardless of their faith, make use of Church of England parish churches for marriages, funerals etc. The church could therefore be seen as an integral part of the community as it is providing a spiritual service to all, regardless of belief in God.

Is Christianity a major cause of personal and social problems?

YES

Prejudice

Teachings to 'love thy neighbour' appear to have been distorted to apply to only certain groups who hold the same beliefs and values as Christians. Dawkins points to the fact that Christianity played a major role in the criminalization of homosexuality (which was *illegal* in the UK until 1967). Religion fosters widespread prejudice, and the inability to consider objective evidence on situations such as whom a person should marry means that this indoctrination is inescapable.

Also, one only has to read chapters 9 and 10 in this book to understand the prejudice and discrimination women have faced as a result of the Christian church, and to see that the argument is still valid even with the rise of the feminist society. In many denominations, women are still viewed as second-class citizens who cannot represent Christ (e.g. Roman Catholicism).

Violence

Richard Dawkins identifies many Old Testament stories such as those of Noah (God flooding the earth and destroying the whole of humanity), and of Abraham (God testing Abraham's faith by requesting he sacrifice his son – yet did not go through with this once he knew Abraham was willing to do anything for his faith). God sets out his covenants for the world based on these two events, so the whole relationship between God and humankind is based on an act of violence. One should also consider the term 'An eye for an eye' (Leviticus 24:19–21). This was part of God's law given by Moses to ancient Israel and was quoted by Jesus in the Sermon on the Mount (Matt. 38). It meant that, when dealing with wrongdoers, the punishment should fit the crime, with the rule being applied to deliberate injurious acts against another person. Regarding a wilful offender, Mosaic law stated: 'Fracture for fracture, eye for eye, tooth for tooth, the same sort of injury he afflicted should be afflicted on him' (Leviticus 24:20). Christianity has a history of supporting slavery, colonialism, oppression of women, and violence in the Crusades and other wars.

Illusion and alienation

Feuerbach explains how God is a creation of the human psyche. What we wish to be, we make our God, in order to seek hope and meaning. In this way, religion forces people to feel inadequate and to project their life's meaning onto somebody/something else. This means we are living in an illusion and, in order to shatter this illusion, one must place meaning in oneself, rather than projecting this onto God. Hope and comfort can be found in humanism, rather than transferring all of our meaning and purpose onto a divine being.

Guilt

The NT's focus on Jesus' sacrifice for the forgiveness of the sins of humanity (arguably as a result of Eve's actions in the Garden of Eden) could encourage a collective guilt and a view that the whole of humankind is fallen. This negative and debasing outlook could give way to an obsession with suffering, sacrifice and sin.

NO

Hope and comfort

Some would argue that Christianity actually solves social and personal problems. The belief in a divine power and an afterlife may bring comfort to those who have lost loved ones – the comfort that they are in heaven and that death is not the 'end'. As Kelly Kapic points out: 'Not all is good in the world. God, in his sovereignty, has recruited us into his war against darkness and death, and lament brings us back to our dependence on him in that fight. This lament does not undercut divine authority and care but rather beseeches the presence and comfort of God into the most wounded parts of our souls' (Kapic, *Embodied Hope: A Theological Meditation on Pain and Suffering*, Inter-Varsity Press, 2017, p. 33).

Here, it is clear that it is God that gives a person motivation to fight against 'darkness and death', so religion can provide the motivation to behave in a moral manner in order to make a difference to the darkness of the secular society, whilst also providing comfort for our pain and distress. Thus, humanity is reclaiming the attributes and values projected onto the divine according to Feuerbach, and living in a 'Christ-like' way.

Jesus' and Christianity's contribution to society

If one focuses on Jesus' portrayal in the NT – one of love, hope and forgiveness – as opposed to the violent, punishing God of the Old Testament, one can see the positive impact this has had throughout history: for example, the Civil Rights Movement, education of the poor and introduction of food banks during recent times of austerity. Also, some have argued that Christianity has not only made a difference to the moral thinking of society, but also influenced art, culture and philosophy. Dawkins himself acknowledges how the cultural richness and value of Christianity has been interwoven within British society, although he sees this value as cultural, not true in the claims Christianity makes.

Humanity not Christianity

Some Christians would argue that issues such as stigmatizing homosexuality and female circumcision are contrary to the teachings of Jesus, who preached agape love and compassion. It is humankind's misinterpretation of religious texts and beliefs that lead to this corruption of predominantly positive Christian teachings. Just because some get it wrong, one should not tar the whole of Christianity with the same brush. Religion cannot be blamed for the mistakes of humanity, and therefore should still play a role within politics and education.

Is secularism an opportunity for Christians?

Many Christians argue that secularism provides an opportunity for Christians. One argument is that it allows them to engage with all aspects of society, as opposed to hiding their beliefs away. Indeed, Archbishop Rowan Williams believes that procedural secularism has been a Christian idea from the start. The earliest Christians saw themselves as living in a secular state and were not opposed to it. Williams states:

> ([Procedural] secularism or secularity poses no real problems to Christians; on the contrary, it is quite arguable that the phenomenon of the Christian church itself is responsible for the distinction between communities that think of themselves as existing by licence of a sacred power, on the one hand, and political communities on the other. Early Christianity demystified the authority of the Empire and thus introduced a highly complicating factor into European political life – the idea of two distinct kinds of public loyalty, one of which may turn out to be more fundamental than the other.
> (Williams, *Faith in the Public Square*, Bloomsbury Continuum, 2015, p. 3)

Here, he points out that early Christians were living with both religious laws and state laws, so this debate about religion vs state is nothing new. Williams argues that procedural secularisation means Christians can be open about their religion and challenge the dangerous assumptions of programmatic secularisation. This also provides Christians room to evangelize and spread the word of God whilst also recognizing the authority of the State.

Also, secularisation has led to the emergence of newer Christian-rooted religions, such as the Unitarian Universalists, who hold commitments to intellectual freedom and religious pluralism. In *A Chosen Faith*, John Buehrens states followers to be:

> Neither a chosen people nor a people whose choices are made for them by theological authorities – ancient or otherwise. We are a people who choose. Ours is a faith whose authority is grounded in contemporary experience, not ancient revelation. Though we find ourselves naturally drawn to the teachings of our adopted religious forebears, these teachings echo with new insights, insights of our own.
> (Buehrens, *A Chosen Faith: An Introduction to Unitarian Universalism*, Beacon Press, 1998, p. 11)

Whilst some may argue that they have abandoned fundamental Christian beliefs, many argue that Christianity has held on to far too many outdated beliefs that defy modern thinking, and that this social reform is exactly what the Church needs.

Others may view this idea as opposed to Christianity, and indeed believe that secularisation does not provide any opportunity for Christianity. In *The Death of Christian Britain*, Callum Brown states:

> It took several centuries (in what historians used to call The Dark Ages) to convert Britain to Christianity, but it has taken less than forty years for the country to forsake it. For a thousand years, Christianity penetrated deeply into the lives of the people, enduring Reformation, Enlightenment and industrial revolution by adapting to each new social and cultural context that arose. Then, really quite suddenly in 1963, something very profound ruptured the character of the nation and its people, sending organised Christianity on a downward spiral to the margins of social significance. In unprecedented numbers, the British people since the 1960s have stopped going to church, have allowed their church membership to lapse, have stopped marrying in church and have neglected to baptise their children.
> (Brown, *The Death of Christian Britain*, p. 1)

In an increasingly secular world, some may argue that it is the right time to stand up and make Christianity heard again, as opposed to re-branding the truths to adapt to the changing, secular society. Although *Redemptoris missio* (Pope John Paul II's letter on the urgency and necessity for missionary activities and endeavours in the world, in order to spread the word of God) appreciates the need to respect other religions and worldviews, it highlights the fact that Christians should be proud of their religion and must speak out to ensure their beliefs are not relativized.

Many also see the secularisation of society as posing the danger of Christianity being sidelined and replaced by materialism and **capitalism**. In a 1995 survey of 7,000 people in 6 countries, 88 per cent of people questioned could name the Shell and McDonald's trademark, with only 54 per cent recognizing the Christian cross (www.marketingweek.com/mcdonalds-bigger-than-jesus-christ). This led to a Ronald McDonald Crucifixion parody causing uproar amongst Christians. The statue, which portrays Ronald McDonald on the cross, was intended to represent what many people view as a cult-like worship of capitalism (www.abc.net.au/news/2019-01-15/ronald-mcdonald-mcjesus-statue-sparks-protests-in-israel/10715544). In 2013, it was claimed that Ronald McDonald was the most recognized name among young people

Capitalism: The idea that society works best in a free-market economy

in the USA, and that they recognized that name before they recognized their own. It was further stated that, although there are approximately nineteen churches to every McDonald's restaurant, the latter has a much greater influence on young people (philcooke.com, 26 Feb. 2013: 'McDonalds: More Influence than Christianity?').

FURTHER READING

Callum G. Brown, *The Death of Christian Britain*. 2nd edn. Christianity and Society in the Modern World. Routledge, 2009

Callum G. Brown and Michael Snape, *Secularisation in the Christian World*. Routledge, 2016

S. J. D. Green, *The Passing of Protestant England: Secularisation and Social Change, c.1920–1960*. Cambridge University Press, 2012

Hugh Mcleod, *Secularisation in Western Europe, 1848–1914*. Palgrave, 2000

Matthew Sharpe, *Secularisations and their Debates: Perspectives on the Return of Religion in the Contemporary West*. Sophia Studies in Cross-cultural Philosophy of Traditions and Cultures. Springer Press, 2016

Bryan S. Turner, *Religion and Modern Society: Citizenship, Secularisation and the State*. Cambridge University Press, 2011

E. K. Wilson, *After Secularism: Rethinking Religion in Global Politics*. Palgrave, 2011

Thought Points

1. 'We live happier, more just, lives without the superstition of religion. Religion can be perceived as dangerous or harmful to civilized society.' Discuss this statement.

2. Richard Dawkins believes that teaching children about religions is wrong. To what extent might you disagree with him?

3. 'The Christian family does not exist.' Discuss.

4. To what extent is it possible to define humanism as a religion?

5. 'As long as Christianity grounds its belief in a patriarchal tradition, it cannot be ethical.' To what extent do you agree with Daphne Hampson's statement?

6. 'All of Christianity's beliefs are outdated and should be regarded as useless.' To what extent do you agree with this statement?

7. 'Since the 1960s, British people have forsaken the Christian church.' Make a list of reasons why this statement might be true.

CHAPTER 12
Liberation Theology and Marx

LEARNING OUTCOMES
In this chapter, you will be learning about
- the relationship between Liberation theology and Karl Marx:
  - Marx's teaching on alienation and exploitation
  - Liberation theology's use of Marx to analyse social sin
  - Liberation theology's teaching on the 'preferential option for the poor'

What is Liberation theology?

Liberation theology is a twentieth-century development in Christian thought and action that arose in South America. It began when a number of Latin American theologians committed themselves to what they believed to be the Gospel imperative to bring social justice and political freedom to the poor. This imperative was based not only on biblical teaching but also on political writings, especially those of **Karl Marx** (1818–83) and his idea of **alienation**.

In the colonial days of the seventeenth, eighteenth and nineteenth centuries, Christian evangelists and missionaries in South America, such as **Bartolomé de Las Casas** (c.1484–1566) and **Antonio Vieira** (1608–97), preached that the indigenous populations were treated badly by the political powers. These criticisms had little force until the 1960s, when, in a wave of religious renewal, many lay people and clergy took their social responsibilities seriously and became committed to working with and for the poor and oppressed. Many of the priests and missionaries working with the poor populations of South America found that the doctrinal theology they had

Alienation:
This happens when a person is treated as an object rather than as a valued individual

learned from the Catholic church was not relevant for their situation. This theology was all about Church teaching, but had little relevance for the physical and spiritual needs of the many people living in the slums of South American cities.

Young Roman Catholic theologians such as **Juan Segundo** (1925–96) and Gustavo Gutierrez began to think in terms of practical theology (**orthopraxis**), rather than just teaching the doctrines (**orthodoxy**) of the Church. Their emphasis began to focus on the practical needs of the poor people. Gutierrez, arguably the founder of Liberation theology, identified its origin in the 'premature and unjust death of many people'. The crucial shift was pointed out by Gutierrez in his 1983 book *The Power of the Poor*: 'The question in Latin America will not be how to speak of God in a world come of age, but rather how to proclaim God as Father in a world that is inhuman. What can it mean to tell a non-person that he or she is God's child?' (Gutierrez, *The Power of the Poor*, SCM Press, 1983, p. 57).

Another Liberation theologian, **Jon Sobrino** (1938–present), a Protestant, spoke out against the European traditional church's emphasis on 'explaining' faith and reflecting on the 'truths' that appear in the Bible. Sobrino argued that this approach risked irrelevance in the Latin American context and achieved little for the liberationist struggle to survive. Many Latin American Christians were very poor and were being oppressed by the rich. For centuries, the Church had supported the wealthy and powerful minority of the community, rather than caring for the poor. Simply repeating traditional doctrine was of no practical value to the poor; action was necessary if they were to be supported in a Christian way. Sobrino argued that doctrine and faith must be supported by practical discipleship.

In the 1960s, the Christian Church in Latin America was approximately 90 per cent Roman Catholic, and made up approximately 40 per cent of the world's population. Many Christian theologians had spoken out against the military dictatorships that wielded political control. Two of these theologians were Camilo Torres Restrepo and **Oscar Romero** (1917–80).

Camilo Torres Restrepo was a radical thinker and was often pictured with a gun. He was a priest in Colombia and had been influenced by the Marxist idea that social change through slow

> **Orthopraxis:**
> The practical expression of church teaching needed to bring aid and liberation to the poor and oppressed

> **Orthodoxy:**
> The official teaching of a religious group

Oscar Romero was a leading figure in Liberation Theology in El Salvador. He was assassinated during Mass in 1980

political means would not work, so the people must become revolutionaries. Torres Restrepo was shot and killed in a battle and became a martyr. He believed that political and military revolution was the only option to bring about social change for the many poor people in Colombia.

Oscar Romero was a Jesuit priest who became Archbishop of El Salvador. His weekly radio programme became very important for the Christian population. This was the most listened-to radio programme in the country, and people saw Romero as a reliable political commentator. He began to speak out against the political hierarchy, as he believed them to be cruel and unjust towards the ordinary people. Romero died in 1980 and was canonized by Pope Francis on 14 October 2018.

Use of biblical teaching

> **Preferential option for the poor:** Liberation theology's catch-phrase for their principal aim of giving practical help to those in society who need it the most

Liberation theologians wished to look carefully at what the Bible had to say about the injustices inflicted on the poor in Latin America. They argued that the Bible supports the **preferential option for the poor**.

One of the key biblical passages is the story of the Exodus of the Hebrews from Egypt. The Hebrews had been slaves for many years, downtrodden by their Egyptian masters, and forced to work long hours in very difficult circumstances for little or no reward. Their story of oppression rang true for Liberation theologians such as Gutierrez. He believed that liberation takes place in two stages. First, there has to be social and economic action before it can come about. In the Exodus story, Moses, the leader of the Hebrews, petitioned the Pharaoh to let the people go free because they had been oppressed for too long and their God was demanding their freedom. The Hebrews were desperately in need of liberation. They believed that their God had the power to deliver them from oppression and poverty and give them a land of their own. Egypt was, at the time, one of the most powerful nations in the world, just as the wealthy landowners of South America were powerful. For Liberation theologians, Moses was both a religious and political leader, and this is why they understood the Exodus story as a model for their wishes and desires for the oppressed people of South America. They saw their own situation mirrored in this foundational biblical story. This central event in early Jewish history was understood by the Liberation theologians as the precursor of an urgent and necessary transformation in the lives of many millions of people in Latin America in the present time.

The theological roots of Liberation theology

Gustavo Gutierrez understood the symbolic meaning of the Exodus story to be the deepest meaning of the Bible's revelation and as a paradigm for interpreting the whole Bible. He laid out a theological vision grounded in the Bible, in which history must be read through the joint lenses of redemption and liberation.

The biblical God heard the cries of Israel (Exodus 3:7,9) and led them out of Egypt through the wilderness to the promised land. They knew that the journey would be filled with problems, but that God would help them to solve them. It would take a long time, but they knew that God would lead them to freedom. Their freedom would be a symbol of God's power, justice and favour for his people. The same favour would be shown to the poor and oppressed people of Latin America.

The Council of Latin American Bishops at Medellín, Colombia, in 1968, spoke of how God sent his only son Jesus to liberate all people from the slavery of hunger, misery, oppression and ignorance. They spoke also of how the 'preferential option for the poor' could already be seen in the Prophets of the Old Testament (for example, Isaiah 1:17, Amos 8, Micah 6:8 and 7:2–3), and also in Jesus' teaching about the kingdom of heaven on earth for those on the margins of society. His parable of the sheep and goats in Matthew 25 judges disciples on the basis of 'what you do for the least of these my brothers'. Good news for the poor is heard throughout the Bible in its consistent teaching about poverty and justice (e.g. Leviticus 19:15), and in Jesus' teaching on the dangers of wealth (e.g. Matt. 5:3, 6:1–4, 25:31–46, Luke 1:46–56, 4:16–20).

Theological motivation for the preferential option for the poor

In their book *Introducing Liberation Theology* (pp. 44–6), summarized by M. Wilcockson (*Christian Theology*, Hodder Education, 2011, p. 108), the brothers Leonardo and **Clodovis Boff** (1944–present) outlined five theological motivations to justify a preferential option for the poor:

(a) *Theological motivation*: the God of the Bible is alive and immanent in the world, involved in human history. God hears the cry of his people (Ex. 3:7) and seeks justice for them. When the Church imitates God, it must hear the cry of the poor and seek justice on their behalf.
(b) *Christological motivation*: Jesus sided with the poor and acted in solidarity with those who had been marginalized by society.
(c) *Eschatological motivation*: God's judgement of the world will be based on whether a person has sided with the poor, according to Jesus' parable of judgement (Matt. 25:31–46).
(d) *Apostolic motivation*: after Jesus' death, the first apostles organized a general levy on all Christian groups to raise money for the poor. They did not distinguish between Christian and non-Christian poor.
(e) *Ecclesiological motivation*: all Christian members of the Church should, as a matter of faith and commitment, seek the transformation of society.

> **Exercise**
> Draw two columns, labelling one 'Bible' and the other 'Liberation theology'. Fill one column with the key ideas from the Bible, and link them with the relevant ideas from Liberation theology in the other column.

The preferential option for the poor

The third meeting of the leading Liberation theologians took place in the Mexican state of Puebla in 1979. It was at this meeting that Gutierrez' phrase 'the preferential option for the poor' was established as the key phrase for the Liberation theologians to rally round and to focus their purpose as a group. It was aimed not at the poor themselves, but at all Christians who were in a position to help the disadvantaged, poor and oppressed in Latin America. It applied primarily to church leaders and teachers, and others who were not poor. These were people who could not only show solidarity with the poor, but had the means and influence to produce practical help for them. In a way, the key term in the phrase is 'option'. This meant that the privileged could 'choose' to show solidarity with the poor, but also become 'poor' with them, in the sense that they could cast off any sense of their own superiority or arrogance. If successful, the result for the Church was that it could become 'radically egalitarian', which was what the message of Jesus had been about: 'We affirm the need for conversion on the part of the whole church to a preferential option for the poor, an option aimed at their integral integration' (Puebla Final Document, point 1134).

Daniel L. Migliore notes:

> For Latin American liberation theologians, knowledge of Christ is inseparably linked to following Christ. Faith affirmations and Christian praxis are inseparable. We will never rightly understand Christ or his proclamation, ministry, death, and resurrection until we find ourselves where he placed himself – in the company of those who are afflicted and unjustly treated and who cry out for the justice and freedom that they have lost or never known. Sobrino argues that 'the only way to get to know Jesus is to follow after him in one's own life; to try to identify oneself with his own historical concerns; and to try to fashion his kingdom in our midst. In other words, only through Christian praxis is it possible for us to draw close to Jesus. Following Jesus is the precondition for knowing Jesus.'
>
> (*Faith Seeking Understanding: An Introduction to Christian Theology*, Eerdmans, 2014, p. 203)

> **Exercise**
>
> In Luke 4:18, Jesus announced a kingdom that meant 'good news to the poor' and 'freedom for the prisoners', and to 'set the oppressed people free'.
> Explain what you think this means and how it relates to Liberation theology.

The Mexican Liberation theologian **José Porfirio Miranda** (1924–2001) used the Bible to highlight the inadequacies of Marx's view. He accepts Marx's analysis that social injustice is located in the control of the means of production and private property. Yet the failure of Marx's historical materialism lay in its underestimation of sin and idolatry within humans. Materialism offers a shallow account of why greed, self-deception and the love of 'mammon' (material possessions and wealth) leave humanity without any understanding of God's gift of life and the natural resources to be found in the environment.

Another example of how the teaching of the Bible has been used by Liberation theologians is seen in the life and work of Jon Sobrino. He spent over fifty years teaching and ministering amidst the violence and bloodshed in El Salvador. He survived an assassination attempt in November 1989 when members of the Salvadorian military broke into the rectory and murdered six of his fellow priests.

The influence of Karl Marx on Liberation theology

> **Karl Heinrich Marx (1818–1883)** Marx was born into the family of a successful Jewish lawyer in Trier, Germany. He studied Law in Bonn and Berlin, but became increasingly interested in the philosophical ideas of Hegel and Feuerbach. He was awarded a doctorate in Philosophy at Jena University in 1841. He moved to Paris in 1843, where he became a revolutionary communist and came under the influence of Friedrich Engels (1820–95). The two lifelong friends were expelled from France and moved to Brussels, where they published their pamphlet *The Communist Manifesto* in 1848. This argued that all of human history was based on struggles between the classes, but that eventually the struggle would disappear when the **proletariat** were successful. In 1849, Marx moved to London, where he spent the rest of his life. Gradually, he wrote his most significant work, *Das Kapital*. Only the first volume of this work was published in his lifetime, but his friend Engels edited and published the other volumes. Marx did not live to see his ideas come to fruition, but he had a huge effect on political, economic and philosophical ideas that continues to the present day.

Proletariat: Marx's term for the workers who are alienated from production because they have no ownership

Marx's teaching on alienation and exploitation

Marx taught that everything in the world is governed by material forces. There is nothing 'spiritual' or 'other-worldly' in Marx's worldview. Human beings are part of the physical world and can affect it – for instance, by taking materials such as trees and minerals from the earth and transforming them into objects or substances that are useful to humans. They are also limited by the material world, however, and so are essentially powerless in the face of nature 'red in tooth and claw'. Climate change, earthquakes and tsunamis are frightening events, and people feel anxious because they cannot stop them from happening and harming or killing many thousands of people. People do not feel in control of the world because of their lack of understanding of how it works.

Marx had a **dialectical view of history**. He borrowed Hegel's view that the world is progressing through a series of stages to achieve a more complete view of itself. Systems replace one another by challenging, and being challenged by, their opposite. Marx agreed that each system would be challenged and replaced, but, whereas Hegel had proposed a philosophical basis for this, Marx believed that the basis was economic. His view is now generally known as **historical materialism**.

Marx believed that all economic systems are essentially flawed because they contain different classes of people. This mix will ultimately lead to problems

Dialectical view of history: The Marxist view that the world operates through conflict, then resolution, then conflict, and so on

Historical materialism: A Marxist theory that describes and analyses historical processes that develop by way of conflict, then harmony, then conflict, and so on

- SLAVERY
- FEUDALISM
- CAPITALISM

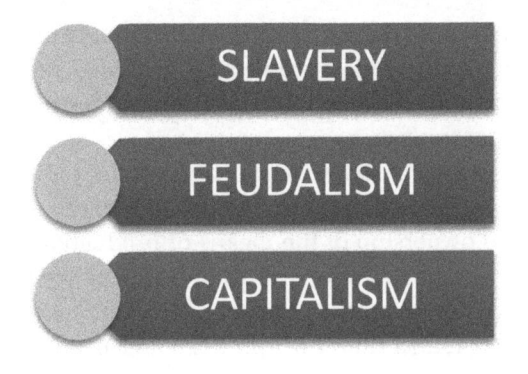

in the society, which will over time cause dissension. At some point, one group, almost always the 'lowest' in society, will challenge the economic set-up and suggest a new one. This will cause discontent in the society, with some wanting to retain the status quo and others wishing to embrace the new system. Eventually, a compromise will be reached and a new way of existing as a society will emerge and be followed.

Marx referred to this process as thesis, antithesis and synthesis. One example that Marx discusses is that of slavery.

Slavery was based on the idea that one class / race / economic status of people was superior to another. It was eventually replaced by feudalism, and this by capitalism. This was a positive progression for Marx, as the slaves were paid for their work, and workers in a capitalist system could, to some extent, choose their employer. To a large extent, however, the workers in a capitalist system (the proletariat) were still exploited by the wealthy minority (the bourgeoisie).

Alienation

Marx said that this exploitation alienated the working class from society. They felt detached from decision-making, powerless and anxious about the future.

> **Exercise**
> Think of examples of people or groups who may feel alienated from their society and discuss possible reasons for this. You might want to begin with minority groups.

Marx believed that human beings created alienation. For him, material forces determine everything that happens in the world. Human actions contribute to the state of the world, and are also affected by it. Marx wanted to know why society became unstable. He observed that there had been times in history when societies had worked well, noticeably when no sector of society was being exploited. These were times when new ideas and new ways of doing things emerged. Society started to disintegrate, however, when surplus foods and other products were created. This showed people that some had more than others, and jealousy created disputes between different societal groups. Class divisions became evident and created disputes over land, housing, families and products. As Marx said: 'In feudal landownership we already find the domination of the earth as of an alien power over men. The serf is an appurtenance of the land. Similarly the heir through primogeniture, the first-born son, belongs to the land. It inherits him. The rule of private property begins with property in land which is its basis' (Karl Marx, *Early Writings* [1833–4], Penguin, 2000, p. 318).

Because the serfs (workers) do not own the land they work, and are dependent on the lords (owners) for it, they must sacrifice some of their produce to the lords. This means that they are alienated from the land and, because of this, they feel undervalued and degraded. They become objects, not subjects.

Marx discussed several difficulties with society in relation to alienation and exploitation. The advent of capitalism was, in Marx's view, a turning point for society. It changed the dynamic between people and ownership of the means of production. In previous societies, the worker had at least some control over what was produced – food, other goods. In a capitalist society, however, that control was taken away because the workers did not have the right to sell their own produce and make a profit. They were forced to pool their produce along with that of others. They were powerless to determine the price of their goods or to whom they were sold. They lost control of all this and became 'an appendage of the machine' (*The Communist Manifesto*, ch.1). Individuals were not able to make decisions about what crops to grow. In factories, workers could not make suggestions about what to produce – they just did what they were told. They became alienated from their work and developed very negative feelings about their employers, the place of work and the products. In a factory, any worker only saw one part of the finished product, so he had only a partial understanding of how his labour made a contribution to the whole enterprise. Workers (the proletariat) became dehumanized and felt unfulfilled and exploited by the owners (the bourgeoisie).

Marx also observed that the proletariat had sometimes revolted against their bourgeois overlords to attempt to gain their freedom. Marx predicted a class struggle between the workers and the other groups in society. If a fair society for all was to be made a reality, there must be a violent reaction by the workers against the ruling classes. Only then would exploitation of the workers cease.

Marx criticized the role of religion in society as one of the most important causes of alienation. He wanted to get rid of religion altogether because it was so harmful to everyone in society. He rejected God's existence – 'religion is the **opium of the people**'. (The full passage is: 'Religion is the sigh of the oppressed creature, the heart of a heartless world, and the soul of soulless conditions. It is the opium of the people' – *A Contribution to Hegel's Philosophy of Right*, 1844). Many capitalists believed in God's existence and thought that the deity was in control of history, including the idea that God had a plan for all people and what kind of lives they would lead. Marx rejected this idea completely, calling it false-consciousness on the part of religious believers. He declared that the forces of history are blind. To think otherwise only leads to false hopes and disappointment. Marx also declared that religion gives power to the ruling elite to control the

Pie in the sky is what some Christians believe heaven will be like

Opium of the people: Marx's judgement on the harmful role of religion in society

ordinary people, inculcating the doctrine that God ordained some to be rulers to govern the majority of people, who were to be servants. The apparent unfairness of this would be resolved after death, when those who have suffered in this life would be rewarded in heaven.

> **Info**
> You may have heard the phrase 'pie in the sky when you die' used to paraphrase the view above. It comes from a popular song, 'The Preacher and the Slave', composed by Joe Hill in 1911, which parodied a well-known hymn.

Praxis: For Marx, this describes a belief that, because the world is in a constant state of change, people can understand why it changes and alter things for the good of all

One other key idea in Marx's views on alienation and exploitation is **praxis**. This is the ancient Greek word for 'action' or 'practice'. Marx says that this is one of the most important lessons that come from historical materialism. For him, praxis describes a belief that, because the world is in a constant state of change, people can understand the reasons why it changes, and alter them for the good of all people. If there is unemployment or injustice, the causes can be analysed and a change made to improve the situation. Marx famously stated: 'Philosophers have only interpreted the world in various ways; the point is to change it' (Marx, *Theses on Feuerbach XI*, Prometheus Books, 1998).

Liberation theology's use of Marx

Liberation theology arose in Latin America at a time when the very wealthy owned all the land and the vast majority of the population were exploited. The poor saw this situation as an intolerable burden. According to Liberation theologians, the people were alienated from God by their poverty and oppression. The people saw themselves as voiceless pawns in an uncaring capitalist society, working hard to make money not for themselves, but for the already wealthy landowners. The Liberation theologians wanted to restore dignity and self-worth to the poor by providing a mechanism that would give them some control over their own lives and destiny. Engaging with Marxist thought provided some positive ideas and strategies for how to effect change.

Several of the most important Liberation theologians used Marx's views. For example, Leonardo and Clodovis Boff, Jose Miranda and Juan Segundo explicitly discussed how Marx's ideas related to Christian beliefs. Others, such as Gustavo Gutierrez and Jon Sobrino, however, used Marx's ideas more implicitly.

It should be clear that all Liberation theologians rejected Marx's analysis of religion. As we have already seen, Marx taught that religion ('the opium of the people') had a negative effect on people. For him, it made believers acquiesce in the status quo of remaining subservient to the ruling classes, rather than taking matters into their own hands and initiating a revolution to claim back their livelihood and their freedom. Instead, the people believed religious teaching about an idyllic afterlife, when all their worries and suffering would disappear, and they would live happy lives with God forever.

Liberation theologians accepted that the Church had been at fault in the past, because it had not always sided with the poor and oppressed. It had also been guilty of contributing to the oppression of the poor. For example, in many churches, the rich sat at the front, in special seats, separate from the poor; sometimes they received the eucharist separately, with higher-quality wine than was offered to the rest of the congregation.

The birth and development of Liberation theology took place in the context of political and social turmoil in several of the Latin American countries. Marxism was the prevalent political ideology. The Liberation theologians saw an opportunity to use some aspects of this ideology to bring greater understanding of Christianity to the ordinary people. They believed that Marx's analysis was useful because they could use it to move away from traditional theology to a modern restatement of Christianity's key beliefs. Traditional theology had emphasized abstract ideas such as 'sin', 'redemption' and 'salvation'. For the indigenous population, in their situation, these abstract terms meant little. Liberation theologians used Marxist ideas and vocabulary to refocus peoples' understanding of the Christian message in terms of their well-being in the present, not on poorly understood concepts that referred to the future.

None of the Liberation theologians wanted to take over Marxist ideas totally. They thought that using some aspects of Marx's teaching could be useful in refiguring Christian beliefs for the Latin American situation. Selective use of Marx's teaching could be very beneficial for the Christian communities in that part of the world. There was not a uniform approach among Liberation theologians in their use of Marxist teaching. Some used it explicitly, while others used it only for their analysis of the economic situation. Others used it more radically to reinterpret some fundamental Christian beliefs. As Leonardo and Clodovis Boff wrote:

> Therefore [Liberation theology] uses Marxism purely as an instrument, it does not venerate it as it venerates the gospel. And it feels no obligation to account to social scientists for any use it may make – correct or otherwise – of Marxist terminology and ideas, though it does feel obliged to account to the poor . . . Marx (like any other Marxist) can be a companion on the way, but he can never be the guide, because 'you only have one teacher, the Christ' (Matt. 23:10).
>
> (Boff and Boff, *Introducing Liberation Theology*, p. 28)

Another leading Liberation theologian, Gustavo Gutierrez, found Marx's ideas of alienation and exploitation useful, and also the idea that humans have the power to change the world they live in. The poor of Latin America, Gutierrez said, had a deep-seated longing to be free from the strangulating burden of capitalism. Christians, he says, have to stand up and be counted alongside those who were being oppressed: 'In Latin America, to be the Church today means to take a clear position regarding both the present state of social injustice and the revolutionary process which is attempting to abolish that injustice and build a more human order' (Gutierrez, *A Theology of Liberation*, p. 265).

Gutierrez believed that it is impossible for a Christian not to get involved in politics, for not to do so would effectively be a vote in favour of Marxism. It is the sacred duty of every individual Christian, and of all churches in Latin America, to denounce every situation that would result in injustice. The Church must speak out against alienation and exploitation. Orthopraxy (doing the right thing) must always come before orthodoxy (believing the right thing). Liberation theology is about having an active faith, not a passive one. The official doctrines of the Church must come second to helping needy people in their own situation.

Another influential Liberation theologian, José Porfirio Miranda, used Marx's dislike of ownership of private property as the foundation of his version of Liberation theology. Marx taught that ownership of property led to injustice, because it made the owners think they could treat the workers on their land as objects, not as subjects. Marx wrote in the first *Theses on Feuerbach* that, when people objectify the world, they treat it as their own possession, and this causes suffering for other people.

Miranda linked Marx's teaching here with an idea that is central to the Bible's teaching: that Jesus preached his message not to the wealthy, but to the oppressed, the poor and suffering. For Miranda, it was essential that Christians should be taking this message to the poor and needy in Latin America.

Miranda spoke of how this Christian message is more important and more powerful than Marxist ideology. Marx had taught that the oppression of the poor was the result of economic forces. Miranda counters this by affirming that the Bible gives a more complete analysis of human nature and reasons why humans oppress others. Miranda also states that Marx gives an inadequate account of how private ownership develops. Miranda refers to the second Commandment, against idolatry: 'You shall not make for yourself an image in the form of anything in heaven above or on the earth beneath or in the waters below. You shall not bow down to them or worship them' (Ex. 20:4–5 NIV).

For Miranda, this means that, if people do not treat God with the respect he deserves, they will fall into 'idolatry'. The Western world has done this for centuries because they have taken capitalism and imperialism as their gods instead.

Variation among Liberation theologians' use of Marx

While all Liberation theologians are aware of the influence and importance of Marxism, there have been differences of opinion about the extent to which Marx's ideas should be engaged with. Some, such as brothers Leonardo and Clodovis Boff, José Miguez Bonino and José Miranda, used Marxist ideas in an explicit way as a tool to analyse the problems experienced by the poor communities in Latin America. Others, such as Gustavo Gutierrez and Jon Sobrino, take a much more cautious approach in their use of Marxist ideas. Gutierrez consistently made it very clear that Christianity and Marxism could not be combined, even though they shared some common elements.

> **Info**
> Shortly after being elected in March 2013, Pope Francis rejected accusations from right-wing Americans that his teaching is Marxist, defending his criticisms of the capitalist system and urging more attention be given to the poor. The Argentinian pontiff said the views he had expressed in his first apostolic exhortation in November 2013 were simply those of the Church's social doctrine.
>
> He said that 'the ideology of Marxism is wrong. But I have met many Marxists in my life who are good people.'

CHALLENGES

Too much interaction with Marxism

Cardinal Ratzinger (1927–present), later to become Pope Benedict XVI, held the position of Cardinal-Prefect of the Congregation for the Doctrine of the Faith, a role formerly known as the Roman Inquisition. His primary remit was to ensure that Roman Catholic doctrine was upheld around the world, and to censure anyone who spoke or acted against church doctrine. In 1984, he summoned Leonardo Boff, a professor of Systematic Theology and Philosophy at Petropolis, Brazil, to Rome, and imposed an official order of silence on him and a suspension of a year, because of Boff's 1981 book, *Church, Charism and Power*, in which he had used Marxist ideas in a way that 'endangered the sound doctrine of the faith' (Congregation for the Doctrine of the Faith, 'Notification on the book "Church: Charism and Power" by Father Leonardo Boff O.F.M.').

In the 1990s, Boff left the priesthood so that he could continue to write freely concerning Liberation theology and other important issues, such as ecology.

Cardinal Ratzinger used his judgement on Boff to make a considered analysis and condemnation of Marxism and of the use of Marxist ideology by Liberation theologians. Ratzinger's document ('Instruction on Certain Aspects of the Theology of Liberation') begins with positive discussion of 'theologies of liberation'. He understands 'liberation' to mean justice for the weak in society, but becomes highly critical of 'certain forms of liberation theology which use, in an insufficiently critical manner, concepts borrowed from various currents of Marxist thought'.

The 'Instruction' was generally supportive of the idea of 'liberation' itself, but criticized the way Liberation theologians had narrowed its use in several important ways:

- Liberation theologians are very selective about which ideas they take from Marxism. This is a dangerous precedent
- The idea of liberation is at the heart of Christianity, but this does not mean focusing

Karl Marx argued that religion was 'the opium of the people'

on economic means of bringing it about – rather, it is about a spiritual liberation from sin
- Liberation theologians focus only on political freedom, but there are many other kinds of freedom that should be included in the discussion
- Liberation theologians interpret sin in social and political terms, but this diminishes the part that God's grace plays in salvation
- Oscar Romero criticized Liberation theologians who taught about practical liberation. Romero argued that spiritual liberation must precede liberation in practice

Too little interaction with Marxism

In his book *Marx and the Failure of Liberation Theology* (SCM Press, 1990), British theologian **Alistair Kee** (1937–2011) criticized both the Vatican's view and that of many Liberation theologians. In his view, the Vatican was almost entirely wrong to claim that Liberation theologians had been insufficiently critical in their use of Marx. He criticized the Liberation theologians because they had been highly selective in their use of Marx, using only the parts of his economic analysis that helped their project. In essence, Kee argues that Liberation theology has been too timid in its analysis of Marxism. Marx developed a radical analysis of society that could have helped the Liberation theologians if they had been open to engaging with it wholeheartedly, rather than only selecting the elements they wanted.

Liberation theology's teaching on 'The preferential option for the poor'

One of the most significant ideas developed by Liberation theologians was the 'preferential option for the poor'. The beginnings of this idea may be seen in discussions that took place during Vatican II, when bishops and archbishops from around the world assembled in an attempt to inject energy and drive into the Church. Discussions were centred on the Bible as the ultimate source of authority in Christianity. One group of attendees, led by the Brazilian Bishop (later Archbishop) **Helder Camara** (1909–99), met in secret in the catacombs of Rome, where Christians had been martyred in the early years of Christianity. They agreed on thirteen points that encouraged priests to live a life of evangelical poverty, i.e. to live simply, as Jesus had done, and to identify with the poor, rather than with the wealthy landowners and politicians. As early as 1936, Camara had begun to talk of the 'unjust structures of poverty'. He said that the Church needed to work not just for the people, but *with* the people. He wrote: 'When you live with the poor, you realise that, even though they cannot read or write, they certainly know how to think.' These ideas played an important role in the later formulation of Liberation theology.

When, in 1968, Camara was made Bishop of Orinda and Recife in Brazil, he helped to organize a historic meeting of Latin American bishops at Medellín in Colombia. The bishops openly decided to reject the Roman Catholic church's historic support of the rich and powerful, and make a 'preferential option for the poor'. They publicly identified themselves with the poor and downtrodden of society. This was a huge victory for the Liberation theologians, because the decision was put into practice in most Latin American countries. One statement from the meeting proclaimed: 'Justice is a prerequisite for peace . . . in many instances Latin America finds itself faced with a situation of injustice that can be called institutionalised violence . . . We should not be surprised, therefore, that the "temptation to violence" is surfacing in Latin America' (Daniel C. Hellinger, *Contemporary Politics of Latin America: Democracy at Last?* Routledge, 2015, p. 71).

> **Info**
> Archbishop Camara was a great storyteller. One anecdote he recounted with great glee concerned Mother Teresa. When she asked him how he managed to retain his humility, Camara replied that he had just to imagine himself making a triumphant entry into Jerusalem, not as Jesus but as the donkey who carried him. Years later Mother Teresa reminded Camara of this conversation, saying that she had adapted his advice to Indian conditions by thinking of herself serving God as an old cow.
> (Obituary for Archbishop Helder Camara, *The Independent*, 2 September 1999)

José Porfirio Miranda explicitly used Marx's suspicion of and antagonism towards private ownership as the basis of his writings on Liberation theology. He argues that the fall of human nature and sin account for why people exploit each other, and that idolatry of capitalism rather than belief in God has led to oppression within society.

Stretch and challenge: Black Liberation theology

Liberation theology in Latin America became very successful in achieving its aims of bringing justice to the poor and oppressed of that part of the world. It is important to note, however, that Latin America was not the only part of the world where liberation from oppression was something that had to be fought for. **James H. Cone** (1938–2018) was a central figure in the development of Black Liberation theology in the USA in the 1960s and 1970s. He was a professor at Union Theological Seminary in New York City for many years. As **Martin Luther King Jr** (1929–68) had done in Georgia and other southern states, Cone argued that racial justice had to be achieved, and that an understanding of the Christian message would ensure that the voices of the oppressed were heard.

Dr Cone was an academic theologian, minister and author. He described Black Liberation theology as 'an interpretation of the Christian Gospel from the experiences, perspectives and lives of people who are at the bottom in society – the lowest economic and racial groups'. Cone himself had experienced the intense racial segregation of the 1940s and 1950s, when he was growing up in the racially segregated town of Bearden, Arkansas. He said: 'Christianity was seen as the white man's religion. I wanted to say: "No! The Christian Gospel is not the white man's religion. It is a religion of liberation, a religion that says God created all people to be free." But

I realized that for black people to be free, they must first love their blackness' (*New York Times*, Obituaries, 29 April 2018: 'James H. Cone, a Founder of Black Liberation Theology, Dies at 79').

Cone's definition of Black theology was: 'Black theology, therefore, is that theology which arises out of the need to articulate the religious significance of [the] black presence in a hostile White world. It is Black people reflecting on the Black experience under the guidance of the Holy Spirit, attempting to redefine the relevance of the Christian gospel for their lives' (*The Cambridge Companion to Liberation Theology*, p. 81).

He spoke forcefully about racial inequalities that persisted in the form of economic injustice, mass incarceration and police shootings: 'White supremacy is America's original sin and liberation is the Bible's central message. Any theology in America that fails to engage white supremacy and God's liberation of black people from that evil is not Christian theology but a theology of the Antichrist' (Cone, *Said I Wasn't Gonna Tell Nobody: The Making of a Black Theologian*, p. 54).

His first book, *Black Theology and Black Power* (1969), is thought of as the founding text of Black Liberation theology. Cone wrote that he had 'wanted to speak on behalf of the voiceless black masses in the name of Jesus, whose Gospel I believed had been greatly distorted by the preaching theology of white churches' (*Black Theology and Black Power*, p. 22). In this book, he challenged the dominant white theological norm. Cone laid out his specific argument for God's radical identification with black people in the United States. He described Black Liberation theology as a belief that God is concerned with the poorest and weakest members of society. In most cases, Cone said, those people were black. He said that doing Black theology was to understand the Christian Gospel as seeking justice for the poor, believing that God is active in the world, freeing Black Americans from exploitation and slavery and leading them to freedom.

Cone often said that Malcolm X and the Revd Martin Luther King Jr were his main sources of lasting influence and inspiration. Malcolm X, although he was an atheist, gave Cone's Black theology its black identity. Martin Luther King gave Black theology its Christian identity. These two sources allowed Cone to give structure to his thoughts and actions.

FURTHER READING

Lillian Calles Berger, *The World Come of Age: An Intellectual History of Liberation Theology*. Oxford University Press, 2018

Leonardo Boff, *Church: Charism and Power – Liberation Theology and the Institutional Church*. Orbis Books, 2011

Leonardo Boff and Clodovis Boff, *Introducing Liberation Theology*. Orbis Books, 1987

Robert McAfee Brown, *Gustavo Gutierrez: An Introduction to Liberation Theology*. Wipf and Stock Publishers, 2013

James H. Cone, *Black Theology and Black Power*, 50th Anniversary Edition, intro. Cornel West. Orbis Books, 2019

James H. Cone, *Said I Wasn't Gonna Tell Nobody: The Making of a Black Theologian*. Orbis Books, 2018

Gustavo Gutierrez, *A Theology of Liberation: History, Politics and Salvation*. SCM Press, 1971

Christopher Rowland, *The Cambridge Companion to Liberation Theology*. Cambridge University Press, 2007

Richard D. Wolff, *Understanding Marxism*. lulu.com, 2019

Thought Points

1. Explain and evaluate the statement: 'No Christian could ever accept Marxist philosophy.'

2. 'Liberation theology was useful in a Latin American context, but would never work anywhere else.' Discuss.

3. 'Liberation theologians engaged too much with Marxist philosophy.' Critically evaluate this statement.

4. 'The "preferential option for the poor" was the best idea to come out of Liberation theology.' Discuss.

5. Compare and contrast James Cone's 'Black Liberation theology' with Latin American Liberation theology.

6. 'Liberation theology leads to action: action for justice, the work of love, conversion, renewal of the church, transformation of society.' To what extent do you think that Leonardo Boff's statement was fulfilled?

7. 'Jesus preached peace and love, so Christians should never use violence, whatever the cause.' Discuss.

Study Skills and Assessment

A Level is a step up from GCSEs and the essay-writing at its heart calls for a range of skills and techniques as well as fluency in your style. Mastering technical terms, providing examples and having a good grasp of the strengths and weaknesses of theories are all part of the mature essayist's work. In short, taking the mystery out of exam success is our aim in this section.

Planning lots of skeleton outlines to exam-style questions will help you to take a broad question and focus it down to a relevant and well-crafted argument. Practice trains you to pick examples, provide reasons and select evidence. It also keeps you focused, stops you going off on tangents and avoiding fallacies, and helps you to spot gaps in your revision. Timed essays in class will also train you to allocate minutes in proportion to the marks available and to work out how many paragraphs you can reasonably write in the 2 hours available for planning and writing three essays.

This section will give you a good idea of what examiners are looking for in the answers of top candidates, and it should serve as a guide as you learn to research and plan your essays. Irrelevance and running out of time are two major reasons for under-performance, so essay skills are at the heart of your success in this subject. Making essay plans and structuring them in paragraphs will help to hone your skills as an essay writer. We begin by flagging up some key elements in essay-writing.

Crafting your essay argument

- Interpret the focus of the question, together with any terms or value judgements implicit in it.
- Decide on your thesis (the broad argument you are going to advance, taking into account any qualifications you might offer to the terms of the question – e.g. 'In my assessment, this is not an either–or situation, but a both–and one').
- Weigh up the *extent* to which you agree with any assertion made in the question – is it true of all or some forms? Are you aware of other *perspectives* or *viewpoints* that could be taken?
- Be clear on the counterargument, key reasons and examples opposed to your thesis + evaluation of strengths and weaknesses. Showing your awareness of this increases the credibility of your own position.
- Then set out the reasoning of key thinkers and arguments *for* your thesis and evaluation of their strengths and weaknesses.

- Evaluate arguments and counterarguments and (if you have time) discuss their relative merits.
- Make your personal response explicit, with phrases like 'it is my contention that', or 'in my assessment, there are obvious strengths in Augustine's view of human nature because . . .'
- Summarize the reasons for your concluding judgement.

Dialogue not monologue

Aristotle commented that 'it is a mark of the educated mind to be able to entertain a thought without accepting it'. One of the lessons to learn as you move from GCSE to A Level is that arguments that oppose your own conclusion deserve a fair hearing, and their criticisms of your position require you to respond to them. Avoid setting up straw-men opponents that are easy to demolish. Try to understand the weaknesses of your position and arrive at a well-reasoned and balanced conclusion.

Essential skills and strategies for success

Please note that all comments concerning techniques, strategies and skills necessary for success at AS and A Level are the views of the authors, not of OCR.

Interpretation
    Analysis
        Evaluation
            Personal response

One of the important ways in which AS and A Level differ from GCSE is in the technique for formulating and writing essays. At GCSE, there is much more of a focus on knowledge learning. To some extent, it is possible to prepare answers in advance, remember the information, then write it in the examination. This is a strategy that will definitely not work at AS or A Level.

If you wish to achieve high marks in the essays you write at this level, you will need to learn a number of important new skills and techniques.

Reading and planning your essay

Homework essays are time-consuming and labour-intensive. It is tempting to skim-read in preparation, or even to write them straight off without research and planning. But teachers and examiners can tell apart those students who have taken the time to read and plan their essays from those who have not done so. Reading builds your vocabulary and understanding of concepts. It sharpens your writing style and offers you a wider range of examples. If this all seems too much like hard work, there are lots of good online audio/visual resources to listen to and watch.

Essay strengths

- Your own personal response as you analyse and evaluate arguments and demonstrate independent reasoning and judgement
- Close attention to the wording of questions and key words
- Clear, practical examples and a sound ability to engage critically with theory
- Good grasp of concepts and distinctions, e.g. a clear understanding of theological terms and their range of meaning and contexts
- Achieving a balance between breadth and depth as required by the demands of the question
- Clear logical structure and tightly argued paragraphs that are relevant to the question
- Clear analysis of strengths and weaknesses of rival positions when assessing their merits
- Excellent engagement between theological theory and its implications

Essay weaknesses

- Pre-rehearsed answers that ignore the specific wording of the question. Irrelevance and poor timing are the key reasons why students underperform
- Generalizations – e.g. 'all Christians believe the Bible is literally true' – or lists of ideas without explanation
- Incoherent or long-winded arguments that do not develop the essay thesis from paragraph to paragraph. Your essay should weave the threads of the argument together coherently
- Evaluation left until the conclusion rather than woven throughout the essay in the analysis of strengths and weaknesses
- Confusion or conflation of ideas belonging to two distinct thinkers, e.g. Aquinas and Barth

Elements of essay writing: consider how you can sharpen these in making an informed, coherent and persuasive argument

- A *sentence* is a grammatical structure ending in a full stop. Try to put just one idea into each sentence, to keep it clear and straightforward. This will make it easier for your teacher and examiner to understand and will help you to explain ideas properly.
- A *paragraph* is a collection of sentences grouped around one purpose or theme. Single-sentence or full-page paragraphs sound alarm bells when examiners scan essays because it usually means that you do not fully understand what you are writing about. You should organize your argument into a step-by-step logical sequence.
- To do this, it is best to structure your essay into a series of steps and then to shuffle your paragraphs to find the most logical order for your essay. For example, you might begin with the *weaker position* or the one you disagree with, noting its strengths and the critical questions it raises for the position you wish to advance. You can then follow this with the position you believe to be stronger.
- Every view deserves a *fair hearing*, so do not be too quick to dismiss opposing positions and to assert the strengths of your own view. A critically considered conclusion will carry more credibility.
- *Introduction.* Interpret the question's key words/phrases and set out your broad position in the essay. Unpack the question and set out your thesis point by point.
- Think of essays as *dialogues* between ideas – not monologues or, much worse, rants. Be concise and clear in your structure.
- *Links/transitions* between paragraphs. Avoid a repetitive style. Try to avoid the same stock phrases – your *style* of writing is important.
- *Evidence.* Your general argument needs particular examples, both to illustrate it and to give weight to the reasons. These can take the form of academic authorities who advance a position, or demonstrations of how a theory proves to be more or less workable in practice. Balanced arguments can give you more credibility through your impartial handling of the evidence.
- *Include examples.* These illustrate your essay and develop a more engaging style.
- *Quotations* are important. For each essay topic, learn a few short quotes that will enhance your style by showing a familiarity with primary sources.
- *Paragraphs*
  - *Signposts at the beginning* – This will help the marker get a clear sense of your structure. State your main argument in the opening sentence of the essay.
  - *Intermediate conclusions at the end* – Stay on course with the focus of the question. Recapping what your examples, evidence and reasons have established in a sub-conclusion (one or two sentences) allows you to move the argument forward. You may even take a different course, persuading the reader that, though the initial position had its merits, it was mistaken, inadequate or needed revision.

- ○ *Sub-conclusions* establish shifts in the argument, like switches that move your train onto a new set of tracks.
- *Fluency with technical vocabulary.* Be aware of key vocabulary from glossaries and indexes in the textbook and have a clear idea of trigger words in questions (see below).
- *Scholars, textual sources, statistics.* Be accurate and selective – let the reasoning drive the essay. Evidence and examples ought to make an essay's reasoning more persuasive and engaging. Read textbooks – they will make you more fluent with ideas.
- *Arguments and counterarguments.* These should form a dialogue in your essay. At times this can lead to a layering of a weakness identified, a response, then a further weakness that clinches the argument in favour of one side. If you were asked whether Augustine was more successful than Bonhoeffer in explaining the basis of human nature, for example, you could present strengths and weaknesses separately but also have a paragraph where some dialogue and debate entered into the argument. This layering of reasons and responses creates a dialogue rather than a monologue, and builds more credibility for your evaluative conclusions.
- *Theory summaries – the way to tame the abstract.* Bullet point the key elements of abstract theories in your revision notes and define the meaning(s) of key concepts clearly. Use these concisely in exam essays. Do not ramble because this only shows that you do not know the material well.
- *Conclusion.* This is where you summarize your argument rather than embarking on a new one. Every paragraph in the essay should lead logically to the conclusion.
- *Review your homework essays.* It may seem like a novel idea, but if it is a homework essay, do not hand it in without first re-reading it! When you do this, check it for errors in spelling and grammar. Then ask yourself whether your explanations are clear in their understanding of concepts and theories. Also try to be self-critical about whether you have addressed the question relevantly, reflected a range of perspectives, and structured a well-evidenced argument in the right order. If not, then edit it. It is tempting to think that it is your teacher's job to rewrite your essay for you, but this is not their job – it is yours! You are learning to be an INDEPENDENT thinker, so critical self-review is the way to mature as an essay writer.

Transitional phrases

As mentioned above, one element of becoming a good essay writer is to move from one paragraph to the next in such a way as to lead your reader through the steps in your thought. This avoids repetition, makes your logic clearer and ought to make it more persuasive. Structure, substance and style all help to engage an examiner and make their job easier. Whilst you do not need to have a formal stock of transitional phrases up your sleeve, you do need to work on the style and structure of your homework essays so that you mature as an essay writer, offering a logical progression from one paragraph to another. Below is a list of exemplar phrases that illustrate this process. Be sure, though, to select from, and deploy, your pre-rehearsed material in the right way, so that you address the exact terms of the question presented to you, otherwise you will lose marks.

Scaffolding your essay

To facilitate this, it is useful to have in mind some scaffolding to your essay.

Structure shows through in paragraphing (with signpost sentences at the start, and sub-conclusions at the end).
Interpret the key terms in the question.
Set up the contrasts and comparisons in your mind.
Weave evaluative judgements about strengths and weaknesses into every sub-conclusion of your essay – do not leave it until the final concluding paragraph.

If you find it helpful, here are some examples of transitional phrases to bring your personal response to the forefront of:

- *your opening thesis statement*
- *sub-conclusions at the close of each of your paragraphs*
- *your main conclusion.*

Introductions

The key terms of the question are contested by different philosophical ideas / theologians, and it is my contention that . . .
My thesis in this essay will be that the terms in the question . . .
At the outset of this essay, I wish to clarify the contested terms in the essay title.
Several scholars interpret the phrase 'X' in the essay title differently . . .
With respect to the term 'useful' / 'helpful' / 'successful', I will argue that X theory is, by comparison with Y theory, preferable because . . .
In this essay, I will argue that . . .

Setting out your personal thesis/assessment

I agree with theologian X who makes a strong case for . . .
Personally, I would argue that a weakness of X's theory is that . . .
I find the argument of X more persuasive than that of Y because . . .
In my view, X's example of . . . is a useful starting point for considering the . . .
Although this is a matter of debate, and is certainly unprovable, I would argue that . . . because . . .
I am persuaded by X's more radical approach to this issue because . . .

Regardless of the individual criticisms that can be made of X's proposal, I still think that it holds up under scrutiny.

In my assessment, this theory has the advantage(s) that . . .

In my judgement, X cogently defends the view that . . .

Expressing what you see to be difficulties with a position / positions

In my estimation, X does not properly account for . . .

It may be objected to X's position that . . .

I consider X's position to be indefensible at the point at which . . .

X's assumption that . . . does not, in my judgement, hold up to criticism and is easily disproved.

In applying this theory to the issue at hand, its weaknesses become evident.

Not all arguments presented by X have survived scrutiny . . .

Several problems appear with this position. Firstly . . .

That argument needs to be made cautiously, given the . . .

The argument is undermined by the fact that . . .

A more fruitful line of argument is . . .

A different position / contrasting view

While all of this may be logically valid, I side with the opposing position set out by X . . .

After evaluating the evidence, I would argue that X is correct in asserting that Y was wrong when he insisted that . . .

On the other side of the issue, X contends that . . . and I find her argument persuasive.

As for Y . . . , I am still more persuaded by X's argument.

In my judgement, while this is a strong argument, it ultimately fails because . . .

This may initially sound like a plausible idea, but I would argue that it fails to explain . . .

In contrast, an alternative argument, which, in my opinion, is a stronger one, is put forward by X . . .

Conclusions/summaries

The contrasts and comparative assessment that I have set out lead me to conclude that the position/theory of X is more useful/practical/principled/consistent and rational / ethically robust than that of . . .

In concluding, it has been my contention in this essay that . . .

Despite the counterarguments to my opening thesis, I see no compelling reason to doubt the view that . . .

In summary, I have tried to make a case for . . .

Note-taking throughout the course

As you work through the course, keep brief notes on comparisons and contrasts, similarities and differences, between theories. You need to be conversant with these. Also write down questions you have regarding the material your teacher covers, or that you would ask of theories and thinkers. Bring these up in lessons for discussion. Much of evaluative essay writing involves the requirement to:

- *Compare* common ground between theories and
- *Contrast* distinctive features / contested approaches to practical theological issues to form evidence-based judgements

Evaluate strengths and weaknesses throughout the essay

Strengths	Weaknesses
Reasons + evidence and examples	Reasons + evidence and examples
Similarities	**Differences**
Reasons + evidence and examples	Reasons + evidence and examples

---

Exercise

Select several opinion or editorial articles from quality newspapers, then . . .

1. Ask yourself whether the writer has been fair in assessing different or opposing viewpoints, rather than misrepresenting them (the straw-man fallacy).
2. Highlight key words and phrases from each paragraph to identify the basic outline of the argument.
3. Critically evaluate whether you think other evidence or information about context or more specific examples / case studies are necessary to support the author's argument – are more conclusions made than are justified by the evidence produced?

Be strategic about your planning and preparation

- Think about your style – be concise and target the focus of the question
- Make sure your information is accurate and relevant. Arrive at your concluding judgement(s) only after a balanced comparison of the strengths and weaknesses of theories.
- In preparing revision diagrams on topics, collect as many past-paper questions as possible (here it may even be worth looking up past papers from other exam boards or the previous OCR Specification to see if there could be a broader range of questions to test your knowledge).

- Work through mark schemes and level descriptors to see precisely what examiners were looking to reward in past exam questions.
- Search books and web links for examples and case studies to illustrate your essays (though let the reasoning drive the essay, not the examples).
- Use mind maps or other diagrams to select the essential terms or ideas on a topic so that they can be seen in an easily memorable way.

Why essays make you employable

Essay writing might seem like a real chore. Yet in developing transferable skills of persuasiveness, analysis and creative thinking, you are becoming more employable. As you read around theories, you will understand them better, and consequently your confidence and fluency will improve. It is precisely these skills in selecting and deploying relevant and precise evidence and arguments that make graduates in the humanities so employable.

Not losing sight of the wood for the trees – seeing the big picture of your argument

To use an analogy, you can get lost in the woods of concepts and abstract arguments with no visible way out. Equally, you might feel the need to airlift your wayward argument out of the forest in the concluding paragraph as you realize that you have not relevantly addressed the terms of the question. Yet a safer way out of the forest may be to leave stores of food there: to have well-rehearsed key points ready to go once you have selected what is relevant to the question. Excellent selection and deployment of relevant reasons, examples, thinkers, strengths and weaknesses are crucial in achieving a high grade.

Before you actually start writing an essay, whether as homework or in an exam, it is important to think carefully about both the content and its structure. This will be easier if you have used mind mapping techniques or some similar way of noting the information for a topic. Set out key terms, examples, key quotes, relevant thinkers, arguments and analytical points. Doing this will prepare you for any essay on any topic that you may be set.

Doing well in exams is a feat of memory – use bullet points, acronyms and mnemonics to help your recall become exam-proof.

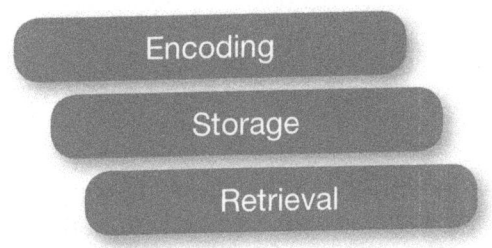

Encoding

Storage

Retrieval

Exams are not just about understanding theories and being able to explain them. They are also timed tests of your recall. Under such pressure, you need to find a process or system for encoding the information that will make it easy to retrieve. Lists of key principles and concepts in theories, as well as evaluative lists of strengths and weaknesses, should be memorized. This is best done in a concise orderly way using mind maps or bullet points, or with the aid of acronyms and mnemonics.

The two websites listed below may assist you in generating acronyms and mnemonics.

Acronym	*Mnemonic*
An acronym is an abbreviation using the first letter of each word. For example AIDS is an acronym for Acquired Immuno-Deficiency Syndrome	A mnemonic is a short phrase that you use to help remember something. So 'Richard Of York Goes Battling In Vain' helps me to remember the colours of the rainbow – red, orange, yellow, green, blue, indigo, violet
Acronym generator: www.cs.uoregon.edu/Research/paracomp/anym/	Phonetic mnemonic generator: www.remarkablemarbles.com/memory/phonetic-mnemonic-generator

Assessment

AS Religious Studies and A Level Religious Studies

You will choose to study either AS Religious Studies **OR** A Level Religious Studies. These are two separate qualifications that are self-contained. In both cases, the AS and A Level Developments in Religious Thought component of Religious Studies amounts to 33.3 per cent of the course, alongside the other two sections of the course, namely Religion and Ethics, and Philosophy of Religion.

A summary of the major differences is provided here:

	AS Level	*A Level*
Course studied over	1 year	2 years
% of marks for AO2 Analysis and evaluation	50%	60%

For students taking an AS Level course, the end-of-course exam will be made up of 30-mark questions (you answer two questions from three options). A possible question for the AS Level Developments in Religious Thought component of the course could be:

1. 'If the Fall did not actually happen, then Augustine's views on human nature are incoherent.' Discuss. [30]

For students taking an A Level course, the end-of-course exam will be made up of 40-mark questions (you answer three questions from four options). A possible question for the A Level Developments in Religious Thought component of the course could be:

1. Assess the view that gender equality is desirable but unattainable. [40]

The key difference between AS and A Level questions is that, whereas at AS Level the descriptors only go to level 5 (for Very Good), at A Level there is an extra descriptor – level 6 (for Excellent). This recognizes the greater level of maturity that students may have developed in their second year of study. The weighting also shifts from 50-50 to 60-40 in favour of AO2 (Analysis and evaluation).

There are two Assessment Objectives (AO1 and AO2). Learning to understand what these Assessment Objectives mean will help you a great deal in the way you write essays. They will help you to interpret and analyse information and to assess and evaluate theories. You will need to develop an independent mind and critical awareness of strengths and weaknesses so that you can make your own response to the question you have been asked.

| AS Level | 75 minutes | Two 30-mark questions | 60 marks in total |
| A Level | 120 minutes | Three 40-mark questions | 120 marks in total |

| Assessment Objectives ||
AS Level	A Level
AO1 50%	AO1 40%
AO2 50%	AO2 60%

Getting to grips with AO2 skills

You will have to sharpen your skills of interpretation and analysis of the terms in the question. Thorough knowledge and understanding ought to be the foundation of your success. Experience of doing past-paper questions will sharpen your skills in:

- interpreting key terms, trigger words and value judgements over rival positions
- selecting and deploying relevant theories and thinkers, examples and arguments

- seeing how your judgement may rest on interpreting the question precisely
- evaluating the strengths and weaknesses of rival positions concisely
- making focused and concise comparisons and contrasts and supplying good relevant examples
- identifying fallacies, assumptions, errors or claims that are scientifically or rationally unsound or just incoherent
- coming to a personal response regarding, for example, whether a theory is the 'most useful', 'best approach', 'effective in applying principles'
- using technical language fluently.

So, after you have learned each section of the course, you need to practise, practise, practise essay technique. Test and homework essays are not just for consolidating your knowledge. Rather, they are where you develop as a thinker and sharpen your skills of selection and structuring a coherent argument. Essays are where you learn the discipline of sifting, sequencing and assessing the material in front of you. In guiding the reader/examiner through the process of your thinking, it is helpful to use transitional phrases that *explicitly* set out your *personal response* to the question for the reader, together with *your own* interpretation, analysis, argument and evaluation of the question. Setting out a clear plan and structure to your argument avoids repetition, makes your logic clearer and ought to be more persuasive. The use of good examples or astute analysis and comparison of theories and ideas identify high-grade candidates. Remember that you do need to bring *your personal response* to the question to the forefront of your essay.

For AO1

An **excellent** demonstration of knowledge and understanding in response to the question involves the following:

- fully comprehending the demands of, and focusing on, the question throughout
- excellent selection of relevant material which is skilfully used
- accurate and highly detailed knowledge which demonstrates deep understanding through a complex and nuanced approach to the material used
- thorough, accurate and precise use of technical terms and vocabulary in context
- an extensive range of scholarly views, academic approaches and/or sources of wisdom and authority are used to demonstrate knowledge and understanding.

For AO2

An **excellent** demonstration of analysis and evaluation in response to the question involves the following:

- excellent, clear and successful argument
- confident and insightful critical analysis and detailed evaluation of the issue
- views skilfully and clearly stated, coherently developed and justified
- answering the question set precisely throughout

- thorough, accurate and precise use of technical terms and vocabulary in context
- an extensive range of scholarly views, academic approaches and sources of wisdom and authority used to support analysis and evaluation.

Assessment of extended response: There is an excellent line of reasoning, well developed and sustained, which is coherent, relevant and logically structured.

A Level candidates achieving excellence in their answers (the level 6 descriptors listed above) show a familiarity with scholarship informed by wider reading. This gives them fluency with technical vocabulary and allows for an intelligent interpretation of the question to produce a thoroughly relevant answer that pays close attention to its wording. Level 6 candidates will show skill in selecting and deploying material, along with a nuanced understanding of thinkers. These candidates understand classic theologians and their contemporary interpreters so well that they can present a nuanced account of how their thought may apply to modern debate.

Accomplished essay writers exhibit accuracy, precision and depth of understanding, together with a breadth of perspective that allows for a variety of views to be compared and contrasted in a sophisticated way. They have fingertip familiarity with a range of scholarship, but have digested it to the extent that they can advance their own thesis and position on any given question, arguing cogently for their own judgements in a persuasive way. Most importantly, they understand that assessment and evaluation should be woven throughout the whole essay, not just restricted to the concluding paragraph.

A discerning writer makes informed judgements as to the relative strengths and weaknesses of theories throughout the essay. Their critical analysis is coherent and persuasively argued from a clear thesis statement to a successful conclusion.

Glossary of Key Terms

Act agapism Fletcher's version of a kind of Act Utilitarianism, making ethical decisions on the circumstances of an individual's situation, not on laws
Agape Jesus taught that selfless love was the highest form of love
Akrasia Aristotle's word for weakness of the will, related to the moral life
Alienation This happens when a person is treated as an object rather than as a valued individual
Amsterdam Declaration Seven statements agreed at the World Humanist Congress in 2002, setting out the minimum aims of modern humanism
Apostles Jesus' twelve disciples minus Judas Iscariot
Apostles' Creed One of the most important Christian statements of belief, the current version dates from the eighth century
Arianism The beliefs of a heretical group founded by Arius, who preached that Jesus was not God by nature, but aided in the process of salvation
Autonomous Christian ethics Person-centred ethics. Used by Fletcher in his Situation Ethics
Barmen Declaration A document, largely composed by Karl Barth in 1934, setting out the Confessing Church's opposition to the German Christian movement that had accepted Nazism
Beatific Vision Aquinas' view of heaven as a place of perfect happiness
Beatitudes Part of Jesus' teaching about social justice in Matthew 5
Book of Common Prayer Church of England's collection of orders of service and prayers, first published in 1549
Broad exclusivist Church members must be baptized by a priest and receive the sacrament regularly
Cambridge Inter-Faith Programme One of the English focal points of the Scriptural Reasoning Movement, offering meetings, discussion, courses, etc.
Capitalism The idea that society works best in a free-market economy
Caritas Latin word, used by Augustine, for generous love
Catechism of the Catholic Church A book listing all the beliefs of the Roman Catholic church. The most recent edition was produced by Pope John Paul II in 1992
Chalcedonian Definition Definitive statement on the nature of Christ – that he was co-equal with God. Finalized at the Council of Chalcedon in 451 CE
Cheap grace For Bonhoeffer, this was grace that did not have to be worked for and is therefore false

Christa **controversy** A statue displayed in 1984 in St John the Divine Cathedral in New York City that caused controversy because it represents the crucified Christ as a woman

Church tradition The official teaching of the Church on important matters of doctrine, based on what Christians have believed and practised over time

Cognitive/non-cognitive Refer to different kinds of statement: cognitive = facts / alleged facts; non-cognitive = non-facts, e.g. poetry, metaphors, symbolism

A Common Word Between Us and You A 2008 document from Muslim scholars declaring the common ground between them and Christians

A Common Word for the Common Good A document representing Christian views about the value of dialogue with Islam

Concupiscence Augustine's term for uncontrolled desires, including sexual lust

Confessing Church A breakaway group within German Protestantism that disagreed with Hitler's attempt to make churches an instrument of Nazism

Conscience The moral response to the apprehension of God's existence

Costly grace For Bonhoeffer, this is true grace, that sacrifices have to be made for, and is based on 'only Christ, only scripture, only faith'

Covenant A mutually binding agreement between God and his followers

Cupiditas Latin word, used by Augustine, for self-love

Dabru Emet **(Speak the Truth)** A document from Jewish leaders encouraging discussions with Christian leaders to establish common ground and dialogue

Dahlem Declaration The Confessing Church made a declaration in 1934 challenging the legitimate authority of the Reich Church

Decalogue Another name for the Ten Commandments

Dialectical view of history The Marxist view that the world operates through conflict, then resolution, then conflict, and so on

Docetism The belief that Jesus was divine, and only appeared (*dokeo*) to be human

Donatism A movement declared as a heresy

Double Predestination The view that God chooses only a certain number of people to achieve salvation

Ebionites A Jewish-Christian group who believed that Jesus was human, but also the Messiah. They rejected the virgin birth

The Elect In Augustine's view, the select few who would be saved by God

Election The state of being chosen by God, mostly associated with John Calvin's theology. It means the same as predestination

Encyclical This is a letter from the Pope to cardinals, bishops, clergy and, sometimes, to all Roman Catholics. These letters usually concern social issues or church doctrine

Epistemic distance The idea that there is a gap between God's knowledge and human knowledge

Eschatology The doctrine of the Last Things, when God's judgement of individuals would determine their ultimate fate

Exclusivism The view that only Christianity offers the means of salvation

External grace Pelagius' idea that God provides the means to do what is right, but leaves people to make decisions themselves

Extra ecclesiam nulla salus Latin phrase: 'Outside the Church there is no salvation'

The Fall The account in Gen. 3 where Adam and Eve disobey God and are expelled from the Garden of Eden

Fides ex auditu Faith from having heard (the Gospel) – for some exclusivists, this is the only way to achieve salvation

Finkenwalde The seminary community where Bonhoeffer taught

Five Ways Aquinas' five arguments for the existence of God

Formed faith Aquinas' term for faith that a person accepts rationally, and accepts as true for themselves

Gender biology Physical attributes of a person's body

Gender expression The way a person dresses, speaks and generally expresses themselves to the outside world

Gender identity The gender a person views themselves as most comfortably belonging to

General revelation God's revelation of his nature through the natural world

Global ethic Hans Küng defined this as the minimal consensus concerning values, irrevocable standards and fundamental moral principles

Globalization The movement of people around the world, resulting in exposure to different cultures and religious traditions

Gnosticism From the Greek *gnosis*, meaning 'knowledge'. Refers to a number of linked beliefs that claimed to have special knowledge of God, but varied from official church doctrine

Golden Rule 'Do to others what you would wish them to do to you': Jesus quotes Leviticus 19:18 in the Sermon on the Mount (Matt 7:12)

Grace God's unconditional love and gifts to humanity. An important term for Augustine

Group for the Ministry of Women A group set up by Daphne Hampson, offering support to women and campaigning for the ordination of women in the Church of England

Hades Latin name for hell

Heaven In Christianity, the 'place' where those saved by God would reside for ever

Hell The 'place' where the damned will spend eternity, traditionally described as punishment and extreme suffering

Heresy A belief that is at variance with the offical view of the Church

High Christology Looks at Jesus 'from above', declaring his divine origins

Historical materialism A Marxist theory that describes and analyses historical processes that develop by way of conflict, then harmony, then conflict, and so on

Imago Dei Latin for 'in the image of God'

Immanence The idea that God is present in the world and can interact with it and with humans

Immediate revelation God makes himself known to humans directly

Inaugurated eschatology The NT idea that the Kingdom of God has already begun during Jesus' lifetime

Incarnation A high Christological term meaning that Jesus was God 'in the flesh'
Inclusivism The view that, although Christianity is the normative means of salvation, 'anonymous' Christians may also receive salvation
Inter-faith dialogue The process of learning to understand and communicate with people of different faiths
Internal grace Augustine's view that God works within the human soul, forcing it to do good and avoid evil
Jehovah's Witnesses A Fundamentalist sect who believe in Double Predestination
Kingdom of God Jesus' teaching that people, following their repentance, would enter God's kingdom
Knowledge There are two kinds of knowledge - natural and revealed
Liberalism Individuals can believe whatever they like and their views should be tolerated by everyone, as long as they do not threaten society
Logos Title for Jesus - the 'Word' in John's Gospel (1:1)
Low Christology Looks at Jesus 'from below', focusing on the things Jesus did and said, e.g. parables, healing, etc.
Magisterium The teaching authority of the Roman Catholic church
Male entitlement Daly claims that men feel entitled to do whatever they want to retain power and subdue women
Mediate revelation People learn about God indirectly
Memetics Richard Dawkins uses this term to explain how ideas like religion survive for a long time, just as genes mutate and multiply
Mulieris dignitatem This papal document, 'On the Dignity and Vocation of Women', was a response in 1988 to the first two waves of feminism
Multi-faith A society in which members of different religious faiths live
Narrow exclusivist Believers in Double Predestination, adding that those who are not chosen will go to hell and eternal damnation
National Socialism The Nazi Party
Natural Law Aquinas defined this as 'right reason in accordance with human nature'
Natural Theology God may be known through reason and the observation of the natural world
Noumenal Hick used Kant's term for the world as it really is
Old Roman Creed An early Christian creed from the middle of the second century
Omnibenevolence God's central characteristic of being all-loving
Omnipotence God's central characteristic of being all-powerful
Omniscience God's central characteristic of being all-knowing
Opium of the people Marx's judgement on the harmful role of religion in society
Orthodoxy The official teaching of a religious group
Orthopraxis The practical expression of church teaching needed to bring aid and liberation to the poor and oppressed
Papal Infallibility This is a dogma, not a doctrine, teaching that Papal statements made *ex cathedra* cannot contain error. Declared at the First Vatican Council, 1869–70

Glossary of Key Terms

Parousia The Christian belief that Jesus will return to earth to judge every human who has ever lived, selecting those who are worthy to live with God forever

Particularism Another name for exclusivism

Pelagianism The view of a British theologian who argued that Original Sin did not ruin human nature, and that humans are still able to choose freely to do good or evil

Perdition A Calvinist word for hell

Phenomenal Hick used Kant's term for the world as humans see it

Pluralism The view that there are many ways to salvation, of which Christianity is one way

Pluralism The co-existence in one place of many different groups: nationalities, religions, ethical viewpoints, class, sexuality and gender

Praxis For Marx, this describes a belief that, because the world is in a constant state of change, people can understand why it changes and alter things for the good of all

Predestination The idea that some people are chosen before their birth, by God, to be saved, and others not

Preferential option for the poor Liberation theology's catch-phrase for their principal aim of giving practical help to those in society who need it the most

Procedural secularism The role of the State is to take into account the interests of all citizens and institutions

Programmatic secularism The role of the State is to be purely secular; all religious practices should be excluded from public institutions, including governments, schools and hospitals

Proletariat Marx's term for the workers who are alienated from production because they have no ownership

The Prophets A major part of the Old Testament is made up of prophetic writing. It took various forms, such as messages about social justice, or criticism of the Old Testament Jews when they had gone against God's laws

Purgatory A post-biblical idea referring to a state of cleansing after death, before entering heaven

Quest for the historical Jesus A historical/theological search to ascertain who Jesus really was

Redemptoris missio A Roman Catholic Encyclical in response to questions about how Roman Catholics should interact with people of different faiths

Religionless Christianity Bonhoeffer's hope for a bold new reformation whereby barriers between denominations would be broken down and Christians could focus on Christ

Restrictive inclusivism The view that God considers non-Christians, even though they may practise ethical lives, as not capable of salvation, unless they become Christians

Resurrection Being brought back from death

Revealed theology God may only be known when he allows himself to be known – e.g., through the Bible. Also known as 'special revelation'

Salvific The idea that Jesus' death saved humans from their sins

Glossary of Key Terms

Scriptural Reasoning Movement A forum for Christian, Jewish and Muslim people to meet and discuss theological and other issues to foster mutual understanding

Second Vatican Council (Vatican II) An important and influential council of the Roman Catholic church that met in Rome between 1962 and 1965. Its aim was to energize and modernize the Church

Secular humanism This ideology believes that people can live moral lives without the need for religious adherence

Secular positivism The idea of a society based on scientific reasoning and without the need for religion

Secularisation The view that public and private life should be entirely separate. Religious belief should not be in the public domain

Semen religionis Seed of religion – Calvin's view that all humans have a sense of God, though some are unaware of it because of sin

Sensus divinitatis Calvin's view that all humans have an innate sense of God, drawing them towards God

Sermon on the Mount A compilation of Jesus' teaching on morality in Matthew 5–7

Sharing the Gospel of Salvation A 2010 Church of England contribution to the discussion of inter-faith dialogue

Sheol In late Jewish theology, it was thought that, when a person died, they descended to an underground pit, where they would stay for an undefined time

Situation Ethics Joseph Fletcher's liberal theory of ethics, based on Jesus' command to 'love' one's neighbours, based not on laws but on the situation at the time

Sola scriptura Some Christians attempt to derive moral principles from the Bible alone

Son of God One of the Christological titles for Jesus

Sophrosyne Aristotle's word for showing self-control, moderation and a deep sense of one's self, resulting in true happiness

Soteriology The doctrine of salvation

Soul For Christians, this is the immaterial, spiritual part of a human being, which is potentially eternal

Special revelation Another name for Revealed theology

Stewardship According to Augustine, God gives humans special responsibilities to look after the earth

Structural inclusivism Karl Rahner's view that believers in any religion whose structures allow openness to God's grace are capable of salvation

Supercessionism Where one group or religion supersedes or succeeds over another

Suzerainty treaty This was an ancient Hittite treaty between two unequal partners – the more powerful suzerain and the less powerful vassal, who must submit to the suzerain. The Ten Commandments are written in this form

Synderesis Aquinas' view, as part of his Natural Law theory, that good is to be done and evil avoided

Theodicy A justification of the righteousness of God, given the existence of evil

Theology of religions Alan Race's proposed solution to the difficulty of talking to members of non-Christian religions

Theotokos   Title for Mary, mother of Jesus, who gave birth to God (*theos*). The term means 'God-bearer'

Torah   The first five books of the Old Testament

Tradition   How the Church has reacted to an ethical problem in the past. It is an important source of authority in the Roman Catholic church

Transcendence   The idea that God is not part of the world and is independent from it

Transcendent theism   Hick's term for the view that Christianity needs to move away from a Christ-centred view to a God-centred theology. This would lead to the recognition that all religions revolve around God

Unformed faith   Aquinas' term for the belief of a person who can intellectually accept another person's faith in God, but cannot accept it as true for themselves

Unholy trinity   Mary Daly's shocking charge against the Church, whose treatment of women has produced 'rape, genocide and war'

Universal Consent argument   Cicero's argument that humans have a natural instinct to believe in God

Universal salvation   Roman Catholics believe that non-Christians, and those who have rejected Christianity, will have an opportunity of salvation while in purgatory

Universalism   Roman Catholic view that universal salvation must be achieved within the Church, because they believe that there is no salvation outside it (*extra ecclesiam nulla salus*)

Unlimited election   Calvin's view that all people are called to salvation, but not all will be chosen

Virgin birth   The doctrine that Jesus was born to Mary without the normal methods of procreation

Westminster Confession of Faith   A compilation of the beliefs of Calvinistic Protestant churches

Widerstand   The resistance movement that Bonhoeffer joined

Windrush Generation   An example of the movement of (mostly Caribbean) people from one part of the world to another (Britain)

Wisdom   From the Greek word *sophos*, refers to knowledge that comes separately from sense experience and fosters an understanding of one's place in society and how a person should live their life.

Yada   A Hebrew word meaning 'able to know'

Zealots   Revolutionary Jewish group who wanted to take up arms against the Romans, to reclaim Israel for Judaism

Illustration Credits

The publishers would like to thank the following for permission to use copyright material:

Page 5, Wikimedia Commons / Musée Thomas Henry; 14, ZU_09 / iStock; 23, BibleArtLibrary / iStock; 29, Wikimedia Commons; 34, Wikimedia Commons / Gustave Doré; 51, Wikimedia Commons / Pinacoteca di Brera; 56, Goddard_Photography / iStock; 60, FatCamera / iStock; 79, rothivan / iStock; 82, Wikimedia Commons / Casa Rosada; 91, Wikimedia Commons / Bundesarchiv; 110, Wikimedia Commons; 116, Maarten / Flickr; 126, AleksandarNakic / iStock; 153, Wikimedia Commons; 157, Wikimedia Commons / Mim Saxl; 169, Yvonne Hemsey / Contributor; 174, Maor Winetrob / iStock; 175, shcherbak volodymyr / iStock; 176, Wikimedia Commons / Max Halberstadt; 190, Wikimedia Commons; 196, iStock; 200, Wikimedia / John Jabez Edwin Mayal

Index

A Common Word Between Us and You 132, 135, 219
A Common Word for the Common Good 132, 219
Amsterdam Declaration 180, 218
anonymous Christianity 117
Apostles' Creed 55–6, 71, 113, 218
Augustine, Saint vii, 3–20, 23, 24, 33, 44, 85, 88, 113, 114, 209, 218–20, 223
   conversion 6
   Donatism 9
   the Fall 12–14, 16
   human nature 11–16
   Manichaeism 6
   Original Sin 14
   Platonism 7–8
autonomous Christian ethics 84

banning of religious symbols 174
Barmen Declaration 78, 99, 218
Barth/Brunner debate 52 52
Beatitudes 66, 78, 218
Beauvoir, Simone de 150, 154
Black Liberation Theology 202–3
Boff, Leonardo and Clodovis 192
Bonaventure 42
Bonhoeffer, Dietrich ix, 90–2, 94, 98, 101–3, 106
Book of Common Prayer 24, 218
British Humanist Association 182
broad exclusivism 114, 218

Camara, Helder 201, 202
Cambridge Inter-Faith Programme 134, 218
capitalism and secularisation 187
Cardinal Ratzinger's criticisms of use of Marx 200, 201
caritas 12, 13, 218
Catechism of Catholic Church 30
cheap grace and costly grace 102–4, 106, 219
Christa controversy 168–9
Christian Moral Action v, ix, 90–105
   Barmen Declaration 99, 218
   Bonhoeffer, Dietrich ix, 90–2, 94, 98, 101–3, 106
   cheap grace and costly grace 102–4, 106, 219
   Dahlem Declaration 98, 218

Finkenwalde 91, 101–3, 220
   relevance of Bonhoeffer 105
   Widerstand 93, 224
Christian moral principles v, ix, 75–89
   autonomous Christian ethics 84 84
   Beatitudes 66, 78, 218
   church tradition 75, 219
   Fletcher on Situation Ethics 87–8
   Hauerwas, Stanley 84
   heteronomous ethics 80
   Kung, Hans, global ethic 85
   Magisterium 75, 82, 83, 85, 86, 89, 221
   Natural Law 48, 54, 75, 83, 84, 88, 118, 221, 223
   Prophets 47, 59, 76, 77, 87, 192, 222
   Tillich, Paul, on agape 86
   Torah 23, 24, 76, 110
Christological controversies 57
Church of England 24, 112, 129, 132–3, 138, 139, 159, 167, 180, 182, 184, 220
   inter-faith dialogue 132–3, 138, 139
   Synod 132, 160, 167, 223
   women priests 159
church tradition 75, 219
concupiscence 14, 219
Cone, James H. 202–3, 204
conversion 5, 8
Creation 1, 12
   Augustine on 11–18, 19, 22, 25, 26, 28
   Barth/Brunner debate 52–3
   Dawkins on 19, 183
   Lightfoot on 17
   Paul, Saint, on 44, 45
   Ussher on 17
   Ward on 17–18
cupiditas 12, 13

Dabru Emet (Speak the Truth) 130–1, 219
Dahlem Declaration 98, 219
Daly, Mary 146, 154, 156, 161, 169
Dante 28
Dawkins, Richard 19, 173, 178, 180, 182–4, 188, 221
de las Casas, Bartholomé 189
dialectical view of history 194, 219
Donatus 9

Index

Election, limited 32, 33
Election, unlimited 34
exclusivism 109, 111, 112, 113, 222
  broad exclusivism 114
  Hick on 121
  narrow exclusivism 114
  restrictive access exclusivism 111, 113–14

faith and reason ix, 51, 52
  Kierkegaard on faith and reason 52
Fall, the 3, 10–16, 83, 102, 111–14, 144, 145, 159, 162, 202, 215, 220
Farquhar, John Nicol 130
feminist theologians ix, 156, 162, 168
  Daly, Mary 146, 154, 156, 161, 169
  Hampson, Daphne 157–8, 167
  Ruether, Rosemary Radford 156, 161, 165–9
feminist waves 149
Feuerbach, Ludwig 176, 185, 186
fides ex auditu 113, 116
Finkenwalde 91, 101–3, 220
Firestone, Shulamith 150
Fletcher, Joseph, on Situation Ethics 87–8
Ford, Professor David 131, 134
Freud, Sigmund, on religion 176, 222

gender and society v, 143–55
  Beauvoir, Simone de 150, 154
  feminist waves 149
  Firestone, Shulamith 150
  gender expression 143, 220
  gender identity 143–5, 220
  gender roles ix, 143–7, 149, 152, 158–60
  Mulieris dignitatem 149–51, 155, 221
gender and theology v, 156, 157, 159, 161, 163, 165
  Christa controversy 168–9
  role and status of women in history 159–61, 169
  Ruether on Jesus' challenge to the warrior messiah 165–7
grace 11, 13
Gregory of Nyssa 30
Group for the Ministry of Women 167
Gutierrez, Gustavo 68, 69, 190–1, 193, 197–9, 204

Hampson, Daphne 157–8, 167
Hauerwas, Stanley 84
heaven 21, 22, 24, 26–8, 29, 32
hell 21, 22, 27–35, 37, 38, 110, 114, 120, 220–2
heteronomous ethics 80
Hick, John 18
  criticism of inclusivism 119, 123
  on pluralism 121
historical materialism 193, 194, 197, 220
Hitchens, Christopher 61
human nature 4, 5, 9, 11–13

immediate revelation 46, 47, 220
Incarnation 24, 60–1, 67, 113–14, 117, 122, 162, 221
inclusivism 109, 112, 116–18
  criticisms of 119
  restrictive inclusivism 115–16, 118
  structural inclusivism 115, 116, 117
inter-faith dialogue 125, 127–8, 134, 136–7, 139, 221
  A Common Word Between Us and You 132, 135, 219
  A Common Word for the Common Good 132, 219
  Dabru Emet (Speak the Truth) 130–1, 219
  Ochs, Peter 133, 139
  Scriptural Reading Movement 125, 131, 133–4, 136, 139, 218
  Sharing the Gospel of Salvation 132–3, 223

Jehovah's Witnesses 114, 221
Jesus' miracles 61
Jesus' resurrection 62–3
Jesus' use of parables 65
John of Damascus, Saint 130, 190, 193–4, 197, 199
Justin Martyr 129

Kee, Alistair 201
Kierkegaard on faith and reason 52
Kingdom of God 25, 34, 35–7, 66, 68, 70, 78, 93, 220, 221
knowledge of God ix, 55, 58, 60, 116, 124, 220
  Barth/Brunner debate 52
  Bonaventure 42
  faith and reason ix, 51, 52
  immediate revelation 46, 47, 221
  mediate revelation 46, 47, 221
  Natural Theology 43, 45, 46, 50, 52, 54, 221
  Revealed Theology 43, 46, 47, 50, 52, 54, 222, 223
Kung, Hans, on global ethic 85

Liberation theology v, ix, 198–204
  Boff, Leonardo and Clodovis 192
  Camara, Helder 201, 202
  Gutierrez, Gustavo 68, 69, 190–1, 193, 197–9, 204
  Kee, Alistair 201
  Liberation theology's use of Marx 197–200
  Miranda, Jose Porfirio 193
  orthodoxy 190, 221
  orthopraxis 190, 221
  preferential option for the poor 68, 69, 189, 191–3, 201, 202, 204
  Romero, Oscar 190
  Segundo, Juan 175
  Sobrino, Jon 190, 197
  theological roots of Liberation theology 191, 192

Liberation theology (*cont*)
  use of the Bible in Liberation theology 197, 198
  Vieira, Antonio 189
liberator, Jesus as 55, 68–71
life after death
  Dante's vision of hell 28
  Election, limited 32, 33
  Election, unlimited 34
  heaven 21, 22, 24, 26–8, 29, 32
  hell 21, 22, 27–32, 33–5, 37, 38, 110, 114, 120, 220, 221, 222
  Kingdom of God 25, 34, 35–7, 66, 68, 70, 78, 93, 220, 221
  parable of the sheep and goats 35
  Parousia 25, 222
  predestination 10, 32, 33, 114, 219, 221, 222
  purgatory 175
Lightfoot, John 17

Magisterium 75, 82, 83, 85, 86, 89, 221
Manichaeism 6
Marx, Karl 189, 191, 194–7, 222
  on alienation and exploitation 195–6
  on historical materialism 193, 194, 197, 220
  influence on Liberation theology 194–5
mediate revelation 46, 47, 221
memetics 180, 221
Miranda, José Porfirio 193
Mulieris dignitatem 149, 150, 151, 155, 221

narrow exclusivism 114, 221
Natural Law 48, 54, 75, 83, 84, 88, 118, 221, 223
Natural Theology 43, 45, 46, 47, 50, 54, 221
noumenal, the 121

Ochs, Peter 133, 139
Original Sin 10, 11, 14, 15, 16, 33
orthodoxy 190, 221
orthopraxis 190, 221

parable of the sheep and goats, Matt. 25 35
Parousia 25, 222
Paul, Saint 44
Pelagius 10, 11, 16
person of Jesus Christ v, ix, 55–71, 122
  Apostles' Creed 55–6, 71, 113, 218
  Christological controversies 57
  Incarnation 24, 60–1, 67, 113–14, 117, 122, 162, 221
  Jesus' miracles 61
  Jesus' use of parables 65
  Jesus' resurrection 62–3
  liberator, Jesus as 55, 68–71
  Son of God 26, 37, 48, 55, 57–62, 67, 159, 223
  teacher of wisdom 55, 65–7
  virgin birth of Jesus 61
phenomenal, the 121

Platonism 4, 7, 8, 129
pluralism 112, 113, 119, 120, 123, 125, 126
predestination 10, 32, 33, 114, 219, 221, 222
preferential option for the poor 68, 69, 189, 191–3, 201, 202, 204
procedural secularism 10, 32, 33, 114, 219, 221
programmatic secularism 192, 193, 201
Prophets 175
Purgatory 175

Rahner, Karl 47, 59, 76, 77, 87, 192, 222
  on anonymous Christianity 21, 29–32, 35–8, 112, 115, 222, 224
  Rahner on exclusivism 31
Redemptoris missio 128, 187
relevance of Bonhoeffer 117
Restrepo, Camilo Torres 128, 222
restrictive exclusivism 68, 190–1
resurrection 109, 111–14, 118, 121, 124
Revealed Theology 118
  revelation through the Bible 24, 25
  revelation through faith 43, 46, 47, 50, 52, 54, 222, 223
  revelation through grace 49–51
role and status of women in history 48–9
Roman Catholic church 30, 75, 80–1, 150, 160, 161, 165, 218, 221, 222, 224
  encyclicals 60, 82, 128, 219, 222
  exclusivism 114, 118
  inclusivism 112, 116, 117–18, 221, 213
  inter-faith dialogue 128
  women priests 160
Romero, Oscar X, 68, 190, 191, 201
Ronald McDonald crucifixion 159–61, 169
Ruether, Rosemary 187
Ruether on Jesus' challenge to the warrior messiah 190

Scriptural Reading Movement 165–7
secular humanism 156, 161, 165–9
secular positivism 125, 131, 133–4, 136, 139, 218
secularisation 180, 223
Segundo, Juan 173, 223
Sermon on the Mount 175
Sharing the Gospel of Salvation 190, 197
Sobrino, Jon x, 190, 193, 194, 197, 201
Son of God 132–3, 223
structural inclusivism 26, 37, 48, 55, 57–62, 67, 159, 223
supercessionism 132, 218 130

teacher of wisdom 116–18
Tertullian 130, 223
theological roots of Liberation theology 55, 65–7
Theology of religions 130, 159
Tillich, Paul, on agape 191, 192

Torah 111, 123
Tradition 86
transcendent theism 23, 24, 76, 110

universal access pluralism 22, 26, 28, 52, 60, 66–7, 75, 80–1, 82–4, 94, 101, 127, 135–6, 138, 145, 147, 160, 163, 177, 178, 181, 188, 219, 224
universal salvation 120
universalism 111, 113, 114
use of the Bible in Liberation theology 24, 34, 115, 224
Ussher, James 17

Vatican Council II 30, 220
Vieira, Antonio 17
virgin birth of Jesus 57, 61, 66, 219, 224

Ward, Keith 17, 20, 112
Westminster Confession 61
Widerstand 17–18
Williams, Rowan 112, 132, 186
Windrush Generation 127, 224